Refractions of the National, the Popular and the Global in African Cities

Edited by Simon Bekker, Sylvia Croese and Edgar Pieterse

AFRICAN
MINDS

Published in 2021 by African Minds
4 Eccleston Place, Somerset West, 7130, Cape Town, South Africa
info@africanminds.org.za
www.africanminds.org.za

The views expressed in this publication are those of the authors.
When quoting from any of the chapters, readers are requested to acknowledge the relevant author.

ISBN (paper): 978-1-928502-15-9
eBook edition: 978-1-928502-16-6
ePub edition: 978-1-928502-17-3

Copies of this book are available for free download at:
www.africanminds.org.za

ORDERS:
African Minds
Email: info@africanminds.org.za

To order printed books from outside Africa, please contact:
African Books Collective
PO Box 721, Oxford OX1 9EN, UK
Email: orders@africanbookscollective.com

Contents

Preface

Urban scholarship is a forte of social science in Africa and a proper response to urban change and innovation. Africa south of the Sahara has been very under-urbanised for a long time but currently is undergoing rapid urbanisation, sometimes, as in Congolese Kinshasa, with a problematic originality of massive urbanisation without any substantial industrialisation or other economic development. Recent years have witnessed an urban building boom from Dakar to Dar es Salaam. Lagos, Luanda, Nairobi and others have set out the goal to become 'world-class cities.'

This volume arises from a conference hosted by the Stellenbosch Institute for Advanced Study (STIAS) in 2017, with the kind and decisive support of its then director Hendrik Geyer, and the African Centre for Cities (ACC) of the University of Cape Town. The conference brought together over 30 scholars representing a range of different disciplines from across the African continent and beyond, including a number of young talented African scholars. It was a conference on African cities which looked at the refractions of the national, the popular and the global, analysed in my global study, *Cities of Power*, of which the conference was also an African launch.

The national refers to the constitution of nation-states, of states representing the nation, and not a colonial empire or a local king. It meant a nationalisation of cities, in their layout, organisation, architecture and symbolism. In Africa, and in the whole vast ex-colonial zone, the nation-state was established through independence from the colonial power. In most of Europe, it meant a peoples constituting itself as a nation independent of the king. South Africa was set up as a settler state, like the Americas and Australia, as a nation of European settlers making themselves independent of their motherland. The country became an African nation-state only in the 1990s, with the fall of racist settler rule.

Popular moments have occurred when popular forces challenge the rule of the national elite, demanding cities built for and serving the mass of ordinary people. 'Popular forces' are non-ruling nonelites whose ranks may comprise different characteristics, of class, caste, ethnicity, gender, occasionally religion, as in the ongoing conflict in Bahrein between the Sunni dynasty and the Shia majority of the people. From an urban studies perspective, a popular moment is not quite the same as the rise of a protest movement. The former refers to successful challenges and protests which have an effect on the city.

Global moments happen when global status and attraction become predominant city aspirations. Historically there have so far been two such moments in modern times. The first had its zenith in the decades around 1900 and was a globalisation of nationalism. Cities 'worthy of the nation' had to be built, all over Europe, the Americas, and a few Asian cities, like Tokyo. Paris of the second empire was then the main urban model, with London offering the best infrastructural example, of sanitation, sewage, clean water and electricity. In most of Asia and in the whole of Africa there were then no nations with states, so here the first global moment passed by. The second urban global moment arrived in the late 20th century in the wake of industrial outsourcing, de-industrialisation, footloose financial capital, globalised real estate markets and mass tourism, as the global moment of capital. Attracting foreign investment, foreign business headquarters and solvent tourists became primary big city goals. Becoming a 'global city' or a 'world-class city' has replaced the previous moment's 'city worthy of the nation.'

Both global moments have meant importing global influences and aspiring to global recognition and fame, by national and local politicians and capital. They are not actively imposed from the outside by global forces. The editors have then done a tremendous job turning the conference into a publication. In its geographical scope, from Cairo to Johannesburg, and in its thematic range, from efforts at national city impregnation in Yaoundé, national-local government relations in Cairo, Addis, Kinshasa, Tshwane and Johannesburg, to popular rebellions in Nairobi and Harare, and further to top-down globalist planning in the local contexts of Lagos and Luanda, this is a major example of the vigour of African urban scholarship.

Thanks go out to STIAS, to its then Director Hendrik Geyer, to Christoff Pauw, Programme Manager, and Nel-Mari Loock, Programme Administrator, for making the conference happen. Thanks also to those who presented and participated in the conference but could not participate in the publication, especially Eduardo Moreno, Frederick Golooba-Mutebi, Philip Harrison, Susan Parnell, Sophie Oldfield, Ntombini Marrengane, Glen Robbins, Lindsay Sawyer and Ngaka Mosiane. Thanks go out to NRF funding for the South African Research Chair in Urban Policy, held by Edgar Pieterse, which allowed for the translation into English of two chapters originally written in French. Thanks for funding of this publication go out to STIAS, the NRF South African Research Chair in Urban Policy at the University of Cape Town, and Stellenbosch University. Appreciation is extended to the Partnership for African Social and Governance Research (PASGR) that enabled the research for chapters 9 to 11. A special thanks to Sylvia Croese and Simon Bekker for pulling everything together.

Göran Therborn, University of Cambridge

CHAPTER 1

Introduction

Simon Bekker, Sylvia Croese & Edgar Pieterse

> The urban is old: cities have existed for thousands of years, but they have been transformed by the arrival of nation-states over two centuries ago ...
>
> The future of globalism looks pretty sure and well laid out ...
> The main difficult question is the future of the people.
>
> – Göran Therborn, *Cities of Power* (2017: 1, 356)

Scholarship on African cities has been proliferating over the past two decades. This is testament to the growing acknowledgement of the importance of cities in an increasingly urban age. This Introduction commences with an outline of Africa's urban reality today. Subsequently, an overview of contemporary urban scholarship calling for Global South and African approaches to this reality is offered before turning to that proposed by Therborn's *Cities of Power*. The principal framework to structure this volume and its various case study chapters is based upon his publication. Its primary theme of seeking relationships between the national, the popular and the global in capital cities today is outlined and the notion of refractions of these forces introduced. The chapter concludes with the structure of the volume.

In sub-Saharan Africa, urbanisation has grown exponentially. From 1995 to 2015, Africa's urban population doubled from 236 million to 472 million. Over the next decade, this population is projected to become larger than Europe's (559 vs. 555 million). It will also be larger than that of Latin America and the Caribbean (536 million) (Moreno 2017; UNDESA 2019).

Urban growth has been associated with social, economic and political development. In 1900, life expectancy in Africa was estimated to be 24 years – today it has reached 63 years. Literacy rates tripled from 23% in 1970 to 65% in 2010. Gross Domestic Product (GDP) multiplied by five times from 1995 to 2015, with an expanding share of industry and services as part of total GDP. Africa's average GDP growth was about 5% per annum (1996–2015) – substantially higher than in the 1970s and 1980s. The resource boom of the first decade of the 2000s brought a renewed sense of hope for the continent, translated in the notion of 'Africa rising.' Two-thirds of African governments now encourage different forms of political participation and 40% have strengthened their safety and the rule of law (2000 to 2012). It is clear that Africans living in urban settings will remain a force driving socio-economic transformation. At 40% urban, African cities contribute 50–70% of the continent's GDP (Moreno 2017; UN-Habitat 2018).

It is, however, only a few who benefit from the advantages of urbanisation. Cities fail to provide sustainable space for all – physically, as well as in the civic, socio-economic and cultural dimensions attached to collective space. Africa's primarily youthful labour force is projected to expand from 400 million to 1.2 billion between 2000 and 2050 but its economies are unlikely to produce enough jobs for this rapidly expanding population. A majority of the urban population continues to live in sprawling slums and informal settlements. Half of the countries on the African continent have a slum incidence of at least 60% and more urban residents are poorer today than in 1990. Urban planning in these cities has not been able to keep up with urban growth and development. Only 56% of this growth in African cities is currently planned, while this was 68% in 1990 (Moreno 2017). At the same time, efforts to plan and transform cities into 'world-class', 'smart' or otherwise 'modern' cities through mega housing and infrastructural development projects have increased (Croese et al. 2016).

As a result, African cities have fragmented and polarised (Bekker & Therborn 2012). Seven of the ten most unequal countries in the world are located in Africa, most of them in southern Africa (Moreno 2017; UNDP 2017). Global trends such as the rise of new global powers from the South, corporatisation, the digital revolution and climate change have important implications for the performance and social polarisation of African cities and the ways in which governments are able to address developmental agendas and challenges. Political decentralisation has been incomplete at best, and stagnant or regressive at worst, while popular protest has been on the rise (Mo Ibrahim Foundation 2017).

Contemporary urban studies in Africa manifestly locate their investigations within a postcolonial context. Many scholars argue that there is a need to turn away from the modernist approach of mainstream European and American scholarship which has typified Northern cities as modern and developed and African cities as developing along the same modernising route – attempting to catch up whilst struggling with rising inequalities, absence of proper planning and pervasive informality, both in shack settlements and in the informal sector. A Global South approach is called for that could lead both to multiple modernities as well as multiple rationalities that underpin contemporary life (Harrison 2006; Pieterse 2010; Parnell & Robinson 2012).

Schindler (2017: 198) has proposed a Southern urbanism approach, focused particularly on 'a persistent disconnect between capital and labor, which gives rise to urban governance regimes geared toward the transformation of territory rather than the "improvement" of populations.' Mbembe and Nuttall (2004) have called for the writing of the social back into our understanding of African 'life forms.' And Ananya Roy (2011) has called for 'subaltern urbanism,' revealing the subaltern spaces and subaltern classes in the cities of the South.

The most influential disciplines in these contemporary African urban studies are human geography and planning. The doyen of these studies, Mabogunje (1990), laid the foundations for a pluralist approach to urban studies incorporating spatial analyses with post-modernist methodologies. His work also proposed a pro-market and developmental policy agenda at urban level, particularly to address poverty and high inequalities in African cities (Filani & Okafor 2006).

The pervasive informality in African cities has been illuminated by two geographers who argue that formal local planning has been notoriously lax in many of these cities and, as a consequence, has led to the 'sprawling of illegal and extra-legal land uses and practices, with the informal business and housing sectors overtaking the formal sector in many cities' (Kamete & Lindell 2010: 911). The term 'informal' has been used in many discourses. 'Moreover, informality takes on different forms at different times and in different places, making each interpretation of the term highly specific ... Alternative ways of framing these developments are called for' (Bekker & Fourchard 2013: 9).

Nevertheless, the inequalities flowing from this complex informality have been illustrated above. These inequalities, moreover, have been shown to widen further by using the concept of spatial justice where space in the African city is defined as including both its local representations in maps and symbolic artefacts, as well as its physical attributes. Confinement of life in an informal settlement is hereby given local meaning (Gervais-Lambony & Dufaux 2009).

Myers, in his publication entitled *African Cities* which bears the subtitle, *Alternative visions of urban theory and practice*, argues that, despite this title, it would be incorrect to promote the idea that African cities make up one unique type. He also remarks that

> Strangely, political science seems only an occasional presence in African urban studies, when it ought to be a central field in our analyses, because these are such fascinating years for urban politics in Africa. (Myers 2011: 198)

In like vein, Freund (2007: 165) has argued that most scholarship on African cities has been that of social scientists rather than historians. He shows convincingly that cities in Africa have been established and endured for all of recorded history. His publication offers an overview of African urban life during the colonial period and summarises scholarly approaches to postcolonial Africa in a fashion similar to that reviewed above. Furthermore, he concludes his historical overview with three historical city case studies that illustrate both the divergencies as well as continuities of postcolonial urban Africa. These are Touba in Senegal, Abidjan in the Ivory Coast and Durban in South Africa.

The inspiration for this book draws on the works of Göran Therborn, in particular, from his publication *Cities of Power* which addresses the urban at a global level and bears the subtitle *The Urban, the National, the Popular and the Global*. As will be shown below, there is a fundamental historical point of departure to his analysis: globally, capital cities have travelled down one of four main routes to national statehood. To illustrate his use of the political in the study of cities in Africa, moreover, the following extract detailing the informality and sprawl of many modern African cities is drawn from one of his earlier publications (Bekker & Therborn 2012: 202):

> It was now that Africa became the continent of slums. But the crisis and its effects were nevertheless managed by the state – the central state – not

the city. African capitals and other big cities did not collapse into general misery. They polarised, between the large, impoverished majority and a tiny political clique around the president and around business protégés of the president ... Political power has in this way become the crucial agency of social polarisation. The ruthlessness with which political posts are fought for, even under electoral auspices, is rational, given how much wealth and privilege is at stake.

Cities of power: The urban, the national, the popular and the global

As outlined in the preface to this book, Therborn argues that, historically, nation-states have constituted the drivers of modernity and thereby transformed the nature and function of cities, particularly their capital cities. However, this has not taken place in a uniform fashion. There were, he argues, four main routes to national statehood:

- the European route of 'states of princes' to 'states of nations',
- the New World settler secessionist route,
- the colonial and postcolonial route and
- the top-down route where modernisation was reactive.

The influence of the rise of the nation-state – and its associated institutional and architectural arrangements – upon capital cities has been extensively researched in Europe and European settler states (Hall 1998; Therborn 2002; Le Galès & Therborn 2010). What is less well-known are the similarities and differences of these influences in other world regions.

Rather than distinguishing between cities of the global North and the Global South or, for that matter, insulating cities of Africa as a category of their own, Therborn maps out these four routes to nationhood. This also enables comparisons to be made of cities across continents. Accordingly, *Cities of Power* may be used to outline a context for our study of Africa's capital cities. Most of the fifty-four nation-states on the continent are ex-colonies. Most of these ex-colonies have attempted to 'nationalise colonialism,' either by transforming the colonial capital into a national capital, by opting for a new capital or by building a capital from scratch. However, most capital cities are distinguished by an enduring duality between the ex-colonial and the indigenous city, in turn leading to the emergence of a sharp division between a small political elite and the large popular masses.

As an historical case study in Asia, the postcolonial route followed by Jakarta is illustrative. Indonesia's claim to independence in 1945 descended – particularly in Jakarta, the colonial capital – into violent conflict between nationalists and the Dutch colonisers until 1949 when the Dutch grudgingly recognised their ex-colony as a fully independent Republic. This resulted in 'the first example of victorious rupture with colonial rule,' exemplified in the former colonial capital (Therborn 2017: 116). The first president, Sukarno, was both a militant nationalist and a modernist. Symbolic nationalism in the capital included two monuments, one – the Monas – embodies early Hinduist Javanese culture, the other – the Irian Jaya Liberation monument –

commemorates the Indonesian takeover in 1963 of Dutch colonial Western New Guinea. A new sports stadium, a national independence mosque and a new parliament building represented the turn toward modernism in the built environment of the capital. The colonial names of streets and squares were all changed. Two of Jakarta's central boulevards acquired the names of two heroes of the anti-colonial struggle. During the sixty-year post-independence period, however, little progress has taken place in the burgeoning residential areas of the urban poor – the *kampung*. Recently constructed elevated highways for motor traffic from outlying affluent suburbs into the city centre illustrate the continuing divide between an elite and those living in the *kampung*, '[a] new postcolonial form of urban dualism,' in Therborn's words (Therborn 2017: 118).

Few African countries – Ethiopia being the prime exception – qualify as having been modernised reactively from above, where threats to their independence by European and US imperialism were asserted and led to an imposition of modernity. This is most evident in their capital cities, where traditional hierarchical institutions and cultural continuity from their pasts have endured.

Bangkok may be used as a second case study in Asia, in this case illustrating the top-down route where modernisation is reactive. As capital of Siam in the 18th century, Bangkok became the capital city of Thailand in the early 20th century. Sandwiched between British Burma to the west and French Indochina to the east, the Thai monarchy shared power until the 1950s with both elected as well as military governments. The architectural expression of Bangkok as capital began with palaces, including the Dusit palace built by Italian architects with imported marble. During the 1930s and 1940s, a monument to democracy was constructed and annual Constitutional Celebration Fairs were organised. After a military coup in the 1950s, earlier urban iconography returned with a renewed emphasis upon the monarchy and the king. Today, Bangkok reflects urban dualism, but in a fashion different from ex-colonial capitals: many neighbourhoods include 'still-living indigenous cultural institutions, royal and other, alongside its Westernized lowlife [sic] of fast food, cheap drinks and prostitution' (Therborn 2017: 154).

Nevertheless, across all of Africa, the influence of nationalism upon capital cities – symbolically and politically, architecturally and in terms of urban iconography – has been deep and enduring. In the 21st century, the rising influence of global capitalist forces – particularly as the digital revolution broadens its reach into urban Africa – will alter but not extinguish the influence of the national. Therborn agrees that competition between the global and the national is taking place but argues that the claim of a severe weakening of the nation-state is unwarranted. Globalised shifts in the architectural design of capital cities, including new business districts, new transnational businesses, massive infrastructural programmes and so on, are often driven by 'local nationalists' rather than a global elite. Hence, the 21st century shows not only the intertwining of the national and the global, but also that '[t]hey are distinct but [...] not necessarily incompatible' (Therborn 2017: 355).

The processes of nationalism and of globalisation in turn interrelate with urban communities, both in terms of their life chances and living conditions as well as their possibilities of expressing voice and agency. In nation-states that have followed the two pathways of nationalisation, of colonialism or reactive modernisation, mobilisation from below is particularly difficult to achieve in their capital cities. The reasons are clear: urban dualism in both cases – the deep divide between the elite and the urban poor in the first case and between the elite and communities living out a traditional lifestyle in the second. However, according to Therborn (2017: 356,357):

> [T]here are two reasons for moderate optimism ... the recent return of popular urban revolutions... [and] the possibility of urban reformism ... Ordinary people are not going away. They will continue to disturb the vision of global image capitalism. Their chances of social transformation are better in cities than elsewhere.

Refractions

The overarching theme of this book, as outlined above, involves the relationships between the national, the popular and the global as points of departure in studying capital cities in Africa. Moreover, these relationships are further shaped by the prism of refractions. Indeed, we are not only interested in interrogating how and why within African capital cities we may think about the intertwining of the national, the popular and the global, but also how, as in physics, these forces are amplified, adapted or dispersed and what this means for how power operates, how it is manifested or how it is resisted.

In an age of 'dissonance' (Simone & Pieterse 2017), the boundaries in urban Africa between the global and the national, between the public and the private, and between the formal and the informal are increasingly blurred. While taking into account that Africa has always been global and that it has shaped the rest of the world as much as it has been shaped by it (Hodgson & Byfield 2017), 21st century globalisation has produced different modes and models of 'worlding' (Roy & Ong 2011) that are distinctly local.

Central in shaping such modes and models is the continued 'shadow of hierarchy' or the ways in which the national continues to wield power in spite of discourses and commitments to multi-scalar, collaborative and participatory good governance (Harrison 2017). At the same time, national power is continuously contested by forces that operate both within and outside of the state. These include traditional authorities which operate in urban areas all across the African continent and play an important role, at times challenging, at times complementing, the role and power of the state (Marrengane 2017). Resistance can also emerge from inside the state, revealing its multiplicity and porosity and the constant negotiations that take place within and between different scales of government. Popular protest, in turn, appears both to be on the rise and simultaneously dispersed, showing a spectrum of social mobilisation which, depending on and in response to different acts of the state, can range from formal, organised resistance to leaderless street politics, virtual defiance through social media, and even acts of waiting (Oldfield 2017).

Structure of the volume

This book materialises from a conference hosted by the Stellenbosch Institute of Advanced Study (STIAS) and the African Centre for Cities (ACC) on 1 August 2017, entitled 'Refractions of the National, the Popular, and the Global in African cities.' It draws on a selection of the contributions presented during this conference, which brought together over 30 scholars from across the African continent and beyond. In addition, several young African academics were invited to contribute, especially colleagues who participated in the study on 'African Turn-around Cities,' supported by the Partnership for African Social and Governance Research. Accordingly, the case studies in this volume predate the global Covid-19 pandemic.

The principal framework used to structure this book is taken from Therborn's *Cities of Power* and its three urban themes. In addition, two earlier edited publications have provided the scaffolding for this book: *Capital Cities in Africa: Power and Powerlessness* published by CODESRIA and HSRC Press in 2012, and *Governing Cities in Africa: Politics and Policies* published by HSRC Press in 2013.

The first publication focused on capital cities in a number of African countries, and traced how the power vested in them has evolved through different colonial backgrounds, radically different kinds of regimes after independence, waves of popular protest, explosive population growth and in most cases stunted economic development. The nine different capital city case studies drew attention to the tension between the symbolic power of capital cities on the one hand, and their political powerlessness vis-à-vis their national governments, on the other.

The second publication – on governance – employed a lens focused on the city rather than on the national government. Issues of policy, practice and service delivery were studied both top-down as well as bottom-up, at city level. The book was organised in two parts, the first entitled 'party politics and the politics of identity' and the second 'urban public policies: problematizing informality.' Rather than employing case studies of individual cities, each chapter focused on a specific theme and its manifestation in several cities. Accordingly, each has been written by several authors.

Both publications cover case studies of cities from across sub-Saharan Africa, including former English, French as well as Portuguese colonies.

This volume builds on these characteristics. In addition, it connects the elements of the national and the popular to the global, asking how national, popular and global forces come together, clash or interact in the African capital city and what kind of practices or imaginaries are produced in the process. Each of its three thematic sections comprises a number of case studies of African capital cities. Each section, moreover, is introduced by brief editorial commentary.

The first thematic section addresses how the national and the nation-state is manifested in the capital city. To what extent is the political and the social character of the national-state regime expressed in the capital city and its governance? Featured chapters discuss tensions and contradictions between national and local government, extending this discussion to the city regional level in the north African region. It explores the urban challenges that local governments face and the ways in which these either close off or open up space for other actors within or outside the state to participate and contribute by responding to these challenges.

The second thematic section addresses the nature and impact of popular forces that have mobilised and made themselves heard in the African city in recent years. The chapters analyse different popular forces and practices, including resistance from inside the state by government officials, the changing role of formal civil society and the rise of informal tactics and street politics combined with the use of social media to challenge state power and structures from below.

The third thematic section analyses a range of urban infrastructural development projects and policies in the cities of Luanda, Lagos and Addis Ababa in order to explore how local political interests, politics and priorities relate, incorporate or respond to global urban development plans, policies and imaginaries. The chapters show the different ways in which the global and the local intersect in the contemporary African city and explore the continuities and discontinuities from colonial to postcolonial times.

The concluding chapter seeks to refract through these themes by reflecting on contemporary urban scholarship not only on Africa but also globally as well as on other continents. It draws on the African capital city case studies in this volume to illustrate these refractions without claiming to exhaust the terrain. The continent today is the least urban on an increasingly urbanised globe. Accordingly, in all probability, urban scholars will progressively situate Africa at the start of a process of large-scale urban transformation, a process that will deeply influence its future.

References

Bekker S & Fourchard L (eds) (2013) *Governing Cities in Africa. Politics and Policies.* Cape Town: HSRC Press

Bekker S & Therborn G (eds) (2012) *Capital Cities in Africa: Power and Powerlessness.* Cape Town and Dakar: CODESRIA and HSRC Press

Croese S, Cirolia LR & Graham N (2016) Towards Habitat III: Confronting the disjuncture between global policy and local practice on Africa's 'challenge of slums.' *Habitat International* 53: 237–242

Filani M & Okafor S (eds) (2006) *Foundations for Urban Development in Africa. The Legacy of Akin Mabogunje.* Washington: The City Alliance

Freund W (2007) *The African City: A History.* Cambridge: Cambridge University Press

Gervais-Lambony P & Dufaux F (2009) Justice ... over space. *Annales de géographie* 665–666(1): 3–15

Hall P (1998) *Cities in Civilization.* London: Pantheon

Harrison P (2006) On the edge of reason: Planning and urban futures in Africa. *Urban Studies* 43(2): 319–335

Harrison P (2017) (Dis)ordered hierarchies: The nation through the urban in the governance of large cities. Keynote address. Unpublished paper presented at the Stellenbosch Institute of Advanced Study (STIAS) conference in Stellenbosch, South Africa, 1 August

Hodgson D & Byfield J (eds) (2017) *Global Africa into the Twenty-first Century.* Berkeley, CA: University of California Press

Kamete A & Lindell I (2010) The politics of 'non-planning' interventions in African cities: Unravelling the international and local dimensions in Harare and Maputo. *Journal of Southern African Studies* 36(4): 889–912

Le Galés P & Therborn G (2010) Cities. In: S Immerfall & G Therborn (eds) *Handbook of European Societies: Social Transformation in the 21st century.* New York: Springer. pp. 59–89

Mabogunje A (1990) Urban planning and the post-colonial state in Africa: A research overview. *African Studies Review* 33(2): 121–203

Marrengane N (2017) Maintaining the monarchy in the city of Mbabane, Swaziland. Unpublished paper presented at the Stellenbosch Institute of Advanced Study (STIAS) conference in Stellenbosch, South Africa, 1 August

Mbembe A & Nuttall S (2004) Writing the world from an African metropolis. *Public Culture* 16(3): 347–372

Mo Ibrahim Foundation (2017) *Ibrahim Index of African governance.* Index report. https://mo.ibrahim.foundation/sites/default/files/2020-05/2018-index-report.pdf

Moreno E (2017) Urban Africa in the 21st century: Potential and challenges. Keynote address. Unpublished paper presented at the Stellenbosch Institute of Advanced Study (STIAS) conference in Stellenbosch, South Africa, 1 August

Myers G (2011) *African Cities: Alternative Visions of Urban Theory and Practice.* London: Zed

Oldfield S (2017) From resistance to waiting? Popular urban politics in Southern African cities. Keynote address. Unpublished paper presented at the Stellenbosch Institute of Advanced Study (STIAS) conference in Stellenbosch, South Africa, 1 August

Parnell S & Robinson J (2012) (Re)theorizing cities from the Global South: Looking beyond neoliberalism. *Urban Geography* 33(4): 593–617

Pieterse E (2010) Cityness and African urban development. *Working Paper No. 2010/42.* Helsinki: UNU-WIDER

Roy A (2011) Slumdog cities: Rethinking subaltern urbanism. *International Journal of Urban and Regional Research* 35(2): 223–238

Roy A & Ong A (eds) (2011) *Worlding Cities: Asian Experiments and the Art of Being Global.* Chichester: Wiley-Blackwell

Schindler S (2017) Towards a paradigm of Southern urbanism. *City* 21(1): 47–64

Simone A & Pieterse E (2017) *New Urban Worlds. Inhabiting Dissonant Times.* Cambridge: Polity Press

Therborn G (2002) Monumental Europe: The national years. On the iconography of European cities. *Housing, Theory and Society* 19(1): 26–47

Therborn G (2017) *Cities of Power: The Urban, the National, the Popular, the Global.* London: Verso

United Nations, Department of Economic and Social Affairs (UNDESA) (2019) *World Urbanization Prospects: The 2018 Revision.* New York: United Nations

United Nations Development Programme (UNDP) (2017) *Income inequality trends in sub-Saharan Africa: Divergence, Determinants and Consequences.* New York: United Nations

United Nations Human Settlements Programme (UN-Habitat) & IHS-Erasmus University Rotterdam (2018) *The State of African Cities 2018: The geography of African investment.* (Wall RS, Maseland J, Rochell K & Spaliviero M). United Nations Human Settlements Programme (UN-Habitat)

PART I

The national in urban Africa

Simon Bekker

Four case studies of the role of the national regime in postcolonial African cities are presented.

Successive post-independence regimes in Cameroon employed Yaoundé, the capital city, as the terrain upon which they built a series of national projects: iconographic and architectural examples are provided as well as the political use of urban spaces. These new forms of urban geology which include 'global' projects in the capital city reflect the symbolic power of the Cameroonian nation, as defined by successive regimes.

The next two cases – sited in the Gauteng province of South Africa and the Greater Cairo City Region in Egypt – both consider the rhetoric of their national regimes regarding the need to decentralise power to lower levels of government whilst maintaining authority in national hands, in reality. In the case of Johannesburg and Tshwane, both metro governments in Gauteng, the national regime's promise of fairer treatment of households living in informal dwellings is not realised partially because of little real devolved authority over housing matters. In the case of Greater Cairo, equally, devolution to both regional as well as local scales of state authority are limited partially because of confusing legislation. The recent declaration of a new Egyptian capital city in the desert is an illustration of national authority taking critical urban decisions on its own.

In both cases, moreover, the other major factor inhibiting decentralisation is the limited and variable devolution of financial resources. Examples of local 'popular' initiatives to improve public participation are given and are judged not to have the promise of replication on scale as a result of financial constraints at local urban level. Authority over finances remains largely in national hands, formal legislation and rhetoric notwithstanding.

In our introductory chapter, Therborn defines the postcolonial route to modernity as involving attempts to 'nationalise colonialism' where capital cities are distinguished by an enduring duality between the ex-colonial and the indigenous city, leading in turn to the emergence of a sharp division between a small political elite and large popular masses. This depiction does some justice to the current urban realities in Yaoundé, Cairo and Gauteng. It is also a useful manner to introduce the fourth case study of this part of the book. Kinshasa is the capital city of the Democratic Republic of the Congo (DRC). Located on the southern banks of the Congo River, it has grown rapidly both in population and in area. It was declared a province of the DRC in the 1960s. The geographic area comprises three types of urban settlement: the former colonial centre where many national state activities are situated, the neighbouring planned area where land and urban infrastructure are under municipal administration, and the peripheral area (the largest of the three) where such administration is largely absent.

This case study focuses on the role of chiefs and traditional authorities in Kinshasa. Given a city and a country characterised by a small political elite and large popular masses, traditional authorities – particularly in the periphery of Kinshasa – continue to play important roles in the lives of urban residents. Moreover, in 1996, the national regime decided to establish a state body designed to enable coexistence of state and traditional authority in Kinshasa and in the rest of the country.

These four case studies illustrate the challenges African national regimes face in their capital cities since national leaders and new elites are required to cohabit with residents in slum areas, *bidonvilles* and informal settlements, with newly arrived migrants and with traditional authorities, their chiefs and their clans. 'Nationalising colonialism', to use Therborn's term, is no easy task.

CHAPTER 2

National projects in a postcolonial capital city: The example of Yaoundé

Jean-Pierre Togolo

Introduction

Since achieving independence in 1960, the Central African nation-state of Cameroon has had three different political regimes, each of which used the capital city of Yaoundé to represent not only the emergence of a new nation, but also to reflect the power of the State. This chapter aims to focus on the role of national influences on Yaoundé, the capital city, while the influences of the global and the popular will also be identified. Emphasis will be placed on the illustration of the differing representations of the capital city through examples of changes observed particularly in the built environment of Yaoundé. Each of the three national regimes developed public policies that singled out Yaoundé as the capital city. The implementation of these national policies in the capital city is the first aim of this chapter. Their consequences for city residents in terms of nation-building and state formation is the second.

After a brief historical overview of the emergence of Yaoundé and the introduction of Cameroon's three postcolonial regimes (Section 2), the focus of this chapter will be on the identification and implementation of the differing ideologies of the three regimes regarding the capital city (Section 3). Subsequently, the focus will shift to the consequences of this implementation, in particular by identifying certain forms of monumentality and name changes in the city, as well as the construction of commercial infrastructure by national and international businesses (Section 4).

Before concluding, the use by citizenry of particular sites in the capital city to express political and more general opposition to national regimes is addressed (Section 5). Since the capital city is widely perceived to be where political power is wielded nationally, opposition forces, both symbolically as well as in terms of 'counter-power,' often employ the same venues.

The conclusion (Section 6) assesses the influence of national regime politics on developments in the capital city while indicating that global as well as popular forces have also played a role. In addition, these regime politics employ both indigenous African as well as global urban elements.

A brief history of Yaoundé and the emergence of Cameroon's three postcolonial regimes

Yaoundé is situated in the space that caught the attention of German explorers in 1887. A space between 11 to 15 days of walking from the coast in the middle of a lush forest described as one of 'picturesque beauty.' The city was established in 1889 as a military post by two German officers, Kund and Tappenbeck (Von Morgen 1972), and served as a strategic base for the German administration in southern Cameroon, through which it controlled the hinterland. This security policy, according to official German colonial records, was to counter violent threats from local African kingdoms, in particular from incursions of Ngila, where Chief Vuté was 'famous for his slave trade in the region' (Von Morgen 1972). This policy, far from being limited to the protection of the populations of the region, was also a strategy to provide the military post with greater military protection and to lay the foundations for future conquests into present-day northern Cameroon (Essomba 2005: 258).

After the First World War in 1914, Germany lost its colony of Cameroon to the Allied forces. Great Britain established itself in the western part of what had become a Trust Territory, while France administered the eastern part of the territory – designated Western Cameroon and Eastern Cameroon, respectively. During this phase, until its independence, Yaoundé was the capital of French Cameroon. On 1 January 1960, Yaoundé was confirmed as the capital of postcolonial Eastern Cameroon. One year later, in 1961, French and British Cameroon formed a federal republic and Yaoundé was declared the federal capital.

The population of Yaoundé has expanded rapidly in the years since independence. Its population grew from 89 969 in 1962 during the first postcolonial *federal* regime, to 313 706 in 1976 during the second postcolonial *unitary* regime and then to 2 440 462 in 2015 during the third regime under President Biya. Today, it is the second-largest city in Cameroon after Douala (MINDUH 2010: 21).

According to Debbasch et al., a political regime designates the institutions and political personnel of a state. Accordingly, it is clear that a political regime involves two aspects: the institutional form of power, but also the practices of the leaders linked to the exercise of this power (Debbasch et al. 2001: 357).

This definition leads us to consider two essential changes in Cameroon after independence. The first one was a constitutional change which marked the country's conversion from a federal state to a unitary state on 1 October 1972, both under the presidency of Ahmadou Ahidjo. The second was a presidential transition that took place on 6 November 1982. It marked the end of Ahidjo's presidency and the start of the Biya regime. Thus, the history of postcolonial Cameroon may be divided into three regimes:

1.   the federal regime under Ahidjo (1961–1972),
2.   the unitary regime under Ahidjo (1972–1982) and
3.   the unitary regime under Biya since 1982.

Figure 1: Extension of the city of Yaoundé between 1960 and 2010

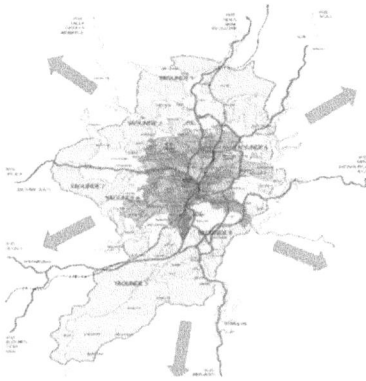

	1962	2010
Area	2 920 ha	31 000 ha
Population	89 969	2 400 000
Average annual growth	1.6%	6.8%

Source: Adapted from Plan d'Urbanisme Directeur Yaounde 2020 (CUY 2008:34)

These different political regimes each developed their own system of ideas, beliefs, opinions and rules that influenced the processes of construction and change of the capital city.

Ideological impact

The ideological impact of the federal regime under Ahidjo on the public policies of the capital city

The system of ideas on which this federal regime was based revolved principally around the assertion of the power of the state over its entire territory. Apart from multiple public services, policies reflected a distinct desire to concentrate most of the power around the president of the republic to whom the government was answerable. This centralisation of presidential power in a federal regime – seemingly contradictory in terms – may be explained by the regime's commitment, in the late 1950s and early 1960s, to put down the 'rebellion' led by nationalists of the Union of the Peoples of Cameroon (UPC) (Eboua 1995: 31–35). Significant military force was employed by the first postcolonial government and this left it with established central authority, albeit in a federal regime.

If public policy is understood to mean the 'interventions of an authority vested with public power and governmental legitimacy in a specific area of society or power' (Thoenig 2014), then the main such policy of the federal regime in Yaoundé began with two urban plans: the Urban Plan (PU) in 1963 and the specific Master Plan for Yaoundé a few years later.

Approved by a decree in December 1963, the PU was developed by the federal regime to ensure the well-being of the population, with focus on three main goals: (1) to improve residential space by extending the urban perimeter, (2) to clean up the working-class suburbs by removing the traditional low-cost shacks and slums, (3) to adapt infrastructures and services in the city to the functions and roles for which they were assigned. In this last aspect, action consisted of reducing or extending residential space, and where necessary, redeploying it along the main roads (Ngwé 1982).

Through these provisions, the federal regime ordered and guided the development of the capital city (and other large urban areas) according to its ideology. The desire to adapt infrastructure to the functions of the city is a testimony to the desire to assert the power it has inherited and exercise it by renewing the urban landscape of the capital city. This is the same vision that seems to be pursued in the second public policy, the Urban Management Master Plan (SDAU), drawn up shortly after the implementation of the first one. The SDAU was an ambitious public policy designed solely for Yaoundé, which aimed at comprehensive implementation by the year 2000. By taking up some aspects of the PU, the SDAU intended to realise the following five goals:

1.   Adapting infrastructure to the function of the federal capital.
2.   Establishing a balance between residential zones and economic activities.
3.   Incorporating peripheral areas through the development of non-urban, urban and suburban spaces.
4.   Creating a city centre in order to accommodate high-level structures necessary to fulfil its role as capital.
5.   Creating structural hubs within the suburbs, adapting and rehabilitating the working-class districts. (Ngwé 1982: 81)

Furthermore, in order to achieve these goals, the federal regime adapted local urban administration by amending the status of the municipality of Yaoundé. In 1967, the urban district of Yaoundé became an urban municipality falling under a 'special regime'. In fact, the functions of an elected mayor at the head of the urban municipality were assigned to a government delegate appointed by presidential decree. The activities of the delegate in the performance of his or her duties were defined by provisions carefully established by the federal regime, which had supervisory authority. Effectively, the delegate exercised the functions generally assigned to the elected mayor of an ordinary urban municipality, but did not preside over the municipal council (Kuoh 1992: 88). Nonetheless, the delegate was granted discretionary authority to manage the capital city according to the ideological orientation of the federal regime.

The ideological impact of the unitary regime under Ahidjo on the public policies of the capital city

The unitary regime period under Ahidjo was from 1972 to 1982. Through the merger of the federal institutions in 1972, the unitary regime under Ahidjo further centralised and consolidated its power, such as by declaring Yaoundé the capital city of the new unitary state (Azevedo 1989). In particular, the ideology of the unitary regime was based upon a single political party, the National Union of Cameroon (UNC) (Bwele 1981). The urban public policies of this party influenced specific developments in the capital city during this regime.

The ideological involvement of Ahidjo in the construction of the capital city can be observed in the departments created for this purpose. Mainly attached to the central government, these departments constituted the spearhead through which the regime controlled urban growth in Cameroon. A status report on Yaoundé drawn up by the urban planning department revealed various urban structures and their features whose fragmented and heterogeneous appearance in both residential as well as commercial zones left the impression of anarchic living. In light of this situation, the government of the unitary state planned to transform the urban space of the capital city by establishing public policies whose implementation was intended to lead to effective operational urban management. These specifically consisted of the Mission for Management and Maintenance of Urban and Rural Lands (MATEUR) and the Société Immobilière du Cameroun (SIC), for property development.

The application of these public policies in the capital city minimised the participation of local administration. Under the unitary regime of Ahidjo, Yaoundé fell under the responsibility of an officer-in-charge appointed at national level to head the urban municipality. In its organisation, the municipality retained the structure established under the federal regime. That is, it was a decentralised public authority with a legal personality and financial autonomy (Kuoh 1992: 86). In practice, the government delegate appointed by presidential decree exercised the function of a mayor, acting as the political authority of the national government (Bwele 1981). Visibly, the Ahidjo regime reframed the status of the municipality through measures that reinforced state authority over local urban government (Law no. 74/23 of 2 December 1974). In addition, the national government had the primary responsibility of establishing the urban planning documents that the local urban government were called upon to implement. In effect, for all urban areas nationally, control over the management of municipalities was provided at national level by the Ministry of Territorial Administration and applied at local level by the governor and the prefect of the territorial administration where the local community was based.

The ideological impact of the unitary regime under Biya on the public policies of the capital city

When Paul Biya took over as president of Cameroon on 6 November 1982 after the resignation of his predecessor, a decisive turning point in the proposed political life of Cameroon took place. Envisaged political changes were conceived within the context of what was called *progressive liberalisation*. Three years later, in 1985, one year after the failure of an attempted state coup, the president established his own political party, the Cameroon People's Democratic Movement (CPDM) and thereby marked an ideological breakaway from his predecessor. The essential aspects of the doctrine of this new party as well as its guidelines for government action are carefully set out in a book that Paul Biya published in 1986, entitled, *Pour le libéralisme communautaire*.

In reality, *community liberalism* is an ideology through which the Biya regime planned to promote a democratic awakening in Cameroon through top-down rule. This ideology is based upon values that promote the sharing of customs of the multiple ethnic groups of Cameroon, each considered an integral part of the Cameroonian nation (Mono Ndjana 1989: 31).

The construction of the nation-state as conceived in the ideology of the Biya regime requires the consolidation of national integration. He asserted this under these terms:

> We must give all Cameroonians a sense of their existential solidarity, the basis of the optimal deployment of the vital forces essential for the acceleration of the general progress of the country. I therefore consider the achievement of national integration, the supreme phase of national unity, to be the main historical and priority work that I must undertake with all Cameroonians. (Biya 1986: 30) [own translation]

Contrary to the ideology of the National Union advocated by the unitary regime under Ahidjo, Biya's national integration 'demonstrates the desire to move from a juxtaposition to a fusion of cultural realities through links that the regime intends to encourage between Cameroonians,' according to Mono Ndjana (1989: 33). To achieve this, the regime needed a strategic location to realise this new orientation of national policy. Yaoundé seemed appropriate because it was the seat of state institutions, and so would serve as a showcase of the country both domestically as well as internationally.

One of the first decisions of the Biya regime regarding the capital city can be traced to the local government reform of 1987. Pursuant to law no. 87-015 of 15 July 1987, a decree was signed to rename the city's municipality into the Urban Community of Yaoundé (CUY). The new name described a decentralised public authority that grouped together and coordinated the activities of the four municipalities of the arrondissements that Yaoundé had by that point.

In effect, urban public policy in Yaoundé was controlled by the administration of the central government. At the level of the different arrondissements of the capital city, responsible for local administration, elected mayors chaired arrondissement councils (UNDP 2002). Many decisions at this level required ratification from the community council of Yaoundé itself. Instead of an elected city mayor, the government delegate, appointed by the President of the Republic, presided over the community council of the city and authorised the decisions it took (CUY 2008: 39). In 2008, this centralised approach to governance in the capital city was concretised in the Urban Master Plan (PDU) of Yaoundé horizon 2020.

Accordingly, it is clear that many of the urban public policies developed and applied in Yaoundé after 1960 were influenced both by the somewhat divergent ideologies of the three postcolonial regimes as well as by the fact that they wished to implement particular policies in their capital city with the intention of symbolising the emergence of an independent African nation-state. It is also apparent that these regimes believed they required centralised authority over their capital city in this endeavour. We will now turn to the visible consequences of these policies on the built environment of Yaoundé.

Transformation of the built environment of the capital city

The two Cameroonian presidents and their central governments – largely by way of their control over Yaoundé's local governments – brought about visible changes in the capital city. Three have been selected for discussion, one during each of the three postcolonial regimes. These cases reflect the use of the capital city in the process of nation-building and of expressing national state power.

The construction of public and commercial buildings in Yaoundé

Changes and additions to the built environments of capital cities, particularly in the years after independence from colonial rule, may fruitfully be viewed in the context of nation-building (Bekker & Therborn 2012). In this regard, Maurice Agulhon states that 'political power aims at being recognised, identified and, if possible, favourably appreciated by means of a whole system of signs and emblems, the principal ones of which are those that strike the eye' (Agulhon 1988). Here, the focus is on the construction of buildings of both national and international significance in Yaoundé as well as changes to the names of boulevards and main streets in the capital city (Pondi 2012; Essono 2016).

1961 was the year of reunification of Western and Eastern Cameroon and the establishment of a federal republic. Accordingly, Yaoundé represented both the capital of the Eastern federated state and the capital of the federal state. It accommodated 2 governments, with 7 ministers for the Eastern State and 20 for the federal state (Ze Nguele 1972: 1096). The city also had two legislative assemblies with their respective administrations (Bwele 1981). In short, in a physical and visible sense, the Federal Assembly of Cameroon, the Supreme Court, and other ministerial buildings, contributed to symbolising the power of the new state in its new federal capital.

At the global level, the confirmation of Cameroon's independence led to the need for the capital city to play a role in international affairs. Yaoundé served as a showcase for independent Cameroon when it hosted the head office of the Common African, Malagasy and Mauritian Organisation (OCAM); the African and Malagasy Intellectual Property Office (OAMPI), which later became the African Intellectual Property Organisation (OAPI); the Regional Bureau of Unesco as well as other bodies (Ze Nguele 1972: 1096). The architectural style chosen for these buildings – a modern mix with German, French and African roots – is also apparent in the headquarters of state and private enterprises: the Société Nationale des Hydrocarbures (SNH) and the, then, Central Information Technology Directorate as well as the head office of Cameroon Radio and Television (CRTV) are examples.

Change of road names in Yaoundé

Many of the main streets in Yaoundé continue to bear names that signal both the period of their construction as well as people of note at that period. First are the names of religious personalities: *Rue Mgr* René Graffin, *avenue Mgr* Vieter, *Mgr* François-Xavier Vogt. Second, the names of French doctors and soldiers: *avenue* Jamot, *avenue* Maréchal Foch, and third, as Cameroon changed its status from Trust Territory to sovereign independence: *avenue* Kennedy, *avenue* Charles de Gaulle, *Rue* Valery Giscard d'Estaing, *avenue* Churchill, and *avenue* Jean Paul II (Pondi 2012).

After independence, a number of boulevards and streets changed their names to commemorate important dates and personalities reflecting the sovereign independence of the nation: the Boulevard *du 20 mai* and the Boulevard *de la reunification* as well as the Squares *de l'indépendance* and *du cinquantenaire* (the 50th centenary of Independence). L'*Avenue Ahmadou Ahidjo* and l'*Avenue John Ngu Foncha* (a former prime minister of Cameroon) pay tribute to two Cameroonian leaders. The table below records a number of the changes that have taken place after 1960, identifying old and new names.

Table 1: Some of the road name changes in Yaoundé since 1960

Formerly	Currently
Abyedege asi/Bilig bi Embumbun	Boulevard du 20 mai
Boulevard Charles de Gaulle	Rue Essono Ela
Carrefour Bouillet	Place Ahmadou Ahidjo
Plateau atemenque	Boulevard de la Réunification
Mfundi assi	Av. Ahmadou Ahidjo
Elig Mballa Enyengue	John Ngu Foncha
Vallée de Dzungolo	Av. Kennedy

The national flag and reunification

The design of the Cameroonian flag predated independence. Adopted in October 1957 by the Legislative Assembly of Cameroon (ALCAM), the legislators selected a tri-colour flag with vertical stripes of equal size from the left to the right, in green, red and yellow. The green symbolised the large tropical forest of south Cameroon, the red indicated power and the blood of the Cameroonians shed during the struggle for independence, while the yellow represents the sun, the Sahelian soil and the savannah of the northern part of the country (Mbarga 2014).

Changes made to the flag after 1960 are evidently related to the country's march towards unification. In 1961, the flag was enriched by two gold stars incorporated in the green stripe, representing the two federated states and, from 21 May 1975, the two were replaced by a single star in the red stripe following the reunification that took place in 1972.

It was in Yaoundé that the flag was hoisted for the first time on 10 November 1957 by the then Prime Minister, André Marie Mbida (Bwele 1981). Subsequently, it has been used in official ceremonies country-wide. It may be seen in front of many public buildings in the capital city and its third expression – that of the reunification of the East and West symbolised by a golden star – was accompanied by the construction of the Monument to Reunification in Yaoundé (see Figure 3).

The capital city as the site of claims to 'counter power'

African capital cities may be viewed as public sites where African governments express 'power over' their citizenry. This 'power over', however, differs from 'power to': most administrations lack the know-how and resources to address the city services and other needs of their burgeoning urban populations (Bekker & Therborn 2012).

Figure 2: Evolution of Cameroon's flag since 1957

| 1957–1961 | 1961–1972 | 1972– |
| State of Cameroon | Federal Republic of Cameroon | |

Source: Essono (2016: 238)

Figure 3: Monument to Reunification

Source: FischerFotos

As a consequence, opposition forces often use sites in the capital city to publicly express their resistance to the national government. The Boulevard *du 20 mai* is an appropriate example. Located in the city centre, the Boulevard *du 20 mai* publicly and symbolically recalls the 1972 transition of the federal state to a unitary nation-state. Accordingly, as is well-known in the capital, it serves each year as the setting for the parades commemorating National Day, National Youth Day, Workers Day and several other national events. It is not surprising, therefore, that opposition forces and opposition national parties use the same Boulevard to publicly express their claims to voice and to 'counter power.' In 1990, a number of political parties demanded of President Biya that the next national elections be multi-party. These demands were publicly expressed and widely broadcast from the Boulevard.

Conclusion

Since independence in 1960, the built environment of Yaoundé has been deeply influenced by national government interventions. The skyline of the central city illustrates modern buildings built to accommodate central state and new private sector edifices, reflecting both domestic as well as global interests. The names of the capital's main streets, moreover, identify both earlier leadership as well as new nomenclature reflecting postcolonial iconic dates and events as well as leadership.

These changes are due in no small measure to the postcolonial ideologies of the three regimes described above. The chronology of regimes from federal to unitary and subsequently from the rule of Ahidjo to that of Biya moreover parallels an increasingly centralised and authoritarian national control over both the capital city as well as the country as a whole. These central government and presidential interventions in Yaoundé have contributed toward the vigorous and sustained urbanisation flows into the capital city. It is somewhat surprising, moreover, that these internal migration streams have not demonstrated superior flows of members of each presidents' ethnic group to the capital during their tenures (Togolo 2019). Rather, the venue of the capital city has been identified – by both competing national political parties as well as by a restless urban citizenry drawn from Cameroon as a whole – as a public area where their opposition and displeasure may optimally be made visible and public.

In conclusion, it is not only the leaders of the central government whose top-down control has marked the urban landscape of Yaoundé but also global interests – as evidenced in their new edifices – as well as the influences of the urban citizenry. It is also worth noting that the nature of these changes to the built environment expresses a mix of African and global values. The monument to reunification, illustrated above, is an example.

References

Agulhon M (1988) *Histoire vagabonde. Tome 2. Idéologie et politique dans la France du XIX e siècle.* Paris: Gallimard

Azevedo M (1989) *Cameroon and Chad in Historical and Contemporary Perspectives.* New York: Edwin Mellen

Bekker S & Therborn G (2012) *Capital Cities in Africa: Power and Powerlessness.* Cape Town: HSRC Press

Biya P (1986) *Pour le libéralisme communautaire.* Lausanne: Pierre-Mar

Bouvier J-C & Guillon J-M (eds) (2001) *La Toponymie urbaine: Significations et enjeux, Actes du colloque d'Aix-en-Provence des 11 et 12 décembre 1998.* Paris: L'Harmattan

Bwele G (ed.) (1981) *Encyclopédie de la République Unie du Cameroun. Tome II. L'Histoire de l'Etat.* Douala: Les Nouvel

Comard-Rentz M (2006) Dénomination et changement de nom de rue: Enjeu politique, enjeux de mémoire. Unpublished thesis, Université Lumière Lyon 2

CUY (2008) *Yaounde 2020 Plan Directeur D'Urbanisme.* Yaoundé: Ministere du Developpement Urbain et de L'Habitat

Debbasch C, Bourdon J, Pontier J-M & Ricci J-C (2001) *Lexique de politique 7e édition.* Paris: Dalloz

Eboua S (1995) *Ahidjo et la logique du pouvoir.* Paris: L'Harmattan

Essomba PB (2005) Voies de communications et espaces culturels au Cameroun sous domination allemande 1884–1916. Doctoral thesis, Université de Yaoundé I

Essono J-M (2016) *Yaoundé une ville, une histoire (1888–2014). Encyclopédie des mémoires d'Ogola Ewondo, la ville aux 'mille collines'.* Yaoundé: Asuzoa

Kuoh C (1992) *Le Cameroun de l'après-Ahidjo (1982–1992). Tome 3 de mon témoignage.* Paris: Karthala

Mbarga G (2014) *Le drapeau du Cameroun, le vexille étoilé.* Paris: L'Harmattan

MINDUH (2010) Urbanisation : les ambitions de nos villes (urban dream in Cameroon). *Cameroon Tribune,* Hors-série

Mono Ndjana H (1989) *Pour comprendre le Libéralisma Communautaire de Paul Biya.* Yaoundé: CEPER

Ngwé E (1982) La croissance démographique accélérée de Yaoundé entre 1957 et 1976 et l'inadaptation des équipements sanitaires, scolaires et culturels. Bordeaux III

Olivier M (2015, 7 mai) Cameroun: Musée national, une machine à explorer le temps. *Jeune Afrique.* https://www.jeuneafrique.com/230961/culture/cameroun-mus-e-national-une-machine-explorer-le-temps/

Pondi JE (2012) *(Re) découvrir Yaoundé! Une fresque historique et diplomatique de la capitale camerounaise, Yaoundé.* Yaoundé: Afric'Evei

Tamo Tatiétsé T & Bidja A (2002) Impact du parc automobile et du linéaire de voirie sur la mobilité urbaine à Yaoundé (Cameroun). *CODATU X.* pp. 483–489

Thoenig J-C (2014) Politique publique. In: L Boussaguet, S Jacquot & P Ravinet (eds) *Dictionnaire des politiques publiques 4e édition précédée d'un nouvel avant-propos.* pp. 420–427

Togolo JP (2019) Yaoundé après l'indépendance: Les changements migratoires dans le processus d'urbanisation d'une ville-capitale 1960–2010. Doctoral thesis, Stellenbosch University

Touna M (2004) *De la planification urbaine à l'urbanisme des projets de lotissements au Cameroun : Impacts sur les stratégies d'accès à la propriété et aux services urbains.* Yaoundé

UNDP (2002) Diagnostic de la délinquance urbaine à Yaoundé. Nairobi: UN-Habitat. pp. 17–18

Von Morgen C (1972) *A travers le Cameroun du Sud au Nord: Voyages et explorations dans l'arrière-pays de 1889 à 1891.* Traduction, présentation, commentaires bibliographie et index de Philippe Laburthe-Tolra. Cameroun: Archives d'histoire et de sociologie de l'Université fédérale du Cameroun

Ze Nguele R (1972) Problèmes démographiques de la croissance urbaine à Yaoundé. *Croissance urbaine en Afrique Noire et à Madagascar. Tome 2.* pp. 1089–1103

CHAPTER 3

Lip service: How voices from informal settlements were sidelined during the first decade of local democracy in South Africa

Liela Groenewald

Introduction

A majority of the South African population has been urban since the 1990s (Kok et al. 2006: 11). Over 22% of this population lives in the province of Gauteng, which, after the Western Cape, was the country's only other province experiencing net in-migration at the time of the last census (StatsSA 2011: 2). Local government in the province of Gauteng includes the three Category A or Metropolitan municipalities, namely the City of Johannesburg, the City of Tshwane, and the City of Ekurhuleni. This chapter provides an examination of the top-down treatment by two of these metros of those living in their informal settlements over the course of the first decade of democratic local government (2000–2010), during which both cities were governed by the country's liberation movement turned ruling party, the African National Congress (ANC).

The City of Johannesburg Metropolitan Municipality is a single tier local authority incorporating a geographical area formerly governed by 11 different local authorities with disparate capacities. Johannesburg had begun as a tent camp that mushroomed there during the gold rush to the Witwatersrand from 1886 but had grown quickly and sufficiently to support travelling traders and several sectors of industry. For most of the city's history, the majority black population has been confined to overcrowded residential areas on the periphery of the city and largely excluded from the white centre.

The City of Tshwane Metropolitan Municipality governs the city of Pretoria and its surrounds. Pretoria had been founded as capital city of the *Boer* republic, the

Zuid-Afrikaansche Republiek, in 1860. The geographical boundaries of the city have changed a number of times over the course of its history. Coinciding with the date of the local government elections that took place just after the period covered by this study, the incorporation of an additional hinterland municipality, Metsweding, made Tshwane the third largest municipality in the world by surface area, at 6 368km^2 (City of Tshwane n.d.).

Municipal expenditure per capita, including investment in infrastructure, is much higher in the metropolitan municipalities than in South Africa's peri-urban and rural areas (SACN 2011). The impressive record of house building in the metropolitan municipalities has, however, been 'over-shadowed by the sizeable, expanding population of these areas compared to the rest of the country' (SACN 2011: 50). The building of record numbers of low-income housing has not prevented substantial proportional growth in the informal settlements of the urban areas of Gauteng and Cape Town, compared to a slight decline in the proportion of informality in the rest of the country.

The ways in which the state takes account of, and acts on, informality presents an important area for considering state-society relations (UN-Habitat 2003). The South African challenge has its roots in colonial and apartheid legislation which impacted decisively the incidence, form and distribution across the landscape and population, of informal housing. The tangible decline in recent electoral support of the ANC in South African metropolitan councils, moreover, raises the question of state-society relations under early democratic rule by South Africa's liberation party. As other research has indicated (Huchzermeyer & Karam 2006; Robins 2002), strategies of the post-1994 government have perpetuated and exacerbated informal settlement.

Democratic South Africa, in constitutional terms, endorses a three-sphere (rather than three-tier) system of government – the national, the provincial and the local – so as to offer equal voice to elected leaders in each sphere. In addition, in the local (and metropolitan) sphere, elections produce an equal mix of proportional representation and ward-based direct representation of individual candidates. Both these constitutional principles are aimed at ensuring that voice is offered to individuals at local level, the first through elected councillors by political party and the second through elected ward councillors representing residents' interests at the micro-level. This is the basis for the national government's pledge that public participation in planning and implementation of policy includes the voice of the poor and of residents in informal settlements.

Along with basic service delivery strategies, legislation that obliges local authorities to consult their constituent communities (Republic of South Africa 2000) has accompanied the consolidation of democratic institutions in South Africa. Ward-level participation feeds into each municipality's Integrated Development Plan (IDP), which becomes a legally binding programme of development and expenditure upon being ratified by a local council (Republic of South Africa 2000). Characteristics of integrated development planning include community participation; a strategic focus to make the most of limited resources; integration between sectors; and to have an outcomes and delivery orientation. The municipalities must prepare five-year IDPs that are accompanied by a financial plan. Every year, the IDPs are also subject to a review process.

This pledge of the national government to ensure listening to popular voices from below through its public institutions, both elected as well as appointed, is the focus of this chapter. An overview of analyses focused on bottom-up participation by urban residents is followed by a short summary of the research methodology used. Subsequently, five constraints 'from above' on real devolved power to the metros of Johannesburg and of Tshwane and to their residents will be identified.

Before concluding, the role that the state plays in the production of urban informal settlements is broached. The conclusion itself will argue that the national state's centralising forces severely limit the extent to which local state institutions are able to incorporate the voices of informal settlement residents into their planning and practice. Accordingly, the national rhetoric of democratic participation, particularly in South Africa's metropolitan areas, is not accompanied by concomitant practice.

Shortcomings of formal participation from the bottom up

State-created mechanisms of participation are what Cornwall (2002) has labelled 'invited' spaces of participation in order to distinguish them from 'invented' spaces of participation in which communities respond on their own terms. Since only genuinely enabled citizens can realise the potential of popular participation to influence government, truly democratic participation spaces are difficult to achieve even in societies with low levels of inequality (Esau 2007).

In the South African context, invited spaces of participation have been criticised by many scholars. These state-created mechanisms of participation may

- tie communities to pre-set agendas (Heller 2009; Putu 2006);
- be dominated by ward councillors' political allies (Sinwell 2010);
- rely on overly technical discourses that ordinary people find difficult to follow (Putu 2006);
- treat as aberrations the differences within communities (Friedman 2007);
- tend to de-radicalise or 'domesticate' social movements (Sinwell 2008: 245);
- privilege the organised over the non-organised (Friedman 2007);
- manage to attract particularly the middle class (Bekker & Leildé 2003); and
- present barriers to the poor, in particular those in the informal sector (Friedman 2007; Mohamed 2006).

These shortcomings of formal participation processes have been offered as de facto explanations for the slow progress with regard to the social welfare of poor communities. In most cases listed here, the focus is upon difficulties regarding the mobilisation of the agency of the poor, both from below as well as via the local authority. Moreover, this planned mobilisation ought to take place within state-created institutions.

Methodology

This chapter draws on a study of the local state housing sector in democratic South Africa as it responds to informal settlement (Groenewald 2012). The research took the approach of studying up to focus on local state approaches to informal settlement in two major cities for the decade after the local government elections held on 5 December 2000. Until 2000, the continued reliance on racially defined voting districts had extended white control at the local level, in what has been termed a 'delayed transition at the local level' (Bekker et al. 1997: 38–43). The period studied therefore represents the first decade of local democracy in South Africa, during which the character of the post-apartheid local state has emerged, together with the kind of urban citizenship that has been constructed under the ANC. The research sites were the local municipalities in the cities of Johannesburg and Tshwane, which, for the period covered by the project, were two of six metropolitan councils among the 284 South African municipalities. In-depth interviews were conducted with 23 senior appointed and elected officials responsible for housing. More detail on these interviews is available (Groenewald 2012).

During the research process it became clear that in each of these two cities a dedicated unit coordinated the planning process and drew up a coherent IDP, taking into account the needs voiced during this annual community consultation process on the one hand, and the electoral promises of the majority party, on the other. Long-term strategic city priorities and sector-specific inputs were also considered when council made adjustments to the IDP. Actors within the local state felt that the legislated obligation to consult communities was indeed being met through an annual round of community meetings. They further reported routinely going beyond the legal requirements of the IDP process. In both cities, the mayor had arranged opportunities for direct engagement with community members, departmental community meetings were sometimes held, and service delivery satisfaction surveys had been conducted. Every participant in the study mentioned instances where they had personally been involved in community consultation. Involvement was therefore limited neither to elected politicians nor to appointed officials; neither to policy decision-makers nor to those responsible for practical implementation. Both elected and appointed staff spent a substantial amount of time in evening and weekend meetings listening to community members. Further consultation of specific communities had also been a requirement of specific court judgments.

A number of the most influential participants in this study were asked to comment on the relative importance of a range of influences over local state policy and practice, particularly regarding participation. In addition to the internal shortcomings of formal participation listed above, five factors that limit the reach of local participation can be distinguished in the accounts of these senior decision-makers within the housing sector. These five structural constraints are

- planning priorities set from above,
- the separation of implementation and accountability,
- the failure of the courts to provide consistent protection to the poor,
- ineffective needs assessment and
- inadequate funding.

Constraints on real devolved power to local metropolitan authorities: Factors from above that impede local state responsivity

Priorities from above determine funding and performance targets

Participants indicated that the intentions of the ruling party played an important part in determining local state programmes. The IDP had to balance needs articulated by communities with the priorities and electoral promises of the ruling party. Councillors and officials described the mechanisms by which ruling party priorities were incorporated into planning in very similar terms. Elected councillors valued their party caucus as a forum that could be used to ensure cohesion in policy and practice, while the Mayoral Committee provided direction with regard to various policy areas. This was the case in both cities.

The participants also explained how their performance management was informed by political priorities. The mayor of a city would pronounce certain priorities during the State of the City address. These priorities would feed into the IDP, which would in turn be used by city departments to develop their detailed scorecards. A city's Annual Performance Plan would include all these detailed targets.

The system mimicked the target development process described by officials in the provincial and national government. At provincial level, the budget speeches of members of the Executive Council would feed into the targets of provincial departments, while at the national level, goals set in the president's State of the Nation Address would be broken down into various ministers' portfolios, and this would be broken down into targets for various sections of a national department. The targets of provincial governments would of course inform their budget allocations to municipalities.

Over and above this, officials in the national Department of Human Settlements were responsible for ensuring alignment between the IDPs, provincial plans and the national planning framework. The Department of Human Settlements conducted imbizos that gave community members the opportunity to talk directly to staff of the department. Actors in the national Department of Human Settlements said that strategic priorities were driven by articulated demand. They expected municipal IDPs to reflect the priorities expressed in the president's State of the Nation address and national and provincial priorities, along with local demand. Central state participants were frustrated when municipal IDPs did not reflect national and provincial priorities which, they argued, were also informed by articulated demand. Projects needed to be initiated by municipalities, but aligned with provincial plans, otherwise they would simply not be funded by the national department. The devil lies in the detail: due to the timing of the financial year-end at municipal and provincial levels, provincial planning is completed earlier in the fiscal year than municipal planning which places municipalities at a disadvantage. All in all, the metropolitan local state was under significant pressure to align its own plans to those of the central and provincial government.

Separation of implementation and accountability

In the local state housing sector responding to informal settlement, the sway of central and provincial government over local government was further entrenched by the fact that accountability was located at a different level of government to that for primary control over funding and implementation.

Participants' descriptions divulge a practical separation between those who are actually responsible for implementing the bulk of housing projects and those who consult communities.

The central government divided the housing budget among South Africa's nine provinces which then had control over the further division of the budget among allocations to municipalities and the provincial government's own operational and capital expenditure, including housing projects. No downward accountability to specific constituencies is built into the design of South Africa's provincial level of government. Instead, all elected representatives come from a party list.

Provincial officials generally described their role as funded delivery. A technical feasibility study, which included a land suitability survey, was conducted as part of the planning of each provincial housing project, and layout plans were advertised for public comment. Provincial plans would usually be presented to affected communities prior to approval. 'Greenfields' projects, in which nobody resided on the land earmarked for development, would involve no community consultation, while other cases might warrant social impact assessment. A dedicated communication division was responsible for handling housing project-related queries from the general public. In some cases, opportunities for direct engagement between the provincial government and the community were arranged by the municipal speaker's office, when the municipality held meetings in informal settlements, or when the central government held imbizos. For example, when the members of surrounding suburban communities had initially objected to a mixed income state-supported development on the grounds that it would affect their property values, these objections had decreased over time, said Ned, a provincial official. Participants in the provincial government sometimes attended community project updates and community consultation opportunities arranged by municipalities so that the relevant background or technical information could be provided. Consultation by the provincial government which exercised the primary control over decision-making about housing was therefore primarily reactive and technical.

City councillors in the study considered their engagement with communities a critical contribution to the housing process, which finds some support in the fact that councillors' knowledge of the grassroots level was both acknowledged and valued by their provincial counterparts. Provincial participants said that they relied on municipalities to conduct in-depth consultation and to provide information about community priorities and preferences. However, the portion of the housing budget controlled by municipalities was small and funded primarily from service delivery, their current account. Although municipalities had the primary responsibility for local planning based on the IDP process, implementation of the priorities identified in the IDP depended on the size of the housing capital budget available at the local level.

Provincial participants experienced this as a functional division of labour; an experience which may well have been moulded by their location within a province where the local and provincial state is governed by the national ruling party which determines the overarching policy framework. The framework removes accountability to grassroots communities from provincial officials who implement housing projects that directly affect those communities, but at the same time, holds accountable local authorities that have limited influence over the distribution of the provincial housing budget. Officials feared that further consultation would add fuel to the fire of already frustrated communities. The leaders who were accountable to the constituencies were therefore not the ones who had real power over implementation.

In summary, a separation was practised between the provincial government responsible for budget allocation and implementation and the local state responsible for community consultation and local planning. The division of competencies between the provincial and local state left ordinary residents without direct access to or influence over the primary housing decision-makers.

Court rulings give inconsistent guidance

The local state is closest to ordinary people. It has, therefore, become the focus of popular contestations over the content of national citizenship. Compared to the rhythm of state planning processes and ruling party meetings, court judgments were ad hoc and relatively unpredictable. Nevertheless, they had a direct influence on the practice of local authorities. Two court cases against the City of Johannesburg, in which the City of Johannesburg and other government departments were challenged with respect to the provision of water and housing led to limited gains for pure communities (see Mazibuko and Others v City of Johannesburg and Others; Occupiers of 51 Olivia Road, Berea Township and 197 Main Street Johannesburg v City of Johannesburg and Others).

The local state could also seek eviction orders from the courts with regard to habitual non-payers residing in social housing, or in cases where public land had been occupied for longer than six months, or seek ownership of a bad building that had been abandoned by the owner. Although this was not raised by participants, the local state in both cities had successfully applied for several eviction orders issued under various circumstances. In the City of Tshwane, the courts were ostensibly also being used to test in which cases the city would be required to formalise or service informal settlements and when they could be evicted or tolerated while being provided with rudimentary services only. This transpired from a comment by Nellie, a Tshwane councillor, who said that legal informal settlements were 'the ones where the court has instructed us to provide services.' Court judgments, therefore, provided neither reliable relief to the poor, nor lasting guidance to the local state.

Metropolitan municipalities lobbied for greater local state control over housing programmes, partly because they had been taken to court by residents with regard to housing and shelter. But despite a number of limited victories for poor communities, the local state had also successfully applied for eviction orders issued under various circumstances. While officials and councillors in this study declared that they had no choice but to adhere to court judgments, they sometimes acted in contravention of the law by evicting residents without a court order. In the case of informal settlements razed to the ground, there was no immediate possibility of return, regardless of court rulings. The series of court cases between city residents and the local state have, therefore, not consistently resulted in the protection of the poor.

One reason for this inconsistency was apparent in the aftermath of one of the early cases of court-based contestation over citizenship that had faced the post-1994 South African government. In the prominent constitutional court case of Irene Grootboom, the provincial government was instructed to provide the funds for the relevant municipality to provide tents, toilets and water to the informal settlement community where Grootboom lived (Grootboom and Others v The Government of the Republic of South Africa and Others). The judgment also recognised the right to housing, but like other cases in which citizens have taken the state to court over services, failed to resolve the question of fiscal responsibility (Huchzermeyer 2004). While popular voices were often validated by court rulings, this did not lead to consistent improvement of the fate of South Africa's poor. A constitution that is globally renowned for obligating the state to progressively realise rights, has not sufficiently challenged a system designed to privilege central control over local spending.

Inadequate funding restricts local state responsiveness

The claim by participants that the allocated funds from the central state were insufficient for addressing the identified housing need is supported by several pieces of evidence. First, as mentioned above, the two metropolitan municipalities in this study exhausted their housing budgets by means of project implementation. Second, the number of houses that can be delivered by the local authorities based on the available subsidies constitute a small fraction of the known housing need. Given the strict criteria for subsidised housing stipulated by the national Housing Code, however, estimates of housing need are likely to underrepresent the population unable to access adequate shelter via the open market. As mentioned above, the state has also placed the burden of self-identification on those who wanted to register their need on the housing demand database. Third, the central budget allocation for Housing has never reached the 5% of the national budget that the ANC envisaged during the transition (Pottie 2003).

Local authorities each have an operating and a capital budget that must be prepared together, since commitments in the capital budget incur operating costs. Increases in operating expenditure need to be considered before decisions are made about capital projects to ensure that the budget will be balanced (ETU n.d.). Capital budgets are for longer-term developments or assets and may be funded from a combination of loans, donations, government grants, public-private partnerships or the operating income in a particular financial year (ETU n.d.). Operating budgets, on the other hand, cover the day-to-day costs and income to deliver municipal services and are funded from the rates and taxes that municipalities collect together with their equitable share of national revenue (ETU n.d.). Since the equitable share depends on the number of poor people within the municipality's area of jurisdiction, rural municipalities benefit more than urban municipalities, although the equitable share covers only a small share of municipal operating expenditure (ETU n.d.). Local authorities are therefore effectively expected to be self-sufficient for the purpose of service delivery.

The severe shortage of funds limits the capacity of the local state to respond meaningfully to the priorities identified by community consultation. These priorities and those identified in the most recent ruling party election manifesto(s) together inform the Integrated Development Plan (IDP) of each local authority. The priorities captured in the IDP determine the order in which the proposed projects for a specific financial year are funded until the budget has been fully allocated. Once the allocations have been depleted, no further projects can be approved. Compared to a properly funded local state where various models of meaningful democratic control over the budget can be pursued, inadequate funding of the local state limits the influence of community consultation to that of prioritising expenditure which essentially pits one poor community against another.

The value of prioritisation is severely diminished by the fact that only a small proportion of the population in need of assistance can be assisted with the available budget. The waiting periods that result from this relationship of need to provision vary widely but have been roughly estimated at a decade. The burden of self-identification placed on the poor has therefore been deepened by the obligation to retain the status of a qualifier for more than a decade by remaining in the lowest income category and continuing to have dependents. Should the ten-year period be sufficient for the state to provide that person's needs, but the dependents reach majority age after nine years, the prospective beneficiary would be disqualified from receiving subsidised housing. The prospective beneficiaries are effectively expected to be patient indefinitely while adequate shelter continues to elude them.

The challenge cannot be expected to dissipate, as contemporary South African cities reflect the trend of previously unparalleled urbanisation taking place across the developing world (UN 2016). In the meantime, local authorities are left with little choice but to turn to partnerships, giving the private sector exaggerated influence compared to ordinary people.

Ineffective needs assessment hinders planning and burdens the poor

In the province of Gauteng, both the high rate of in-migration and natural growth contribute to the need for housing. Local state officials and councillors were aware of projections with regard to the urban growth rate in general, including the rate of household formation in the lowest income categories and the rate of in-migration. Participants in Johannesburg mentioned that in-migration together with the rate of new household formation meant that backlogs were constantly growing. Maureen, a Johannesburg official, gave this account:

> If you look at the City's Growth and Development Strategy, it talks about all these parameters. We have got a Department of Economic Development in the City where we have got senior economists who will tell you that in terms of population growth we are going to be growing at 1.4% year in year out and because Johannesburg is the key economic hub of Africa, the City is supposed to grow at this X amount. But 9 out of 10 (times) that is not necessarily matched with available resources and that is one big challenge. ... So we are going to end up here and we hope by some miracle that we will have a blip. Because Local Authorities' funding is based on the ability to get more revenue for your Council growth and if unemployment goes up and up and up, our ability to increase our revenue base gets eroded as well. ... It sounds like an excuse for a government official to say maybe we must raise

the rates and taxes by 70%, but the truth is if you look at migration into the cities, it is higher than what we can afford.

The degree to which systematic needs assessment and projections influenced planning was explored in interviews. Census data and household surveys conducted by Statistics South Africa would inform national planning priorities and the distribution of funds, but the frequency of the census has been decreased to once every ten years. In addition, the South African census is plagued by questions about accuracy, including undercounting in excess of international benchmarks (Berkowitz 2013; Schultz 2013). Whether accurate or not, these tools appeared to be largely ignored when it came to planning at both the provincial and the local level. Instead, all participants considered principal source of information on housing need to be the housing demand database.

In 2007, the approach to housing needs assessment in the province of Gauteng had changed from that of a waiting list with limited information about prospective beneficiaries and their needs, to a demand database that disaggregated need in terms of the kind of housing that the prospective beneficiary wanted and in terms of the income category of beneficiaries. The participants in government were visibly animated by the cleaning of the demand database which also represented a way to ring-fence the vast and growing need for housing. The original post-1994 housing waiting list had been problematic because it simply contained a list of people who had indicated that they needed state subsidised housing and failed to disaggregate need. The list had not been cross-checked against other government databases to exclude non-qualifiers who had either claimed to earn lower salaries than they actually earned or who had claimed to have dependents who did not actually qualify as dependents, and people who received houses elsewhere had not been removed from the list over time.

The list was shortened by means of data cleaning exercises that removed people who were listed with incorrect ID numbers, who had obtained or applied for housing elsewhere, or who did not meet or no longer met the criteria to qualify for subsidised housing – for example, if their dependents had become adults or their salaries had increased. In addition, prospective beneficiaries on the waiting list were asked to show themselves at state housing offices. Such an indigent approach that shifts the burden of proof of poverty onto marginalised households ignores their lack of resources to prove that they qualify for assistance (McDonald & Pape 2002). For this reason, the burden of self-identification could contribute to a further underestimation of need. Following the clean-up, the total number of prospective beneficiaries in the province of Gauteng on the database had decreased from around 800 000 to over 600 000.

While the new demand database was a more reliable indication of the number of people who had self-identified and qualified for subsidised housing at a given point in time, it could not be expected to accurately reflect the need for assistance with access to shelter. In addition, because the list was not publicly available and because programmes did not respond to prospective beneficiaries in the order in which they had registered, communities had no way of knowing whether they had been bypassed and whether nepotism or corruption played a part in beneficiary selection. Moreover, the demand database was perceived to be applied in a corrupt and arbitrary manner (Rubin 2011).

While the local state broadly relied on regular community consultation to inform the IDP, the demand database where the poor had self-identified their need of housing assistance was the primary mechanism used to assess housing need.

With regard to informal settlements, shack registration exercises were conducted that could also identify where there was a need for intervention. The provincial administration had conducted an audit to identify and record the location of all informal settlements in 2005, an exercise that was mentioned and considered helpful by all the participants in understanding the demand for state-funded housing. However, information on needs assessment was held by the provincial office and did not feature prominently in the planning processes in which provincial administrators were directly involved. Since the participants were animated by the provincial audit, they appeared not to recognise the need for a method that would measure and predict need over time, rather than to provide a once-off snapshot of housing need.

To avoid shacks being used as a 'queue jumping mechanism', the allocation of subsidised housing was linked to a shack number in the city's database when the occupant of a shack became a beneficiary of a government programme, said Maureen, a Johannesburg official. This local state approach therefore served to strengthen the Housing Code focus on individual beneficiaries rather than geographic areas or communities, which in turn limited the scope of state housing assistance. Planning and budget allocations responded to a housing demand database that reflected an overly static understanding of need on the part of the central and provincial state, whose practices placed the burden of identifying need primarily on poor households rather than on the state.

In both cities, the list of people on the housing demand database did not overlap closely with the residents of informal settlements, as indicated by participants and corroborated by staff of Statistics South Africa. A substantial proportion of people living in informal settlements did not qualify for subsidised housing. In addition, many temporary workers and migrants did not want RDP housing in the city, whereas candidates for family units did not want social housing, which could entail a lifetime of paying without owning anything. Participants had taken cognisance of the fact that a one-size-fits-all approach to housing was unlikely to succeed, as many migrants did not require family housing and a substantial proportion of people without adequate housing did not qualify for fully subsidised housing.

Participants in the local state knew that the estimated need for housing was increasing at a high rate due to both internal growth and in-migration. The state actors were sufficiently familiar with the results of needs assessment exercises to be able to summarise the scope of housing backlogs in the two cities. They were aware that the bulk of housing need in the province was concentrated in the two cities and participants in each city knew in which specific parts of their city need was concentrated. Yet, projections did not play an important role in planning, as the budget allocated to the local state did not even allow it to clear housing backlogs. The number of people in need of fully or partially subsidised housing far exceeded the number that could be assisted, given the funds allocated to address informal settlement and housing. The local state did not have at its disposal any housing instrument that could adequately respond to known need or urban growth.

The obliteration of procedural justice is most starkly accentuated by participants' comments about community participation. Housing need was acute and demand was articulated at every community consultation opportunity at the local level, said Gladys, a Johannesburg official. In Johannesburg, where there was no indication of a failure to spend allocated funds, some participants feared that further consultation would serve merely to raise expectations, although no surplus remained to respond to any additional consultation. The phrase 'social exclusion,' used when multiple deprivations associated with poverty push people to the margins of society to the extent that the advantages of citizenship elude them (Abercrombie et al. 2000), can therefore be applied to the residents of informal settlements in contemporary South Africa.

Informal settlement as a product of state policy and practice

Debates about the definitions of informality will be familiar to scholars in this field. Where Huchzermeyer (2004) has argued that informality should be understood not in terms of its lacking physical or top structure, often contrasted to formal dwellings, this argument has not relied on romanticising living conditions in informal settlements. Instead, it has represented a careful and crucial shift of emphasis away from the inadequacy of the dwelling built by the poor, towards the vulnerability contributed by the state (Huchzermeyer 2011). This approach held the key to shifting the state response away from eviction and towards the improvement of tenure security and living conditions of residents of informal settlements. Nevertheless, it is often because of their gains and aspirations that residents of informal settlements exercise a choice for a precarious place in the city over no place in the city at all (Groenewald et al. 2013). Defining informal settlement in terms of its vulnerability, in particular to eviction, avoids degrading descriptions that trample on this agency, and is accurate in locating responsibility with the state.

If residents of informal settlements are unable to extract recognition and responsiveness from the local state, this cements their position of precarity and in particular, extends their risk of eviction. The additional state contributions to precarity identified here, therefore, constitute the state (re)production of informality. The theory that the state produces informal settlement has therefore been strengthened. The centralising tendency of the South African state, therefore, contributes to continued informal settlement.

This interpretation resonates with what I would like to call a Fanonian understanding of the state. Fanon (1963) locates the cause of the native with the coloniser. His argument that colonial administrations are responsible for the existence of the colonised, systematically links a series of characteristics associated with *natives* to a series of ways in which indigenous peoples are subjugated under colonialism. He demonstrates how colonialism dehumanises its subjects by removing the minimum requirements for a humane existence, setting the example of acting in an inhumane manner and casting the subjects as less than human (Fanon 1963). Fanon illuminates the direct causal relationship of colonial subjugation with the failure of postcolonial governments to improve the plight of the majority of indigenous people. While this perspective took time to permeate the mainstream, when it did so, it caused three critical paradigm shifts: social scientists began to include non-physical factors such as economic capacity into their concepts of race; they began to conceive of these non-physical characteristics not as inherent, but as inherited from past discrimination; and there was a growing recognition that race discrimination was the cause of the distinct positions of 'race' groups in society, rather than the other way round (Groenewald 2004). The same advance has yet to materialise in the dominant discourse on informality.

Conclusion

Alongside the various internal constraints of formal participation that have been described in the literature, a variety of factors from above limit the potential of participation processes at the level of the city or local state in South Africa. The influence of participation was severely curtailed by the structural constraints on the autonomy and budget of the local state, as compared to other spheres of the South African state. Consultation has therefore not translated into the ability of those in informal settlements to make their voices and priorities count. Poor communities often take to the streets in an attempt to evoke a degree of urgency over their desperation.

The legislated entrenchment of democratic participation at the local level offers scant comfort, as the little influence that residents are able to exert serves to prioritise project expenditure. Even full participatory budgeting could leave residents frustrated, as only a small portion of priorities can be addressed with the available budget. In sum, the political right to self-management and participation in decision-making by residents of informal settlements has been stripped of substance. Under these conditions, neither the reform of invited participation spaces, nor their abandonment in favour of insurgent revolt, can realise social welfare. The meaningful participation to which the Constitution of South Africa pays lip service, requires a national 'will' to build local authorities with greater autonomy and fiscal clout.

The decentralising rhetoric of the national state diverges substantially from its centralising practice, which helps confine the residents of South Africa's informal settlements both to the periphery of urban areas and to the footnotes of the economy. They form part of a global underclass that is being abandoned, forgotten, or wished away on the outskirts of world cities, disconnected entirely from the potential opportunities of a fourth industrial revolution.

In the context of a declining economy, pro-poor activists will have to weigh up the potential of different strategies to respond to this dilemma. Support of local entrepreneurship, including the informal sector, can help, but may not be enough to counter the effects of rising unemployment. Entering the fierce competition for a larger slice of a shrinking national budget pits poor communities against government departments that already serve them inadequately. Competition for scarce resources at the local level can also pit one poor community against another, whether in formal, invited participation spaces, or on opposite sides of barricades and burning tyres. All of these strategies are important for strengthening local communities, but their respective pitfalls make it more urgent to consider a Basic Income Grant as a viable policy option for giving ordinary people more control over their own livelihoods and dignity, including their options for shelter.

Acknowledgements

Thank you to Ashwin Desai and Margot Rubin for their comments on earlier versions of this text.

References

Abercrombie N, Hill S & Turner BS (2000) *The Penguin Dictionary of Sociology* (4th edn). London: Penguin Books

Bekker S, Buthelezi S, Manona C, Mlambo B & Van Zyl A (1997) Local government transition in five eastern seaboard South African towns. *Politikon* 24(1): 38–56

Bekker S & Leildé A (2003) Residents' perceptions of developmental local government: Exit, voice and loyalty in South African towns. *Politea* 22(1): 144–165

Berkowitz P (2013) Census 2011 numbers: New concerns over the results' accuracy. *Daily Maverick*. http://www.dailymaverick.co.za/article/2013-02-04-census-2011-numbers-new-concerns-over-the-results-accuracy/#.UY4rGaKgKSo

City of Tshwane (n.d.) The City of Tshwane [website]. http://www.tshwane.gov.za/sites/areyeng/AboutUs/Pages/AbouttheCity.aspx

Cornwall A (2002) Locating citizen participation. *IDS Bulletin* 33(2): 49–58

Education & Training Unit (ETU) (n.d.) *Local Government Finances and Budgets.* http://www.etu.org.za/toolbox/docs/localgov/webmunfin.html

Esau MV (2007) Citizen participation and the poor: A participatory approach to achieving political, social and economic freedom? *Politikon* 34(2): 187–203

Fanon F (1963) *The Wretched of the Earth.* London: Penguin

Friedman S (2007) In full voice: Citizen voice and democracy. Paper presented at College of Human Sciences, School for Graduate Studies Seminar Series, University of South Africa, Pretoria, South Africa

Groenewald L (2004) Experiencing racism. MA dissertation, Rand Afrikaans University. http://hdl.handle.net/10210/1317

Groenewald L (2012) Local state constructions of urban citizenship: Informal settlement and housing. Doctoral thesis, University of Johannesburg. http://hdl.handle.net/10210/8295

Groenewald L, Huchzermeyer M, Kornienko K, Tredoux M, Rubin M & Raposo I (2013) Breaking down the binary: Meanings of informal settlement in southern African cities. In: S Bekker & L Fourchard (eds) *Governing Cities in Africa.* Cape Town: HSRC Press. pp. 93–115

Heller P (2009) Democratic deepening in India and South Africa. *Journal of Asian and African Studies* 44(1): 123–149

Huchzermeyer M (2004) *Unlawful Occupation: Informal Settlements and Urban Policy in South Africa and Brazil.* Trenton/Asmara: Africa World Press

Huchzermeyer M (2011) *Cities with 'Slums': From Informal Settlement Eradication to a Right to the City in Africa.* Cape Town: UCT Press

Huchzermeyer M & Karam A (2006) The continuing challenge of informal settlement: An introduction. In: M Huchzermeyer & A Karam (eds) *Informal Settlements: A Perpetual Challenge?* Cape Town: University of Cape Town Press

Kok P, Gelderblom D, Oucho J & Van Zyl J (2006) *Migration in South and Southern Africa: Dynamics and Determinants*. Pretoria: HSRC Press

McDonald D & Pape J (2002) *Cost-recovery and the Crisis of Service Delivery in South Africa*. London & Cape Town: Zed and HSRC Press

Mohamed SE (2006) From ideas to practice: The involvement of informal settlement communities in policy-making at city level in South Africa. *South African Review of Sociology* 37(1): 35–47

Pottie D (2003) Housing the nation: The politics of low-cost housing policy in South Africa since 1994. *Politeia* 22(1): 119–143

Putu M (2006) *The Role of Ward Committees in Enhancing Public Participation in Rustenburg Municipality: A Critical Evaluation*. Cape Town: Idasa.

Republic of South Africa (2000) Municipal Systems Act, no. 32 of 2000. http://www.info.gov.za/view/DownloadFileAction?id=68199

Robins S (2002) Planning 'suburban bliss' in Joe Slovo Park, Cape Town. *Journal of the International African Institute* 72(4): 511–548

Rubin M (2011) Perceptions of corruption in the South African Housing Allocation and Delivery Programme: What it may mean for accessing the state. *Journal of Asian and African Studies* 46(5): 479–490

Schultz D (2013) Was Census 2011 successful? *Mail & Guardian*. http://mg.co.za/article/2013-03-22-was-census-2011-sucessful

Sinwell L (2008) Using Giddens's theory of 'structuration' and Freirean philosophy to understand participation in the Alexandra Renewal Project. *Development Southern Africa* 25(3): 245–258

Sinwell L (2010) Conceptualizing direct action as a form of participation in development: A South African case. *Politikon* 37(1): 67–83

South African Cities Network (SACN) (2011) *Toward Resilient Cities: A Reflection on the First Decade of a Democratic and Transformed Local Government in South Africa, 2001–2010*. State of the Cities Report 2011. https://www.sacities.net/wp-content/uploads/2019/12/towards_resilient_cities.pdf

StatsSA (Statistics South Africa) (2011) *Midyear Population Estimates 2011*. Pretoria: StatsSA. http://www.statssa.gov.za/publications/P0302/P03022011.pdf

UN-Habitat (2003) *The Challenge of Slums: Global Report on Human Settlements 2003*. Nairobi: United Nations Human Settlements Programme

United Nations Department of Economic and Social Affairs, Population Division (2016) *The World's Cities in 2016*. http://www.un.org/en/development/desa/population/publications/pdf/urbanization/the_worlds_cities_in_2016_data_booklet.pdf

Centralised urban governance in the Greater Cairo City Region: A critical understanding of key challenges and responses

Amr Abdelaal, Hajer Awatta, Omar Nagati, Salwa Salman & Marwa Shykhon

Introduction

Egypt, like other countries in Africa, has urbanised with an estimated annual rate of 1.68% between 2010–2015 (CIA 2016). With this exponential urban growth, Cairo, the capital of Egypt and one of the most significant cities in Africa and the Middle East, conglomerated with Giza and Qalyubiyah, its neighbouring governorates, to constitute the Greater Cairo City Region (GCCR) in 1977, Egypt's main urban region. The GCCR's three governorates serve as administrative boundaries that aid in the management of the country's largest metropolis but are physically intertwined and function together as one urban core. It contains between 40–50% of Egypt's university spots, hospital beds, public sector and private sector jobs (Sims 2010), 31% of the nation's economic output (GOPP 2012) and almost a quarter of Egypt's population (UN-Habitat 2011). This undisputedly renders it the most significant region in Egypt. It also captures most of the incoming private and public investment and business enterprises, with 83% of all foreign establishments located in Cairo (Sims 2010). Its location – at the centre of a linear settlement pattern along the Nile Valley and the Delta – means that Cairo is well connected to most of Egypt's smaller cities and towns. Today, the GCCR is the best connected and populated urban agglomeration in Egypt with an approximate total population of 22.9 million inhabitants, representing 25% of the total Egyptian population (CAPMAS 2017).

Ineffective urban governance is the primary challenge facing the GCCR, underscoring all attempts to deal with other, more tangible problems, such as the growth of informality as a parallel system for housing, lack of economic opportunities and inadequate services provision. This chapter posits that such ineffective management of the GCCR is extensively attributable to centrality, resulting in inefficient resource allocation, a lack of coordination and investment in inadequate development projects. Centralisation is synonymous with, but not limited to, population agglomeration, top-down decision-making, and financial and administrative centrality. In this chapter, we use the term in contrast to decentralisation, which instead aims at distributing power among different levels of government and dissolving the concentration of power without jeopardising the sovereignty of the state (Bardhan 2002).

This chapter will explore challenges of urban governance in a context of rapid urban growth, with a focus on centralised governance as a main obstacle to development, through an analysis of the administrative structure of the Greater Cairo City Region (GCCR) in Egypt, and its on-the-ground manifestations as exemplified through three urban intervention case studies that span a range of scales of governance.

First, we discuss policy debates regarding centralised governance in the GCCR and approaches to decentralisation. In this context, we will argue that the city region is ill-defined within the legal frameworks; that both the absence of an administrative body that governs the region as a single unit and the dispersed control over financial resources are inadequate; and that the different conceptualisations of decentralisation at the national level in Egypt exacerbate the problem. Second, we explore three urban projects that highlight the resultant challenges of centrality at different scales of government. To avoid a simplified dichotomy between centralisation and decentralisation as two opposing forms of government, this chapter recognises a spectrum of necessary scales of governance. First, we examine the establishment of desert cities at the national (and most centralised) scale; second, we focus on the Cairo Metro project at the regional (an intermediary) scale, and third, we discuss decentralisation attempts through the lens of a case study at the local (and most decentralised) scale. Altogether, we argue that such centrality in urban governance leads to highly ineffective management of the GCCR, which further complicates the urban challenges increasingly facing the region.

The concluding section highlights the need for administrative solutions that are appropriate to each scale of governance, which, in the present context of the GCCR's administration, necessitates an overarching move towards increased decentralisation. It also connects centralisation and approaches to decentralisation in Egypt to the wider debates on decentralisation as an instrument for development. Rather than advocating a romanticised vision of uncritical decentralisation, which often incorrectly assumes its inherent democracy (Heller 2001), this chapter argues that appropriate scales of government should be carefully pursued towards a cohesive and effective hierarchy of governance.

Urban governance in the case of the GCCR: Centralisation vs decentralisation

Following the Parisian example, developed by Baron Haussmann in the early 1800s, Khedive Isma'il commissioned 'Ali Mubarak Pasha, a French-trained engineer, and reformer, to design a plan for a new Cairo, west of the historical Fatimid Cairo (Rabbat 2011). The new Cairo has come to resemble several cities across Europe that were

Figure 1: Map of Greater Cairo

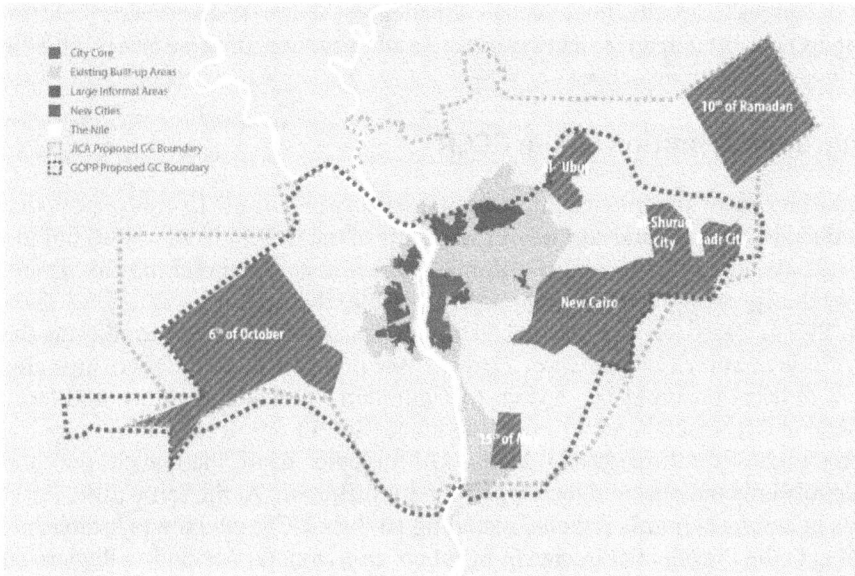

Source: TCID

rapidly redesigned according to a highly spatially centralised model, 'the cutting of two new boulevards in the medieval city's fabric, al-Sikka al-Jadida (the New Street) and Muhammad 'Ali Street, does indeed indicate an intention to enact a system of spatial control and surveillance' (Rabbat 2011: 185). The spatial centralisation of the new Cairo has, in many ways, mirrored the intense centralisation of Egypt's governance structure since the 1800s. This was further accentuated following the Free Officers Movement, in 1952, which overthrew the monarchy and the remains of British colonial rule with the support of a large working class and declared the independence of Egypt. The Egyptian Republic was led by a military government that has since become increasingly authoritarian (Abu-Lughod 1971; Mitchell 2002; Singerman 1995).

The administrative and institutional structure that has developed corresponds to the nature of a regime that primarily seeks 'regime maintenance' (Singerman 1995: 12), ultimately resulting in excessive centralisation that hinders democratic decision-making and maintains power at the national executive level without accountability. The resulting difficulties and inefficiencies in urban governance have spurred discussion and attempts towards decentralisation. While there have been several approaches towards such decentralisation since the 1970s (El Hag 2015), most of these have not surpassed the theoretical level. However, after Egypt's 2011 revolution and the constitution of 2014 the Egyptian President, 'Abdel Fattah el-Sisi, ordered the government to accelerate decentralisation reforms. Accordingly, a new Administrative Law has been proposed and is currently being reviewed and discussed by the Egyptian parliament (Abu al-Mahasin 2018). This section investigates specific forms of centralisation, with a focus on the GCCR, suggesting how centralisation limits the overall capacity for effective urban governance. It also sheds light on current decentralisation approaches pursued to address some of these issues, and the limitations of these approaches.

Incongruent definition of the GCCR

Given the process of incremental interwoven urban expansion and layered growth that has resulted in a vibrant and complex urban fabric of the GCCR, its precise definition is difficult. We identify two methods through which to comprehend the city region: either by the Egyptian Planning System (EPS), or the city dynamics.

The EPS is based on the Unified Planning Law (UPL) no. 118/2008, and the Local Administration Law (LAL) no. 43/1979. According to the UPL, there are three levels of physical planning and spatial configurations; national, regional, and local. The General Organisation for Physical Planning (GOPP) prepares strategic physical plans for each of the three spatial levels.[1] On the other hand, the constitution and LAL identify only national and local types of administration. At the same time, Egypt consists of seven economic regions, including (1) the GCCR, which was established according to the Presidential Decree of Egypt no. 495/1977, (2) Alexandria Region, (3) Delta Region, (4) Suez Canal Region, (5) North Upper Egypt Region, (6) South Upper Egypt Region, and (7) Asyut Region; each region consists of a number of governorates. The inefficient management of resources at the regional economic level is partially a result of the lack of local representation.

The other definition of GCCR is based on spatial dynamics. In other words, it is the manifestation of where economic hubs concentrate, the distribution of industries, the connectivity between different urban areas, and the spatial configurations, etc. The complexity of these dynamics within a region such as Cairo is the primary challenge that confronts the various attempts to draw borders for GCCR. This unclearly defined area, which lies somewhere between the Cairo Governorate level and the GCCR, is not only the country's largest urban area but is considered one of the most populous metropolises in the world with approximately 22.9 million inhabitants (CAPMAS 2017). In 2008, the Japan International Cooperation Agency (JICA) in cooperation with the GOPP conducted a study that suggested a border for GCCR that consisted of an area of 4 367km² and included parts of the north-east governorate, al-Sharqiyya.[2] Four years later, GOPP released, in cooperation with UN-Habitat, a strategy for urban development within Greater Cairo that outlined another border for GCCR that covers an area of only 3 133km². The border was identified based on three factors: the spatial relations between the different neighbourhoods, a common labour market, and the living conditions (GOPP, UN-Habitat & UNDP 2012). These unclear spatial limits of the GCCR further impede effective governance which is reflected administratively in

---

1   The GOPP is the planning arm of the Ministry of Housing, Utilities, and Urban Development (MHUD).

2   There was no justification or methodology given in the JICA study for their demarcation of GCCR.

the lack of a political figure or body that is explicitly responsible for coordinating GCCR-wide development. One of the results of such administrative vs spatial discrepancy is the promotion of executive bodies and companies that override the jurisdiction of local authorities to implement city-wide projects across the governorates. A successful example of this is the ongoing Cairo Metro, which was facilitated by the establishment of separate entities to oversee construction and management, under the jurisdiction of the Ministry of Transport rather than the governorates (NAT and the ECMMO). While this was essential for the success of such a project, it highlights the need for a local administration that spans the governorates, else the direct involvement of the central government will continue to be promoted.

Local administrative structures and national-executive influence

The president, the cabinet, the parliament, and the judiciary altogether form the national level of government, with the cabinet itself formed of the prime minister and thirty-four heads of national ministries, who are directly appointed by the Egyptian president. Altogether they manage the state's administrative and financial resources and determine laws to be implemented by the local-level government (Tadamun 2013). At the local level, Egypt is administered by 27 governorates, of which there are two types: urban governorates, and urban/rural governorates. Spatially, each governorate is divided hierarchically into districts in the urban governorates, and *marakiz* (singular *markaz*) in the rural governorates. The smallest spatial divisions in the governorates are *shiyakhat* (singular *shiyakha*) and villages in the urban and rural governorates, respectively.

The GCCR, which comprises three separate governorates, has a particularly extensive local administrative body. The Cairo Governorate is an urban city-governorate – similar to the city-state concept in the federal systems – that extends over 3 084km² (Cairo Governorate 2016). The governorate accommodates approximately 9.6 million inhabitants living on 188km² (CAPMAS 2017). It consists of four zones, each consisting of a number of districts, in addition to four new satellite cities. Giza is an urban/rural governorate that extends over 1 579km² and accommodates approximately 8 million inhabitants, of which 58.6% are living in urban areas (Giza Governorate 2017). The urban parts of the governorate are divided into 8 districts and 79 *shiyakhas* and 2 satellite cities. Likewise, Qalyubiyah is an urban/rural governorate extending over 1 000km² (CAPMAS 2016); the urban part is administratively divided into two districts and ten *shiyakhas* (Qalyubiyah Governorate 2016), and accommodates approximately 5.8 million inhabitants, of which 44.7% are living in urban areas.

Despite such extensive institutional infrastructure and spatial subdivision, urban governance remains highly centralised. Administratively, each governorate – whether urban or rural – consists of several entities, of which some members are locally elected, that report to the governor. Each governor is appointed by Presidential Decree and, in turn, appoints the Heads of Districts within his governorate.[3] In the special case of Cairo, the governor also designates four deputies at the head of each zone. As such, the entire local administration is inextricably tied to the central government through the state's patrimonial political character.

---

3   Note that the *shiyakhat* administratively follow the district and do not have separate chiefs.

Dispersed finances

While key figures within local administration are directly influenced by central government, often becoming more concerned with pleasing their superiors (Tadamun 2013), the actual capacity of local government to exercise their powers is severely limited by their control, or lack thereof, of financial resources. The local administration structure (as outlined by the Local Administration Law No. (43/1979)) in Egypt gives full executive authority to governors while limiting their financial authority. For example, there are some entities within each governorate, namely the directorates, that administratively follow the governor but financially follow their corresponding sectoral ministries. It is worth noting also that the national budget is unevenly distributed between national ministries and local governorates, with each receiving 90% and 10% respectively. Even where local administration has the financial authority in theory, in practice, budgets were devised by the central ministries and the executive councils of the local administration, and approved by the Ministry of Finance before being implemented by local administrators (Tadamun 2013).

Moreover, local administration is heavily reliant on central government for revenue, with Article 184 stipulating the responsibility of central government to provide the local administration with resources (Tadamun 2013). While local administrations enjoy the legal capacity to collect and spend local taxes, a report by Tadamun has recently shown this independent revenue to be mostly insignificant, with locally elected officials being reluctant to risk the political disfavour of imposing such taxes, thus 'reinforcing the centralised nature of governance' (Tadamun 2013). These dynamics are made explicit when investigating overall public expenditure which highlights the disproportionate expenditure by central administration (79%) compared to that of local administration (12%) (Tadamun 2013). This financial dependency on central government results in the need for approval of expenditures from the centre which often has priorities that are incongruent with local needs, thus reducing local government to a simple administrative role. This is made worse by the patrimonial character of both central and local government administration, ultimately limiting the capacity for effective and accountable local governance.

While institutional mechanisms that facilitate local governance exist, local administration is far from independent from central government. Its primary actors are appointed through direct patronage from primary political figures, while local budgets are significantly monitored and limited by the priorities of the central government. Local administration lacks the combination of executive and financial authority to facilitate effective local governance. In the specific case of the GCCR, incongruent spatial and administrative delimitations lead to an inadequate definition of responsibilities and cross-governorate coherence that encourages reliance on executive boards and companies for the fulfilment of large-scale urban projects. These executive boards, which often enjoy the administrative and financial support of leading politicians, become crucial to facilitating the execution of complex projects but often render urban development responses to exclusive top-down visions rather than a response to local needs. The following section will detail some of the effects of these manifestations of centralisation on the actual urban development plans and projects, highlighting the crucial limitations of such administrative and financial centrality.

Approaches to decentralisation on the national level

Decentralisation has been high on the political agenda in many countries in Africa, as an integral component to development, throughout the last few decades. According to Laila El Baradei (2015: 3), decentralisation involves 'de-concentration, delegation, devolution, and may encompass privatization as well.'

In Egypt, there have been numerous attempts to reform the Local Administration Law and empower local authorities. The 2014 Constitution took the first legislative step towards addressing this issue by supporting decentralisation in Article 176, which stipulates: 'The state ensures support for administrative, financial, and economic decentralisation. The law organises empowering administrative units in providing, improving, and managing public utilities well, and defines the timeline for transferring powers and budgets to the local administration units.' While this was a positive step towards administrative, fiscal, and economic decentralisation, the LAL did not provide the elements necessary for the execution of full decentralisation and thereby limits the role of local authorities. A study that was conducted by Tadamun in 2015 suggests that the law only gave Local Popular Councils (LPCs) an advisory role while the central government and appointed executive councils maintained a monopoly over decision-making. It is important to note that the LPCs' elections have been suspended since the 2011 revolution and were planned to be resumed by the end of 2018 (Ramadan 2017).

On the other hand, the new Draft Law contains 18 new articles, most of which regulate the relationship between different local-level authorities and the central government, and set the basis for local government capacity building. However, affirming that the enactment of the new law would establish the base for a radical decentralisation of governance is still guesswork. Wunsch (2001: 278) explains that the reasons for delays in applying top-down decentralisation reforms include the wearing down of political will at the local level: 'local governance is discouraged by the absence of real decisions, and local civil service administrators can distribute capital resources, often for their comfort and convenience, and manage their local work lives without disturbance from local demands.' This has over time already diminished the capacity of local government to manage decision-making and financial resources effectively, thus rendering the professional capacities of local government themselves an obstacle.

These attempted legal reforms following and guided by the 2014 Constitution offer an example of the possibilities and challenges of top-down steps towards decentralisation. However, while many studies have shied away from analytically questioning the strategies of decentralisation, Heller (2001) divides approaches to decentralisation into two categories, technocratic/top-down approach, and anarcho-communitarians (ACs)/bottom-up approach. He explains that while the technocratic approach 'produces universally applicable blueprints, and decentralisation-by-design promises smooth implementation' (2001: 137), ACs claim that the technocratic approach reproduces the 'elite-controlled characteristics of post-colonial states' (2001: 135). With the absence of a comprehensive top-down implementation of formal decentralisation, non-governmental and local civic organisations can thus, in this context, play a vital role in supporting community participation and offer models for bottom-up decentralisation, which will be reviewed in the next section.

Exploring centralisation at different scales of governance

Within this complex context of administrative and financial centralisation coupled with various attempts towards decentralisation, this section sheds light on the intricate and nuanced effects of centralisation and its practical limitations on urban governance strategies. It provides a series of case studies exploring on-the-ground urban projects at a cross section of scales of governance, unpacking centralisation (and possible decentralisation) at the national, regional and local scales.

The national scale: Desert cities

Desert city expansions have been at the forefront of Egyptian planning policy since the 1970s and are typically high-profile projects with presidential patronage. Conceived at the national scale of governance and directly implemented, they manifest a highly centralised form of urban governance that has dramatically impacted the urban growth of the GCCR over the last few decades. Despite these projects attracting significant criticism, in 2017 the Egyptian government inaugurated the establishment of yet another new city, the New Administrative Capital, 60km east of the centre of Cairo. The vision of the New Capital aims to overcome the shortcomings of the previous experiences of previous desert cities, claiming to focus on best practices in design, ecology and culture and will have a variety of medium and high-density districts to address the issues of land constraints and population density. The New Capital is also planned to host the many public administrative authorities and business centres which aim to work as a catalyst for creating synergistic job opportunities for the country's youth (Capital City 2015).

This project is the most recent in a longstanding tradition of urban desert expansions as a form of city management, which claim that such expansions will result in the movement of populations that would alleviate a variety of pressures within the urban core of the GCCR. In his 2014 book, *Egypt's Desert Dreams: Development or Disaster*, David Sims provides an in-depth economic, social and urban management analysis of the desert urban expansions (new cities) policy. Despite the prevalence of this urban strategy, Sims concludes that 'any desert project whose justification is moving large numbers of people out of the [Nile] Valley should be laughed out of the room' (Sims 2014: 292). Similarly, at the Egypt Urban Forum 2015 (EUF), urban researcher Yahia Shawkat highlighted the relative failures of previous desert expansion projects in response to Asim al-Jazzar's summary of the NSUP 2052 vision. Shawkat suggests that 'more effort should be made to identify those who are willing and unwilling to relocate in order to implement projects more effectively [in the proposed plans]' (UN-Habitat 2016: 32).

Nonetheless, while the existing desert cities, some of which are still under construction and others established over 30 years ago, are still not achieving their targeted populations, there is a continued intention to invest in new towns despite heavy criticism from many in the urban planning field that this investment could be part of the problem (Tadamun 2015). This was particularly highlighted at the EUF, where Asim al-Jazzar, chairman of the General Organization for Physical Planning, summarised the key strategy for dealing with population growth: 'The main vision of the 2052 [National Strategic Urban Plan (NSUP)] is to expand beyond current urban areas and effectively double the current area of inhabited land in the country' (UN-Habitat 2016: 30). It is thus clear that the developmental future of the GCCR remains heavily tied to a vision for the movement of the population away from existing urban cores across the entire country, and the plan includes several expansion projects in other cities.

The persistence of these longstanding urban development strategies, which have proven largely ineffective, are reflective of narrow and linear governance mechanisms that continue to reproduce out-of-touch top-down proposals, without benefitting from the breadth of the national and local institutional network or serving to develop their expertise and capacities. These projects bypass the local administration in the process of their inception, more reflecting the grandiose visions and claims of high-level politicians than a response to studied urban needs and challenges. However, while the adequacy or efficiency of the strategy may be critiqued, the national level of administration through which these projects are proposed and coordinated is appropriate for this scale of urban planning. Through the centralised national-level administration such large-scale urban projects have been feasibly financed and constructed. The specific failures of these desert city projects are particularly revealed at the smaller scales of governance.

When 'new cities' have been implemented within a governorate's spatial jurisdiction, the administrative responsibilities are organised separately from the local government. The seven new satellite cities located within the GCCR, administratively follow the New Urban Community Authority (NUCA) rather than the governorate within which they are located.[4] A city council is formed to operate and manage each new city and is appointed directly rather than being a representative elected body such as the Local Councils established across the governorates. These New Urban Communities report directly to the Ministry of Housing, a national body, leaving these new cities with no institutional mechanism for local governance, let alone an effective one. According to Law no. 59/1979, when this new city development is completed, its administration would supposedly return to the corresponding governorate. However, until now, such transfer of power is yet to happen. The effects of such absence of municipal government and attention was exemplified in the poor management of and inadequate response to severe flooding that severely impacted the desert city of New Cairo in late April 2018.

Conceived, administered and financed separately to existing local administrative structures, the pattern of desert expansion exemplifies the effects of excessive governmental centralisation on urban development. These projects, instead, are manifestations of top-down visions that are removed from everyday realities, and which correlate closely to the kinds of proposals found in the aforementioned urban vision documents. These case studies illustrate and highlight some of the inefficiencies of centralised government as they relate to city management. The resultant condition is excessive investment in projects and proposals that draw on a limited selection of expertise (of the highest-level politicians) and that bypass the authority and potential local experience of local government. Ultimately, this results in a weakening of local administrations, in both their professional capacity and effectiveness in serving as a channel for bottom-up democratic participation.

---

4   NUCA is a subsidiary of the Ministry of Housing and is governed according to Law no. 59/1979.

The regional scale: The Cairo Metro Project

In a 1954 report issued by French experts on the future of transport in Egypt, a proposal for a two-line metro was made as well as the recommendation for the unification of separate transport companies into a single national transportation corporation. Over the next two decades, several studies were conducted by a variety of international parties that unanimously emphasised the necessity to implement a metro system, however, the political and economic circumstances of the time delayed action. In 1969, a growing crisis in public transportation led the Council of Ministers, with support from then president Gamal Abdel Nasser, to reignite serious study of the project, despite the post-war conditions. Accordingly, in September 1970, a tender held by the Ministry of Transportation was awarded to the French company, SUFRETO (now SYSTRA), which proceeded with further studies (MOIC 2016). The 1981–1983 GC master plan was the first to substantially incorporate transportation upgrading within the vision of GCCR's comprehensive development and stipulated the intentions to implement the Metro system and Ring Road to 'improve the efficiency of the transport system' (Word Bank 2000).

The Cairo Metro has since become one of GCCR's fastest and most successful methods of mobility within the congested city, with continuously increasing levels of demand. The implementation of the project also successfully spans across the Cairo and Giza governorates, indicating a degree of intra-governorate efficiency and cooperation not common in urban projects in the GCCR. This success is largely a result of the establishment of separate entities to oversee construction and management who are each under the jurisdiction of the Ministry of Transport rather than the governorates. The National Authority for Tunnels (NAT) was established in 1983 as a governmental agency of the Ministry of Transport to undertake the construction of the Metro system and has since been responsible for other large-scale tunnelling projects. The NAT has also been responsible for conducting the necessary technical and economic research related to the project (NAT 2013).

Such executive regional bodies bypassed an inefficient local administration, and its related limitations, to ensure successful management and implementation across the involved governorates. The project instead relied on an executive form of government stemming from the national and acting on the regional scale. Acting at this regional scale of implementation and coordination, the project was ultimately relatively successful. However, this scale is not integrated within the existing institutional structure but develops as a case-specific solution, highlighting the need for this scale of governance in the GCCR to facilitate projects of this size and complexity. Without the institutionalisation of this scale, which represents a middle ground between the national and local (and the highly centralised and the decentralised), urban projects will continue to fail to coordinate across the GCCR's three governorates or resort to arrangements such as those used in the Cairo Metro project, which are also not without limitations.

A World Bank report (2000) suggests that 'fragmented institutional arrangements' across the transport sector in the GCCR, which is a consistent feature of Cairene administrations, has led to the unclear delineation of responsibilities and reduced overall efficiency. Despite already being a successful and vital element of the GCCR's public transport network, the Cairo Metro's full potential has not yet been realised due to its slow progress and poor integration with other transport systems; an effect of the many bodies addressing transport infrastructure (World Bank 2000). For the Metro to work effectively as a solution to the GCCR's congestion and transportation ills, a comprehensive approach must be taken that allows all systems to work together, and the progress of the metro project should be assessed in relation to other modes of transport, including surface services such as the public buses of the Cairo Transport Authorities (CTA).

While the administrative arrangement of the Cairo Metro project offered an appropriate scale of governance for the project, resorting to such a partnership between national executive administration and private companies was necessitated as a direct result of the forms of centralisation detailed in section two, ultimately resulting in poor coordination with the wider GCCR transport sector. Rather than representing a successful model for project implementation, the more effective lesson derived from this project is the crucial need for this scale of regional governance across the GCCR. Such regional level governance needs to be integrated within the institutional system, with responsibilities towards and communication with both sides of the administrative hierarchy – the national and the local.

The local scale: Participatory approaches

During the last decade, the United Nations have promoted the compartmentship of state, civil society organisation, and private sector, as an alternative to traditional state-led governance/development. This part highlights examples of bottom-up endeavours that try to make up for the lack of local governance and mechanisms through which the local voice can be heard. Within the context of the GCCR explored throughout this chapter, these endeavours attempt to compensate for shortcomings in the local governance structures. Two pilot public space interventions are examined here as approaches to local integration and decentralisation: a public space and environmental upgrading project in 'Izbit Khayrallah,[5] an informal urban settlement in Cairo, by the community development organisation Takween in 2016 (Takween 2017) and a pilot public passageway intervention in downtown Cairo by CLUSTER, a platform for urban research, art and design initiatives (Nagati & Stryker 2016).

In 2016, Takween started a pilot public space and environmental upgrading project in 'Izbit Khayrallah with funds from the Embassy of Switzerland in Egypt and the sponsorship of Cairo Governorate. Takween designed the project to help the local community overcome the negative repercussions of the establishment of a regional ring road that connects Egypt's main roads and different governorates. The Ring Road divided 'Izbit Khayrallah into northern and southern areas, excluding the southern community who depended on the northern area to access different services. After conducting needs assessment and documentation of the current situation, interviews, and workshops with different stakeholders, including the local community, a tunnel

---

5   'Izbit Khayrallah is one of the largest unplanned settlements in Cairo, it falls between four districts: Misr al-Qadima, Dar al-Salam, al-Basatin, and al-Khalifa. For more information, see https://forgottenneighborhoods.wordpress.com/tag/izbit-khayrallah/.

connecting the southern and northern areas has been chosen for development. In a similar vein, in 2014, CLUSTER conducted a participatory workshop to redesign and upgrade two public passageways in downtown Cairo – Kodak and Phillips passageways – in cooperation with the Danish Egyptian Dialogue Institute (DEDI) and the Center for Culture and Development (CKU). CLUSTER has worked with different stakeholders, including property owners and passersby, according to the DEDI website the project '[...] contributes to larger issues related to public space and emerging questions around participatory planning' (DEDI 2014).

While such bottom-up approaches do reach and impact formal government, they usually have minimal impact on national policies and the overall process of decision-making. Their value lies in their enriching of urban interventions and urban governance strategies with the necessary local bottom-up expertise that limits out-of-touch proposals characteristic of those of central government. Through the repeated implementation of these projects, and the necessary collaboration with local authorities, new governance mechanisms can also begin to take shape, affecting institutional mechanisms from below. For example, the passageway renovation undertaken by CLUSTER in downtown Cairo involved an extensive process of consultation and negotiation between different stakeholders, including passersby, passageway shop renters, the building owners and the local authorities (Nagati & Stryker 2016). The maintenance of the project required the establishment of a 'passageway board' that sought to mediate an agreement for the delegation of maintenance responsibilities between relevant parties, ensuring that the key stakeholders in the space both bear responsibility and are represented in the future management of the semi-public space. This method, which can be viewed as a localised form of urban governance, was then adopted by the local authorities when they renovated other nearby passageways, based on CLUSTER's precedent.[6]

In the politically sensitive conditions of post-revolution Cairo, these projects present alternative options for a move towards decentralisation and local representation in government strategies. While their larger effect on existing centralisation is currently relatively small, these forms of urban intervention practice have become a growing sector within the urban studies and practice field, highlighting a possible way forward towards political reform. Perhaps more pertinently, however, the relative productivity and sustainability of projects conducted in such a manner, when compared to the top-down interventions often pursued through national executive bodies, highlights the need for the efficiency of such a scale of governance for effective urban management and investment. Unlike the regional scale, local administration does exist within the GCCR's institutional structure, but as described in the first section of this chapter, it is ultimately ineffective, lacking the combination of administrative and financial authority to fulfil its role, ultimately affecting its capacity as a channel for citizen needs and voices and government accountability.

---

6   The most notable example of this is the renovation of al-Alfi Bey passageway in downtown Cairo, not far from the Kodak passageway intervention.

Conclusion

This chapter has explored some of the administrative characteristics of the Egyptian government and their effect on urban and spatial state-led development practices. The highly centralised nature of the public administration system in Egypt is evident in several regards, most notably in the role of local administration on the governorate level. Limited powers are given to governorates and local authorities in the final planning and budget allocation in matters supposedly within their jurisdiction, and city administrations are often mandated with the development of their region but do not always have full control over the allocation and prioritisation of their financial resources. This leaves the governor, the perceived ultimate authority to the public, burdened by administrative duties and public expectations to address problems in their governorate but they do not have control of their budget.

For a public entity to be effective it needs administrative representation with a clear mandate, decision-making authority, and allocated financial resources. Greater Cairo currently has none of the above, and despite numerous proposals, each area operates within – and is developed by – its own governorate, with little collaboration or coordination between them. Administrative and financial decentralisation in the GCCR are challenges that have yet to be seriously and productively addressed and are found to be an intrinsic hindrance for the region's development. In Egypt, local governments only receive and have experience with relatively small budgets amounting up to 10% of the overall budget, an issue compounded by a general condition of institutional weakness inherent to the state's authoritarian nature, resulting in widespread incompetence throughout all levels of government, that is exaggerated at the local level (Dorman 2007). These are issues that require attention if political decentralisation is to be successfully implemented. The two case studies from TCID and CLUSTER highlight how locally orientated organisations and institutions can play a vital role in offering new models of participation that can add to a more comprehensive bottom-up decentralisation system.

Finally, rather than falling into a simplistic binary of centralisation versus decentralisation, this chapter has argued for a more nuanced understanding of the multiple levels of urban governance, on the national, regional and local scales. The case studies explored within the Greater Cairo City Region offer examples of planning and urban development strategies addressing the three scales and highlighting the particular challenges of excessive centralisation at each. On the one hand, national centralised planning excludes possibilities of local participation, resulting in inefficient urban expenditure and out-of-touch urban interventions and management, thus requiring a form of decentralisation that delegates more decision-making powers to the regional and local scales for specific projects and programmes. Conversely, while small-scale interventions on neighborhood and community scales may provide lessons for direct engagement and bottom-up approaches, they cannot be effectively scaled-up without addressing larger planning considerations, such as traffic, environmental concerns as well as labour and capital flows, which cannot solely be addressed through the local scale of governance. As such, whilst the GCCR requires an overall delegation of administrative and financial authority from the national level, it is also essential that the institutional structure allows for a coordinating governing body across the three governorates and multiple municipalities within the GCCR. Such a move would represent a middle ground between the predominant trend of centralisation and the calls for decentralisation. Through the discussion of examples of urban planning and development projects at these scales, this chapter thus raises the question of which policies, programmes and projects should be assigned to which level of governance, addressing some strategies on a more centralised scale to safeguard the public good, while delegating necessary local decisions through a matrix of decentralised governmentalities to empower communities and enable genuine participation.

Acknowledgements

This chapter comes as a summary of the results of a 2016/2017 joint research project between Takween Integrated Community Development (TICD), and Cairo Lab for Urban Studies Training and Environmental research (CLUSTER). The joint research was under the umbrella of the African City-region Comparative Research for the Gauteng Provincial Government. Thanks is also extended to Beth Stryker and Deena Khalil for contributing to the review and editing process.

References

10 Tooba (2016) *The Built Environment Budget FY 2015/16: An Analysis of Spatial Justice in Egypt.* http://www.10tooba.org/en/wp-content/uploads/2016/06/10-Tooba-BE-Budget-2015-16.pdf

Abdel-Halim K (2017) Urban local governance in Greater Cairo City Region. Interview with A Abdelaal & M Shykhon

Abu al-Mahasin A (2018, 25 December) Minister of Local Development: 'We are working on supporting decentralization'. *Al Dostor.* https://www.dostor.org/2449634

Abu-Lughod IA (1971) *The Transformation of Palestine: Essays on the Origin and Development of the Arab-Israeli Conflict.* Chicago: Northwestern University Press

Aga Khan Trust for Culture (AKTC) (2015) *Cairo: Urban regeneration in the Darb al-Ahmar district.* http://www.akdn.org/sites/akdn/files/Publications/2005_aktc_cairo_regeneration.pdf

Ahram Online (2016, 18 February) Egypt to double underground metro ticket price: Ministry spokesperson. http://english.ahram.org.eg/NewsContent/3/0/187941/Business/0/Egypt-to-double-underground-metro-ticket-price-Min.aspx

Ahram Online (2018, 2 May) Egypt's prosecutor-general summons five officials over last week's floods in New Cairo. http://english.ahram.org.eg/NewsContent/1/64/298764/Egypt/Politics-/Egypts-prosecutorgeneral-summons-five-officials-ov.aspx

Al-Aees S (2016, 27 June) Al Asmarat: The Tahya Misr Fund's relocation of Al-Doweiqa. *Daily News Egypt.* http://www.dailynewsegypt.com/2016/06/27/al-asmarat-tahya-misr-funds-relocation-al-doweiqa/

AlSayyad N (1991) *Cities and Caliphs.* USA: Greenwood

Angélil M, Malterre-Barthes C, Something Fantastic & CLUSTER (2016) *Housing Cairo: The Informal Response.* Berlin: Ruby Press

Bardhan P (2002) Decentralization of governance and development. *Journal of Economic Perspectives*, 16(4): 185–205

Bedīr A (2016) The Ministry of Housing: following up with Cairo governorate al-A'asmarāt project. *Masr Alarabia*. http://www.masralarabia.com/

Cairo Governorate (2016) About Cairo. http://www.cairo.gov.eg/ar/pages/CairoInLines.aspx?CiLID=3

Cairobserver (2014, 12 February) Second print edition of Cairobserver. http://cairobserver.com/post/76427984710/second-print-edition-of-cairobserver#.WEHdHlzpiQ4

Capital City (2015) Vibrant Spaces. http://thecapitalcairo.com/vision.html

Central Authority for Public Mobilization and Statistics (CAPMAS) (1981) *The Census annual book*. Cairo: General organization for government printings offices

Central Authority for Public Mobilization and Statistics (CAPMAS) (2006) *Egypt National Census*. Government of Egypt

Central Authority for Public Mobilization and Statistics (CAPMAS) (2016) *Egypt National Census*. Government of Egypt

Central Authority for Public Mobilization and Statistics (CAPMAS) (2017) *Population of Egypt Now*. http://capmas.gov.eg/Pages/populationClock.aspx

Central Intelligence Agency (CIA) (2016) *The World Factbook*. Washington DC: Central Intelligence Agency. https://www.cia.gov/library/publications/the-world-factbook/geos/eg.html

Cleaver F (1999) Paradoxes of participation: Questioning participatory approaches to development. *Journal of International Development* 11(4): 597–612

DEDI (2014) The Cairo Downtown Passages Design Workshop. https://dedi.org.eg/the-cairo-downtown-passages-design-workshop/

Dorman WJ (2007) The politics of neglect: The Egyptian state in Cairo, 1974–98. Doctoral dissertation, SOAS, University of London

El Baradei L (2015) The case for decentralization as a tool for improving quality in Egyptian basic education. *The Egyptian Center for Economic Studies Working paper* No. 180. http://www.eces.org.eg/cms/NewsUploads/Pdf/2019_1_14-14_19_4720.pdf

El Hag, S (2015) A review of decentralization and local development initiatives in Egypt between the years of 1994 and 2011. Master's thesis, American University in Cairo. https://fount.aucegypt.edu/etds/1114

Ethelston S (1997) *Facts and figures on Cairo*. http://www.merip.org/mer/mer202/facts-figures-cairo

General Organization for Physical Planning (GOPP) (2000) *Greater Cairo Atlas*. Cairo: GOPP

General Organization for Physical Planning (GOPP) (2009) Vision of Cairo 2050 within a National Vision of Egypt. Presentation. https://cairofrombelow.files.wordpress.com/2011/08/cairo-2050-vision-v-2009-gopp-12-mb.pdf

General Organization for Physical Planning (GOPP) (2012) *Greater Cairo Urban Development Strategy*. http://gopp.gov.eg/wp-content/uploads/2015/07/1CFV-EN.pdf

Giza Governorate (2017) About Giza. http://www.giza.gov.eg/Brotocol/about.aspx

GOPP, UN-Habitat & UNDP (2012) *Greater Cairo: Urban Development Strategy*. Cairo: Ministry of Housing and Urban Communities

Government of Egypt (2016) *Egypt vision 2030 – sustainable development strategy.* https://www.greengrowthknowledge.org/sites/default/files/downloads/policy-database/Egypt%20Vision%202030%20%28English%29.pdf

Heller P (2001) Moving the state: the politics of democratic decentralization in Kerala, South Africa, and Porto Alegre. *Politics & Society*, 29(1): 131–163

Informal Settlements Development Facility (ISDF) (2013) *Development of Slum Areas in Egypt.* Informal Settlements Development Facility

Ministry of International Cooperation (MOIC) (2016) *Greater Cairo Underground Metro in Collaboration with France.* http://www.moic.gov.eg/Front/About/StoriesDetail.aspx?MedId=3070

Ministry of Planning (MOP) (2015) *2030 Egypt Vision.* http://mop.gov.eg/MopRep/SDS_Summary_English.pdf

Mitchell T (2002) *Rule of Experts: Egypt, Techno-politics, Modernity.* Los Angeles: University of California Press

Nabil W (2016) al-A'smarat: The residents of el-Dwyqa leave the informal settlements. *Almasry alyoum.* http://www.almasryalyoum.com/news/details/956240

Nagati O & Stryker B (2013) *Archiving the City in Flux: Cairo's Shifting Urban Landscape since the January 25th Revolution.* Cairo: CLUSTER

Nagati O & Stryker B (2016) Cairo downtown passages: A Framework for urban regeneration. In: B Stryker & O Nagati (eds) *Creative Cities: Re-framing Downtown Cairo.* Cairo: CLUSTER. pp. 176–187

Nasir N (2016) Residents of Manshyat Naṣir about their relocation to al-A'smarāt: 'Sisi promises have no substances'. *Masr Alarabia.* http://www.masralarabia.com/

National Authority for Tunnels (NAT) (2013) https://www.nat.org.eg/english/

New Urban Communities Authority (NUCA) (n.d.) 6 October City. http://www.newcities.gov.eg/english/New_Communities/October/default.aspx

Nile TV International (2016, 30 May) El Sisi inaugurates a new housing project in Asmarat area for Doweka residents. http://www.nileinternational.net/en/?p=29294

PDP (2013) Objective and mission. http://egypt-urban.net/objective-and-mission/

PDP (2014, 30 November) PDP inaugurates urban upgrading units in Cairo and South Giza Governorates. *Urban-net.* http://egypt-urban.net/pdp-inaugurates-urban-upgrading-units-in-cairo-and-south-giza-governorates/

Portugali J (2012) Complexity theories of cities: Implications to urban planning. In: J Portugali, H Meyer, E Stolk & E Tan (eds) *Complexity Theories of Cities Have Come of Age: An Overview with Implications to Urban Planning and Design.* Heidelberg: Springer. pp. 221–244

Presidency of the Republic, Statistical Department (1958) *Vital Statistics.* Cairo: General organization for government printings offices

Qalyubiyah Governorate (2016) About Qalyubiyah Governorate. http://www.qaliobia.gov.eg/SitePages/Nabza.aspx

Rabbat N (2011) Special problems in Islamic and non-Western architecture: Cairo, the history of a metropolis. Course notes, Department of Architecture, Massachusetts Institute of Technology

Ramadan B (2017, 3 July) Member of Parliament Ahmed Al-Sigini: Local elections will take place after the presidency elections. *Al-Masry Al-Youm.* https://www.almasryalyoum.com/news/details/1157453

Raymond A (2007) *Cairo: City of history*. Cairo: The American University in Cairo Press

Serag Y (2013) The Haussmanization approach: From a counter revolution urban fabric to a success factor for the Egyptian revolution in Cairo. Proceedings of B13-Cairo, 01-13

Sertich AN (2010) Cairo: A quick intro to the city. *Favel Issues*. https://favelissues.com/2010/09/30/cairo-a-quick-intro-to-the-city/

Shaheen M (2016, December 4) The story of al-A'smarat (Tahya Misr City)

Shawkat Y (2013) *Social Justice and the Built Environment: A Map of Egypt*. The Right for Housing Initiative

Sims D (2010) *Understanding Cairo: The Logic of a City out of Control*. Cairo: The American University in Cairo Press

Sims D (2014) *Egypt's Desert Dreams: Development or Disaster*. Cairo: The American University in Cairo Press

Singerman D (1995) *Avenues of Participation: Family, Politics, and Networks in Urban Quarters of Cairo*. Princeton, NJ: Princeton University Press

State Information service (SIS) (2009, 20 July) Egypt Location. http://www.sis.gov.eg/Story/2?lang=en-us

State Information Service (SIS) (2016) About Egypt. http://www.sis.gov.eg/En/Templates/Categories/tmpLand.aspx?CatID=10

SYSTRA (2016, 22 April) Cairo Metro: SYSTRA named general consultant for phase three of line 3. https://www.systra.com/en/newsroom/article/cairo-metro-systra-named-general-consultant-for-phase-three-of-line-3

Tadamun (2013) A constitutional approach to urban Egypt. http://www.tadamun.co/a-constitutional-approach-to-urban-egypt/?lang=en

Tadamun (2014) Coming up short: Egyptian Government approaches to informal areas. http://www.tadamun.co/coming-short-government-approaches-informal-areas/?lang=en

Tadamun (2015) Egypt's new cities: Neither just nor efficient. http://www.tadamun.co/egypts-new-cities-neither-just-efficient/?lang=en

Tadamun (2015) Masākin `Uthmān. http://www.tadamun.info/?post_type=city&p=5737&lang=en&lang=en#.WERlN1x2Hk8

Tadamun (2016) Egypt's national assessment of progress towards sustainable development goals. http://www.tadamun.co/egypts-national-assessment-progress-towards-sustainable-development-goals/?lang=en

Tahya Misr Fund (2016) Tahya misr city (al-A'asmarāt 1,2,3). http://tahyamisrfund.org/Front/Program/SeeMore?articleId=6297

Takween (2017) Pilot Public Space and Environmental Upgrading in Izbit Khayrallah-Cairo. https://issuu.com/takweenicd/docs/khairallah_booklet_final_113016-shu

Timraz M (2016) Cairo governorate relocates 900 families in al-A'asmarāt 1-2. *al-Youm al-Saba*. http://www.youm7.com/story/2016/11/19/

Unesco (n.d.) *Urban Regeneration Project for Historic Cairo: Second Report on the Activities*. Cairo: Unesco

UN-Habitat (2011) *Cairo: A City in Transition*. Cairo: UN-Habitat Regional Office for the Arab States

UN-Habitat (2016) *The First Egypt Urban Forum 2015*. Cairo: UN-Habitat Regional Office for the Arab States

United Nations, Department of Economic and Social Affairs, Population Division (2014) *World Urbanization Prospects: The 2014 Revision, Highlights (ST/ESA/ SER.A/352)*. https://population.un.org/wup/Publications/Files/WUP2014-Highlights.pdf

United Nations, Department of Economic and Social Affairs, Population Division (2016) *The World's Cities in 2016: Data Booklet (ST/ESA/ SER.A/392)*. https://www.un.org/en/development/desa/population/publications/pdf/urbanization/the_worlds_cities_in_2016_data_booklet.pdf

World Bank (2000) *Cairo Urban Transport Note*. http://www.euromedina.org/bibliotheque_fichiers/espace_organisation/Skhirat_enquete_pays_Egypt2.pdf

World Population Review (2016) *Cairo Population*. World Population Review. http://worldpopulationreview.com/world-cities/cairo-population/

Wunsch JS (2001) Decentralization, local governance and 'recentralization' in Africa. *Public Administration and Development: The International Journal of Management Research and Practice* 21(4): 277–288

CHAPTER 5

Traditional chiefs and traditional authority in Kinshasa

Philippe Ibaka Sangu

Introduction

After gaining their independence, many an African national government has used its capital city to symbolise the emergence of a new nation and to reflect its central authority. However, these two processes have not been uniform since different postcolonial regimes have developed approaches to nation building and to state formation at different stages and in differing ways (Bekker & Therborn 2012). This is true of the Democratic Republic of the Congo (DRC) where, after its independence in 1960, four successive regimes (between 1960 and 2016) have intervened in the built environment of the capital city.

The aim of this chapter is to identify which policies and practices these postcolonial regimes have applied to traditional chiefs in Kinshasa and how traditional authorities in this capital city have adapted to these interventions. Moreover, the ways these chiefs and their authority structures have adapted vary both over time as well as in different zones of the capital city. In other words, the various forms of coexistence of traditional and modern urban institutions are fixed neither in time nor in space (Ibaka 2019).

A concise history of the capital city culminating in the introduction of modern urban institutions will first be presented. This section will include a discussion of the demarcation into three zones of the geographical region of what is now the province of Kinshasa. Subsequently, traditional chiefs and traditional authorities both in the DRC and in Kinshasa will be presented. This is followed by examples of exchanges between central governments and traditional chiefs in Kinshasa during the postcolonial period.

The 1980s establishment of a national legal institution designed to legalise the coexistence (*cohabitation*) of the state and traditional authorities changed the nature of this relationship in the DRC as a whole. Its application to chiefs in Kinshasa will be identified as an important milestone in the process of traditional chiefly adaptation in the capital city. The focus will then shift to a discussion of the different ways in which traditional chiefs have adapted to urban realities in each of the three zones of Kinshasa. Evidence from three case studies including interviews carried out by the author (Ibaka 2019), one in each zone, will supplement this analysis. A key feature of these divergent processes of adaptation is the issue of land tenure.

The informal nature of service delivery for most Kinshasa residents is the context within which conclusions will be drawn. It appears that most chiefly authority in the capital city is diminishing, though a degree of coexistence (*cohabitation*) endures.

The development of Kinshasa as the capital city of an independent DRC

During the period from 1888 to 1910, Léopoldville was the capital of Stanley-Pool, one of the administrative districts of the colonial Belgian Congo. From 1910 to 1930, Léopoldville became the capital of the district of Moyen-Congo and, in 1929, the city became the seat of all colonial state departments. This administrative situation was retained until Congo became independent in 1960 (Kiaku Mayamba Niangi 2015: 33).

Léopoldville did not legally gain the status of a city until June 1941. Earlier, it was designated as an 'urban district' and was divided into two zones: the urban zone and the indigenous zone in the south (Munayi Muntu-Monji 2010: 49). Over the last two decades before independence, the city grew rapidly in size and incorporated the neighbouring settlement of Kimwenza (Kiaku Mayamba Niangi 2015: 34). On 30 June 1960, with a population of 443 000, Léopoldville became the capital of independent Congo and it was not until the Ordinance Law of 1968 that the city took on the name, Kinshasa (Kiaku Mayamba Niangi 2015: 35). Kinshasa was granted the status of a province in 1982, enabling it to receive the same powers and responsibilities as those of all the country's other provinces. As a province, it was governed by an appointed governor at the head of a provincial government tasked with implementing central government directives to modernise the city. In 1982, its population was 2 338 000, a figure that had risen to 12 624 000 by 2017 (Populationstat 2020).

The names of the presidents who have reigned over national governments in the DRC may be used to identify the four postcolonial regimes: Joseph Kasa-Vubu (1960–1965), Joseph Désiré Mobutu (1965–1997), Laurent Désiré Kabila *pere* (1997–2001) and Joseph Kabila Kabange *fils* (2001–2016). As the first president, Kasa-Vubu promoted the ideals of l'ABAKO (Alliance or Association of the Bakongo), an ethnicity-based cultural movement that was transformed into a political party on the eve of independence. Subsequently, during his lengthy period of rule, Mobutu employed the rhetoric of nationalism under single party rule (N'Sele Manifesto 1965: 6). It was during this regime that the National Alliance of Traditional Authorities of Congo (ANATC), a national legal institution designed to legalise the coexistence (*cohabitation*) of the state and traditional authorities, was promulgated. The short and conflictual tenure of Laurent Kabila culminated in his assassination and the presidential regime of his son. Joseph Kabila Kabange employed the rhetoric of 'revolution of modernity' to call for both industrial as well as agricultural reforms in the DRC (Kambila Kankwende wa Mpunga 2017: 131).

The classification of the national economy of the DRC as that of a rentier economy – where access to its enormous natural wealth is controlled by the national government

Figure 1. The three zones defined by urban planning and land tenure, Kinshasa 2011

Source: De Saint Moulin (2011: 28); adaptation (author) 2018

and its associated elites – has been both a shared characteristic and the main driver of development during the last three regimes, those of Mobutu, Kabila *pere*, and Kabila *fils*. Both Kabila presidents have, in this respect, reproduced the Mobutu system of patrimonial governance. The DRC has major ongoing security challenges (especially in north Kivu), an economy that is broadly informal and a history of distrust between ordinary citizens and elites (Trefon 2009: 16). Accordingly, the relationships between chiefs in Kinshasa and DRC presidents were driven by the chiefs' attempts to reconcile themselves with the patrimonial system and to gain where they could from the wealth controlled at the top.

Kinshasa's current economy is also largely informal. The primary sector includes agriculture, animal husbandry, fishing and forestry, industrial sector manufacturing, mining and construction; and the service sector – as may be expected in a capital city – includes hotels and restaurants, repair services, leisure activities, tourism as well as domestic services, utilities, business services, banking and financial services, transport and telecommunications. Nevertheless, the informal non-agricultural and the informal agricultural sector are significantly larger than their formal counterparts.

The postcolonial urban development of Kinshasa began in earnest at the start of the Mobutu regime. On 2 December 1968, a city ordinance was promulgated which incorporated into the city of Kinshasa the traditional Bahumbu and Batéké sectors as well as the Benkana chieftaincy as municipalities. A state decree in 1969 saw the number of city municipalities rise to 24. In terms of this decree, the vast majority of suburban areas neighbouring the former colonial city centre were established as municipalities (Munayi Muntu-Monji 2010: 283). In each, an appointed *bourgmestre* headed up the municipal council which in turn was tasked with the modernisation attempts initiated by the city and, subsequently, the provincial government. By the year 2011, the physical area of Kinshasa (and its resident population) had grown significantly. The population growth was due both to in-migration as well as to the incorporation of rural, traditional communities within new and expanded provincial boundaries. From the 1970s, accordingly, modern urban institutions – the municipal council, the municipality itself and municipal courts (often called peace courts) – were proclaimed to cover Kinshasa's geographical area, with varying degrees of success or failure regarding service delivery.

As shown in Figure 1, the physical area of Kinshasa may be considered to comprise three zones, each defined by city planning and land tenure criteria: the former colonial centre (*ancienne cité*), the planned region outside this centre (*cités planifiées*) and the periphery (*périphèrie*) where neither city planning nor state land tenure regulations in the municipal areas of jurisdiction have been applied comprehensively.

Traditional chiefs and traditional authorities in Kinshasa

A brief overview of the postcolonial legal context of traditional authority in the DRC points toward two forms of access to such authority. The first is the rotating form, in which the different lineages arising from clans having the same origin and a common ancestor rule alternately. The second is the non-rotating or fixed form, in which the descendants of the lineage of the ruling clan are exclusively granted recognition as leaders, without power sharing (Article 15 of the Vade Mecum). After being appointed according to customary rules, leaders are enthroned as chiefs. This distinction has resulted in a number of cases of disputes over power and administration within the chieftaincy. The effective power of the traditional chief consists of three elements: the investiture of the chief who then enjoys indisputable power; the possession of a territory (chieftaincy or grouping) whose boundaries are known to its neighbours and the tenure of which is customary; and the issuing of a decree of recognition by the public authorities, issued by the minister of internal affairs (Article 13 of the Vade Mecum).

When a chieftaincy finds itself in an urban area, three primary challenges to the legitimacy of its authority develop.

The first is simply that the process of urbanisation draws large numbers of migrants from various clans into the territory of the chieftaincy, outsiders who do not recognise the traditional authority of the chief and the traditional institutions of his chieftaincy. The second is the establishment in this territory of modern urban institutions, such as the municipality, its council and court, and its *bourgmestre*; institutions that propose for residents rules other than those proposed by traditional institutions.

Third, and of primary concern, is the issue of land tenure. Chiefs supervise land under communal tenure. As claimed by a chief in 2018: under communal tenure, the role of the chief is not to sell land; he gives it to those who ask for it for their use, at the price of various gifts from the beneficiary. The chief shares the fruit of the sale of the land with his family; the community finds its share in work and other community activities created by the transfer (Ngandoli Musoni, interview conducted in Kinshasa on 7 November 2016). In the urban context, however, land reform promotes state and private ownership of land by using a process of cadastral surveying and registration.

Accordingly, it is apparent that chieftaincies within the boundaries of the province of Kinshasa – whether they have claims as original residents or are migrant chieftaincies – are required to adapt to all three challenges. Before turning to the ANATC – a legal association intended to regulate traditional-state affairs in the DRC – and how chieftaincies have coped with adaption in Kinshasa, the following presents a description of a number of examples of exchanges between central governments and traditional chiefs in Kinshasa during the postcolonial period.

In the decade between 1970 and 1980, the central government under Mobutu planned a number of hillside urban settlements in Kinshasa. They included Cité Salongo in Lemba, Cité Maman Mobutu in Mont-Ngafula, Cité Verte and the Cité de l'Habitat pour l'Humanité (Habitat for Humanity) in Selembao. These cities were built on steep slopes of the hillsides and formed part of what has become the planned zone of the capital city (Lelo Nzuzi 2008: 60). In addition, during the Mobutu period, a presidential stock breeding centre was established in the municipality of N'sele. The president interacted personally with the chiefs of the Nguma and Mabana clans and this breeding centre created employment for local residents.

During the regime of Kabila *pere* (1997–2001), the president established a central Department of National Agriculture and obtained arable land in the municipal area of Kingakati/Plateau-Maluku in Kinshasa. Production was intended for the markets of the capital city as well as for what was called 'strategic reserves.' These developments are reported to have taken place by way of collaboration between the president and local chiefs. Similarly, during the regime of Kabila *fils* (2001–2019), collaboration with local chiefs is reported to have led to the purchase by the president of a farm at Kingakati for personal use. In both cases, agricultural employment for locals had been created (Mudi Nini-Manshwo, interview conducted in Kinshasa on 27 January 2018).

Figure 2. Chief Ebalavo M. Davin, Groupement Kimwenza à Mont Ngafula

Source: Author (Kinshasa, December 2017)

The establishment of the ANATC and its activities in Kinshasa

Prior to the establishment of the ANATC in 1995, the traditional chiefs of Kinshasa had already organised themselves into the Téké-Humbu Committee of traditional chiefs. The aim of this committee was to settle disputes related to traditional rights and to ensure the development of the communal lands they believed belonged to their ancestors, the first occupants of Kinshasa. Toward the end of the Mobutu regime, the central government decided, for the DRC as a whole, to create an Association – the National Alliance of Traditional Authorities of Congo (ANATC) – to oversee the involvement of traditional chiefs in the affairs of the country and to promote grassroots development in their areas of jurisdiction (Article 3 of the Articles of Association). The ANATC is managed by a National Committee that delegates powers to Basic Committees each of which is responsible for traditional affairs in a province (Articles 52–53 of the Articles of Association). Its head office is in Kinshasa.

In 2004, an extraordinary general assembly of ANATC adopted the ANATC's Internal Regulations. Its secretary-general, Chief Pene Mayenge, in his opening address, recalled that the Association had become disorderly due to the lack of competent and effective leadership. 'This situation,' he said, 'has resulted in us missing a lot of opportunities in the face of the political issues of the day. The Alliance has lost all its credibility both inside and outside (Kinshasa and) the country as a whole. This is why we have decided to convene this Assembly, so that we can speak the same language, [...] and set up a new National Executive Committee that can help us reshape our story' (General Assembly 2004: 6). The issue of weak leadership was put down to disagreements, inter alia, in Kinshasa, between traditional chiefs who had entered into bargains with political and administrative authorities in conflict with one another as well as with the guidelines of the Association.

Despite these difficulties, the governor of the province of Kinshasa appointed six members of the arbitration commission of ANATC to deal with customary disputes. Numerous cases have been heard and two recent cases may be mentioned as examples. The first involved disputes in the Kingakati clan in Maluku, and the second in the Mikondo clan in N'sele. The Kingakati case concerned the hereditary Chief Mudi Ferdinand and the self-appointed Chief Munkani who, not being a legitimate successor, was removed from office. Similarly, the Mikondo dispute concerned hereditary Chief Ndola Luzayadio and the pretender, the self-appointed Chief Moba Embama (Esim Eyum, interview conducted in Kinshasa on 4 March 2018).

Within the periphery zone of Kinshasa, some 20 'sectional committees' (associated with ANATC and tasked to identify disputes) in the three peripheral municipalities have been established: ten in Maluku, five in N'sele and six in Mont Ngafula (General Assembly 2004: 24–25). Nonetheless, a number of chiefs of the Téké-Humbu clans of Kinshasa have stated with bitterness that insecurity has become the norm in the city, the actions of ANATC notwithstanding. Chiefs of the Téké-Humbu clan, moreover, called upon urban development agents to provide employment opportunities in the domains of agriculture and road works in their areas of jurisdiction (General Assembly 2004: 25).

Adaptation of chiefs in the three zones of the province of Kinshasa

In Kinshasa, traditional authorities and their chiefs are compelled to coexist with the city's modern urban institutions and with the directives of the central government. In this context, the establishment of ANATC may be viewed as a legal framework defining the coexistence (*cohabitation*) of tradition, state and private sector in an urban environment. Coexistence in this sense is a form of adaptation of traditional authorities to the urban environment.

Adaptation in the ancienne cité of Kinshasa

Urban growth within this section of Kinshasa has led to the displacement of traditional villages. During colonial occupation, sites on the banks of the Congo River were developed for colonial use and the villages of Kintambo, Kinshasa, Kingabwa, and Ndolo (amongst others) were required to resettle to the south, inland from the river. After independence, this urban extension absorbed other villages within its boundaries. In short, rather than being able to adapt, the traditional way of life has been displaced entirely from this zone. Traditional authorities faced with increasing numbers of strangers in their territories, the loss of their communal land, and modern urban institutions imposing new ways of living either attempted to resettle elsewhere in the city or were recognised by the ANATC as honorary chiefs, chiefs in name only.

Adaptation in the planned zone of Kinshasa (the case of Makala-Lemba)

Given rising population densities in the cites of this zone, chiefs and their traditional institutions have had to cope with growing numbers of 'foreigners' who wish to live among the local indigenous people. Formally, these outsiders receive land to occupy by providing gifts to the chief. After having settled down, they enjoy the rights of usufruct under one condition: never interfere in the internal affairs of local customs (Ngandoli Musoni, interview conducted in Kinshasa on 7 November 2016). In theory, the chief and his people learn to live with the newcomers in the village or *city*.

The case of the chief of the Makala-Lemba clan – located in this zone – however, is sobering. He is one among many Kinshasa chiefs who have sold all their land and have no customary village in which to exercise their traditional authority. 'The chiefs in the middle of the city have hardly any space,' states Sabakinu (Sabakinu Kivilu, interview conducted in Kinshasa on 17 January 2017). More generally, in the municipalities of Kalamu and Limete, as a result of land and cadastral surveying by the state, both customary lands as well as private concessions have been 'fragmented,' leading to the loss of viable communal land (Ngandoli Musoni, interview conducted in Kinshasa on 7 November 2016).

In this zone, accordingly, chiefly authority and traditional institutions are faced with all three urban challenges: growing numbers of strangers, modern urban institutional establishment and loss of communal land. Disputes that flow from these challenges may well be addressed by ANATC that recognises the authority of chiefs in this zone but the trend towards the loss of authority is clear.

Adaptation in the periphery of Kinshasa (the case of Maluku and N'sele)

The municipalities of Maluku and N'sele are peri-urban. These former rural areas were part of the traditional Kasangulu territory. As revealed above, from time to time the state has approached customary chiefs in this zone for land to carry out its development and commercial projects within the ambit of the built environment of the capital city. The management of land, particularly in this zone, has become a major bone of contention. Though during collaboration with chiefs in promoting these projects, the state claims to respect communal land rights, realities on the ground differ. As densities in this peripheral zone increase, plots are demarcated, bought and become the property of the buyers. Simultaneously, in areas where communal tenure remains in place and densities are lower, plots are transferred under usufruct. When a non-indigenous person arrives to live among the Téké, for example, a plot for occupation and use is granted free of charge. Arable land is leased over a renewable period of 25 years. When this person leaves the host village, all physical improvements and developments (such as fields, trees, houses, etc.) remain behind for the benefit of the chief and his community. In short, as Kinshasa densifies, the chiefs in these peripheral areas rule over and manage entire villages within which more and more requests for the sale of land (rather than a transfer with usufruct) are made. Insofar as they acquiesce to these offers, they will find themselves in the same position as their colleagues in the city centre: honorary chiefs without land who are chiefs in name only. It is apparent that disputes over chieftaincies and over land in this zone keeps ANATC commissions busy.

Conclusion

The province of Kinshasa and its multiple municipal councils are responsible for the delivery of urban services to their residents. The quality and scope of these services is poor for the majority of this urban population and for a growing proportion of residents as one shifts the lens from the former colonial city centre to the planned zone and subsequently to the peripheral zone (Leclerc-Olive 1997; Trefon 2009; Verdet 2014: 11). Most urban dwellers living in the capital city receive most urban services informally rather than from their municipalities. It is consequently no surprise that many residents consider the traditional institutions of chieftaincies – within the boundaries of Kinshasa – as genuine and worthy of support, even if they do not belong to the chief's clan.

Simultaneously, the precarious nature of urban living in the capital city has led to the proliferation of three forms of chieftaincies that deviate from the generally accepted institutions of traditional authority in the DRC, and accordingly fall outside the ANATC and its legitimisation of the relationship between chief and state. The first, chiefs labelled '*vagabond chefs*' refer to individuals on the streets who claim chief status and apply for authorisation without support from clan members and without claims to communal land. The second, chiefs labelled as 'self-proclaimed' also refer to individuals who claim chief status and apply for authorisation. In these cases, however, there are residents and a number of local municipal officials who swear allegiance to the self-proclaimed chief. In the third place, there are '*des chefs allogènes*' (chiefs who have migrated into Kinshasa from elsewhere in the DRC). Typically, these chiefs enter the province with members of their clans and settle together with a number of them. They are not able to make claims to communal land in Kinshasa and are not authorised by ANATC as chiefs in Kinshasa (ANATC 2015).

The Democratic Republic of Congo has experienced the existence of traditional chiefs and chiefdoms before, during and after colonisation. The province of Kinshasa, the capital city of the DRC, shares this experience. Kinshasa, however, has experienced rapid urbanisation and provides residence today to some 12 million Congolese (Verdet 2014). These urban dwellers are a mixture of locally born and internal migrants from different parts of the country and, accordingly, from various traditional clans in the country. Chiefs in the city comprise indigenous chiefs with clans and claims to communal land falling within the area of jurisdiction of the province as well as other chiefs (ranging from migrant traditional leaders to those that are self-proclaimed or vagabond). New urban institutions operating in the same urban areas include *bourgmestres* and their municipal councils.

The challenge for chieftaincies to adapt to this new institutional urban environment is apparent. As identified above, in fact, chiefs and their chieftaincies' have been living within a national state the leaders of whom have monopolised access to the natural wealth of the country. Accordingly, their relationships with these leaders and presidents have been driven by attempts to reconcile themselves with the patrimonial system and to gain where they could from the wealth controlled at the top.

The process of adaptation has not been uniform: its form depends not only on the nature of chiefly authority but also whether institutions find themselves in the former colonial zone, in the new planned zone or in the peripheral zone of Kinshasa. In the former colonial zone, traditional institutions have disappeared and have been replaced by modern urban state institutions; in the planned zone, they have lost much of their authority; and in the periphery, they tend to coexist with their modern equivalents. With the creation of a national institution called the National Alliance of Traditional Authorities of Congo (ANATC), some of the traditional leaders in the city have been offered a statutory opportunity to collaborate and coexist with modern state institutions.

References

ANATC (2015, août) Secrétaire Général de l'ANATC, Conférence de Presse. ACP. Kinshasa

Bekker S & Therborn G (eds) (2012) *Capital Cities in Africa: Power and Powerlessness.* Cape Town and Dakar: CODESRIA and HSRC Presses

Bolia Ikoli B (2015) *Kinshasa ma ville, ma capitale.* Paris: L'Harmattan

De Maximy R (1984) *Kinshasa ville en suspens. Dynamique de la croissance et problèmes d'urbanisme. Approche sociopolitique.* Paris: ORSTOM

De Saint Moulin L (1971) Les anciens villages des environs de Kinshasa. *Etudes d'Histoire africaine* n° 2: 83–119

De Saint Moulin L (2011) *Atlas de l'organisation administrative de la République Démocratique du Congo,* 2e éd. Revue et amplifiée. Kinshasa: CEPAS

De Saint Moulin L (2012) *Kinshasa: Enracinements historiques et horizons culturels.* Paris: L'Harmattan

General Assembly (2004) Assemblée Générale extraordinaire et élective de l'ANATC, Kinshasa février 2004

Ibaka P (2019) Adaptation des institutions traditionnelles a la gestion foncière de Kinshasa, ville-capitale (1960–2016). Doctoral dissertation, Stellenbosch University

Kambila Kankwende wa Mpunga J-P (2017) *Joseph Kabila Kabange. Essai sur une idéologie du progrès*. Paris, L'Harmattan

Kiaku Mayamba Niangi J-B (2015) *Ngaliema (Kinshasa) commune de paradoxe*. Paris: L'Harmattan

Leclerc-Olive M (1997) Espaces 'métis' et légitimité de l'État : l'expérience malienne. In: *GEMDEV* (éd.) *Les avatars de l'État en Afrique*. Paris: Karthala. pp. 177–192

Lelo Nzuzi F (2008) *Kinshasa: Ville et environnement*. Paris: L'Harmattan

Lelo Nzuzi F (2013) *Kinshasa: Planification & Aménagement*. Paris: L'Harmattan

Mambi Tunga-Bau H (2010) *Pouvoir traditionnel et pouvoir d'Etat en République Démocratique du Congo. Esquisse d'une théorie d'hybridation des pouvoirs politiques*. Kinshasa: Médiaspaul

Mambi Tunga-Bau H (2012) *Pouvoir traditionnel et contrats de cession des terres en République Démocratique du Congo*. Paris: L'Harmattan RDC

Mulendevu Mukokobya R (2013) *Pluralisme juridique et règlement des conflits fonciers en République Démocratique du Congo*. Paris: L'Harmattan

Munayi Muntu-Monji T (2010) *Genèse et évolution des circonscriptions administratives et des entités politico-administratives congolaises (1888–2009)*. Kinshasa: Editions de l'Université Protestante au Congo (EDUPC)

N'Sele Manifesto (1965) Pamphlet 'Le Manifeste de la N'Sele'. Mouvement populaire de la révolution (Zaire) République du Zaïre, 196

Populationstat – World Statistical Data (2017–2020) Kinshasa, Democratic Republic of Congo Population. https://populationstat.com/democratic-republic-of-the-congo/kinshasa

Trefon T (2009) Public service provision in a failed state: Looking beyond predation in the Democratic Republic of Congo. *Review of African Political Economy* 36(119): 9–21

Vade Mecum (2001, août) Des autorités traditionnelles de la RDC. Kinshasa

Verdet F (2014) Schéma d'orientation stratégique de l'agglomération de Kinshasa (SOSAK) et plan particulier d'aménagement de la partie Nord de la ville (PPA). *SOSAK Définitif-S4*, Kinshasa, Août 2014

PART II

The popular in urban Africa

Sylvia Croese

This part of the book explores the role of popular forces in African cities.

The first chapter unpacks the black box of the state and explores the different ways in which state officials in the city of Johannesburg in South Africa have contested plans for mega housing projects directed by national government. The chapter identifies three different repertoires that have been used by state officials at different scales of sub-national government that range from passive-aggressive behaviour, to cattle-trading and feigned compliance to show that the state is no monolith but is comprised of institutional, personal and professional relations, often operating in concert, collusion and, just as often, in contestation, contradiction and working at cross-purposes.

The following chapter shows that, just as the state represents a multiplicity of actors and interests, society is equally pluralistic. Through a study of the role of civil society during the years post-Government of National Unity (GNU) in Zimbabwe, the chapter shows that the role of civil society in representing popular interests can wax and wane. While having played an important role in challenging the ZANU-PF party state, formal civil society weakened in the face of economic hardship, repression and informalisation. This opened up space for a popular politics that went beyond party politics and divides and instead organised around key individuals and issues, played out on the streets and through the use of social media. While unable to effect structural change, it led the way to the fall of longstanding President Mugabe in 2017.

The third chapter looks at protest in the informal settlement of Mathare, in the Kenyan capital of Nairobi, where community members use community meetings to demand water supply and, consequently, to be recognised by city authorities. Important here is the continuation of the neglect of the settlement, which dates back to colonial times, and the strong disjuncture between what the author calls a denial of 'hydrological citizenship' and masterplans which seek to transform the city into a 'world-class African metropolis.'

CHAPTER 6

Local government as the stage for resistance: Strategies and tactics of opposing mega projects in the city of Johannesburg

Margot Rubin

Introduction

In 2014, the Minister for Human Settlements Lindiwe Sisulu launched a new policy direction for the development of human settlements (Ballard & Rubin 2017). The minister said '[w]e need to move from small projects of 200 houses to mega projects of integrated housing mix to cater for different incomes and needs' (quoted in Petterson 2014). Sisulu noted that the Department of Human Settlements would spend 100 days identifying 50 National Priority Projects which would become mega human settlements each one a minimum of 10 000 units (Merten 2014). The call was subsequently taken up by Gauteng's premier and MEC Jacob Mamabolo (2015) with the announcement of the construction of new towns, catering for over 60 000 households: 'In this new vision, we stated two objectives notably, building post-apartheid cities, secondly, completing current legacy projects, or RDP housing development trajectory.'

Provincial Human Settlements officials were alarmed by the announcement: the drive from a national level of the state to institute and push a local project contravened provincial and municipal plans, and long-term projects. These national visions were generally not shared by the 'street-level bureaucrats' tasked with carrying them out. However, despite voicing their concerns to their seniors, officials did not gain any traction and sought ways to deal with this national interference into the local realm.

The following chapter intends to operate on a number of scales: it briefly examines the manner in which the national, in this case embodied by South Africa's National Department of Human Settlements (NDHS), sought to entrench its specific visions in the local. The core focus though is the sets of practices and micro-practices; 'tactics' and weapons that generally low-level or less politically powerful bureaucrats and officials utilised to fend off nationally imposed policies and approaches. These can be conceptualised as the weapons of 'the weak' against 'the strong' (Scott 1985) using the tactics of the *other* (De Certeau 1984). The end result was not a complete 'win' or 'loss' but a set of compromises that make for an unevenly implemented set of policies and practices. The cases open up how and by what forces cities and urban spaces are shaped, the contradictions and contestations that occur within the edifice of 'the state' and how these then become manifest in the cityscape (Hornby et al. 2017).

Beyond the edifice: Inside the bureaucracy

> The work of administration takes place in the fluorescent-lit rooms of drab office buildings where thousands of bureaucrats type streams of information into outdated computers or file handwritten notes in inaccessible archives. From all appearances, this is not an arena of political action at all. Bureaucracy ... obviates individual agency. The humanness of the human condition gets lost in the files, the halls, the shufflings of bureaucratic administration. (Bernstein & Mertz 2011: 6–7)

But it is within these drab shufflings that, if cities are not made, they are certainly influenced. In the hundreds of decisions made by these gods of small things that laminate over time into the materialities of urban spaces. This section assists in chipping away at the 'edifice,' presenting the humanity of bureaucrats and moments of interface and contestation that exist between levels of government and the networks of formal and informal relationships which operate within the state.

Bureaucracies have terrible reputations and have borne the brunt of the critique; caught between a Weberian sense that 'the professional bureaucrat is chained to his activity by his entire material and ideal existence. In the great majority of cases, he is only a single cog in an ever-moving mechanism which prescribes to him an essentially fixed route of march' (Gerth & Mills 1991: 228). In such thinking, bureaucrats lacked agency or even thought and the state was caricatured as a 'vending machine' in which money and resources went in, and through a set of standardised machinery, an assembly line solution produced following the rules of standard procedure (Chipkin 2011). Alternatively, when agency was allowed '[b]ureaucrats at such institutions embod[ied] the spirit of this unpredictable and liminal creature. They [we]re at once inanimate – lazy automatons, blindly serving larger powers – and animate – nefarious, self-interested obstructionists' (Hoag 2011: 82).

However, beginning in the late 1960s a different and more human view was proposed. Lipsky (1969) posited the street-level bureaucrat who questioned whether officials' 'actions in determining whether or not to provide services [operated] according to laws, regulations, and professional norms' (Hoag 2011: 84). Lipsky (1969) saw that bureaucrats were often at the mercy of intersecting forces: political and hierarchical pressure from those above, community groups and social connections, and their own prejudices, politics and sympathies. More recent work takes its inspiration from gender studies and intersectionality based on Haraway and others who reject the idea of a neutral 'cog' in a bureaucratic wheel and 'reclaims vision as an embodied practice, reminding us that all gazes are from somewhere, and a specifically material somewhere' (Lipsky 1969).

As a consequence, daily practices and everyday lives and decisions that constitute the activities of bureaucrats has become an increasing field of interest. How bureaucrats make decisions, their reasons for assigning or not assigning resources, their discretion have been the subject of ethnographic work, examining the sets of social rules that govern exchanges and make them possible. The relationships that exist between 'the public' and the bureaucrats has also become a fertile area of study, particularly in the context of the Global South, where Chatterjee identified 'political society' and the need for platforms of engagement due to the illegality or extra legality of certain urban actors. Where local 'big men' act as mediators on behalf of groups who otherwise would not be able to access the official mechanisms of the state (Chatterjee 2004). Others have noted the informal or so-called 'rude' forms of accountability which, through shame and embarrassment, pressures to maintain reputation and status, and the threat of violence force action and service delivery (Hossain 2010); as well as the institutional structures, which allow front-line bureaucrats to evade responsibility (Chatterjee 2012). Much of the work has focused on the more negative aspects of the bureaucracy and the blame for the failure of state policies. There are fewer attempts which examine the 'will to improve' (Li 2007), and note the 'best intentions' of bureaucrats or take less normative stances, attempting to understand the informal practices of the state at the micro-level. These are attempts to understand the interface between the state and its client, customers and citizens: the state's public guise as it faces outwards.

There is also a burgeoning literature that looks at some aspects of the inward gaze, however, here too it is dominated by more negative accounts with much of the work examining various iterations of corruption. There is a focus in postcolonial and post-communist states on the force of corruption as a driver and shaper of the bureaucracy and its daily function: pointing out the institutional design of bureaucracies to enhance and support lines of personal gain and political patronage (Golden 2003), or the 'politicization of the ministerial bureaucracy to the desire of governing parties to enhance their political control over the formulation and implementation of public policies' (Meyer-Sahling 2006: 274). In general, there is the sense that '[t]he institutional legacies of a relatively weak state, coupled with the emergence of resource-poor and power-hungry political parties, have historically provided a fertile ground for the emergence of patronage politics in many areas of the world' (Bratton & Van de Walle 1997). In Africa, a disturbing line of argument is that 'the state' is a 'pseudo-Western façade' which is still largely captured by society and politics (Chabal & Daloz 1999: 9–16). As such, the state operates within the coils of 'personalised' and 'particularised' relationships with the political and social.

In South African literature authors such as Chipkin (2011, 2013), have taken the bureaucracy as an object of study; Cameron (1996, 2005, 2014) attempting to clarify institutional and structural aspects of the post-apartheid government, and Benit-Gbaffou (2007, 2008) has looked at the interface between the state and modes of engagement. All of which are useful, but it is to Von Holdt (2010) that I turn as he has complexified and unpacked patronage in the South African context, where policies of affirmative action and a culture of deference, coupled with a skills shortage 'generat[e] a powerful culture of moving onwards and upwards' and 'encourages a culture of facing upwards' rather than outwards towards the sites and interfaces of engagement with the public. As a consequence, civil servants are removed from on-the-ground engagement, leading to what is often called 'poor service delivery.'

Facing upwards is not the only way of examining the hierarchy, and urban theorists note that there is no automatic acceptance of national policies into local and daily practice, rather accomplishing such a feat requires the acceptance, and validation of those who need to implement it (Buitelaar, Galle & Sorel 2011). Such acceptance and internalisation is also at the mercy of the informal networks and local cultures that exist. Veron et al. (2003) noted these dissonances in India's bureaucratic architecture, explaining that the lack of validation is driven, at least in part, by the stark contrasts between the levels of government and also the class and educational gaps between the various bureaucrats within the state.

This begins to shed light into the vast differences between those who promulgate policies and regulations and those who implement them. It is into this gap that the following case steps, acknowledging that bureaucracies are key sites of city-making, and that they are not homogenous monoliths, but are comprised of people with their own gaze, histories and politics, much of which is not political or necessarily self-seeking but may come from an opposing or different set of rationalities (Watson 2003). It is these differences, both in vision and position, which act as 'obstacles' to the institutionalisation of national policy (Buitelaar et al. 2011). However, what has been less explored are the mechanisms and modes of contestation within the state through which rebellion occurs. The following sections offer a non-normative account of some of these methods, beginning with an explanation of the national/local contexts and followed by a discussion of the modes and repertoires of contestation.

The national vision in the local sphere: Long-term trajectories

The mega project or mega human settlement vision was first espoused by Minister Sisulu in her 2014 Budget speech:

> MinMec have decided that we will now embark on mega projects, because in this way the economies of scale will be in our favour. In these mega projects there will be a collaboration of all three spheres of government. Local government will ultimately inherit the projects once completed.

In addition, the aim was not only to build new, post-apartheid cities, but to also address issues of poverty, inequality and informality that seemed to be plaguing existing cities and which had been obdurate and unyielding in the face of numerous state attempts (Ballard & Rubin 2017). The idea was that the new cities would somehow stimulate economic growth, offering economic activities and employment, along with a full range of services and facilities. They should also include a range of income groups, moving beyond the current perpetuation of segregated development in these terms (Harrison & Todes 2017: 32–33).

In October 2014, following the initial announcement, the Department of Human Settlements hosted a Housing Indaba. A key moment at the indaba was the unveiling of a social contract which required signatories to commit to '[b]uild 50 catalytic projects and install basic services in all developing towns including revitalising mining towns.' It was apparently also at the indaba that the minister called on all spheres of government and the private sector to submit lists of potential mega projects to national for their consideration.

What followed was a scramble by various departments to support this new policy direction, which in many ways came out of the blue. This is apparently quite normal for South African policy-making: '[This] is a classic case: which is … the political announcement is made first, and then go in and do this' (Narsoom 2016). As such, the Housing Development Agency (HDA) was tasked with making the policy direction viable; a difficult task, since there was 'No consultation initially and although projects were supposed to be decided with relevant local authorities, it was realistically left to the HDA to scramble to devise a process for assessment that could be used to select the relevant projects' (Anonymous HDA officials 1 and 2, 2016). Furthermore, according to an Ekurhuleni Official: 'Private sector developers submitted directly to national without coming via local or provincial,' circumventing local planning processes. This left the HDA in a very awkward position, 'It's very difficult to go back on a political decision or political announcement … how do we almost manage this, what's the word I'm looking for, ameliorate sort of … and it's me thinking with my bureaucratic hat, "oh god this is a disaster how do we fix it up without allowing anybody to have their noses out of joint?"' (Anonymous 3, 2016).

Thus, the HDA was left to devise a process that appeared to legitimate a new set of spatial interventions that circumvented all of the planning legislation and effectively stamped the authority of national on to the local sphere. Also ignored by both national and provincial authorities was the fact that this form of sprawl flew in the face of years of work by the larger metros who had dedicated time and effort to legislating more compact, denser cities, structured along transit-orientated development principles. All of which was disregarded in favour of a model that promoted sprawled urbanisation across the province.

The ministerial pronouncements were taken by officials at all levels, that mega projects would be the new direction of the various Departments of Human Settlements. In Gauteng, the policy was picked up with alacrity and by April 2015, Gauteng launched its own mega projects policy with some of its own provincial ideals. It was argued that the proposed new fully functional mixed income, mixed use towns, built outside of existing cities would effectively deal with the wicked and entrenched issues of apartheid spatial planning, and provide much needed economic impetus to the stagnating provincial economies. Mega projects also satisfied a political agenda, with a premier and high-level ANC officials who wanted recognition for contributing to a radical, transformative project leading up to the ANC's policy conference, scheduled for December 2017.

In some ways, such practice should also be seen within its most recent historical context. After the democratic transition of South Africa in 1994, there was a long-term sustained project to decentralise powers and responsibilities to the local sphere. The South African Constitution clearly designated a number of mandates to local government: planning, land management and infrastructure development. The Constitution also designates three cooperative but autonomous spheres of government, where there are moments of conjoined and independent responsibility. Despite the protections offered by the Constitution, national government has consistently interfered in the operations of municipal government, often seeing it as nothing more than the service delivery arm (Steytler 2005). A number of both overt and subversive strategies have been undertaken in attempts to pull local government back into the central fold (Moya 2008). Moya's (2008) analysis of five dimensions of recentralisation including fiscal and policy-making autonomy, Kroukamp's (2008) examination of the attempted implementation of the Single Public Service Bill as an outright attempt to regain control over the municipalities, whilst Cameron's (2014) analysis of the acts of subversion in the Western Cape all illustrate the strong and indomitable will of the national government's attempts to maintain control over municipalities, especially those wayward enough to elect other parties.

There were also global forces and national political intentions at work. In the South African context, the last few years have seen a loss of legitimacy of the African National Congress on the national and international stage. The allegations of corruption and charges of misconduct against the top leadership have tainted the country's reputation and large infrastructural projects are loaded with political symbolism, intended to 'demonstrate national technological prowess' (Van der Westhuizen 2007: 335). Mega projects, which have generally been constructed within cities, have been used to signify rebranding of cities, making them more attractive and competitive to elite residents and international capital (Hannan & Sutherland 2015). At the same time, there has been a move towards 'new cities' or cities from scratch across the globe. These are often private sector-led housing projects, located on the urban peripheries of existing cities (Herbert & Murray 2015). Cairo, Moscow, Lagos and Nairobi, to name a few, have designed and committed to this urban form, largely leaving the issues of the past behind in the hope of rebranding and marketing these cities locally and internationally.

Thus the implementation of the mega projects vision, initiated by national government and pushed by provincial elites, can be read in light of the longer trajectory of national interference into the urban space and part of an ongoing battle between national, provincial and local structures over land and cities as the powerbases and vote-banks of the major political parties. It was also a political move intended to demonstrate effectiveness and capacity delivery (Ballard & Rubin 2018) and the ability to compete in the international arena. Thus, the timing of the mega projects approach was hardly coincidental since it occurred in the run-up to local elections and the party conference which took place in 2016. With some commentators arguing that prescience born of extensive political astuteness, the mega projects approach was a last ditch attempt by national government to gain control over urban space before it lost the major metros in the next election and appeal more broadly to a disillusioned and disaffected urban constituency.

Nevertheless, local or provincial government officials did not simply take on the national vision. It was within this milieu, where elites were not paying attention to either the procedural deficits of the approach or critiques of the content, that officials began to find ways of contesting the process through various means.

Strategies and tactics: Weapons of the weak

There are two main lines of analytical framing, and one minor one, that become useful when looking at the response and behaviour of state officials. The first originates with De Certeau (1984) who argued that the city was constituted by the strategies of city producers, the state, the government, business and other institutions. It is through these strategies that bounded, codified and ruled space is constructed and dominated. Maps, laws, regulations, and grids constitute the mechanisms and controls of space through which a powerful elite hold on to and pursue power (Jessop 1997). Strategies are used by those within organisational power structures, whether small or large, such as the state or municipality, the corporation or the proprietor, a scientific enterprise or the scientist. Strategies are deployed against some external entity to institute a set of relations for official adversaries, competitors, clients, customers, or simply subjects (Blauvelt 2003) However, everyday practice usurps, contests and destabilises these strategies through the tactics of the *other*, the subaltern and the non-powerful (Mould 2014):

> The place of the tactic belongs to the other. A tactic insinuates itself into the other's place, fragmentarily, without taking over in its entirety, without being able to keep it at a distance. It has at its disposal no base where it can capitalize on its advantages, prepare its expansions, and secure independence with respect to circumstances. (De Certeau 1984: xix)

Scott's (1985) work speaks to the 'subtle but powerful forms of "everyday resistance"', not the grand gestures of coups and rebellion, but the small ways in which the less powerful respond to and contest domination. Scott (1985) importantly identifies non-cooperation, 'foot-dragging, evasion, false compliance, pilfering, feigned ignorance, slander and sabotage' as the everyday counter-hegemonic acts of the 'weak' against the 'strong'.

There is a point of divergence that the following cases surface: both De Certeau (1984) and Scott (1985) conceptualised the state as 'strong,' the entity against which tactics and weapons of the weak are deployed. However, as discussed earlier, 'the state' is no monolith but is comprised of institutional, personal and professional relations, often operating in concert, collusion and just as often in contestation, contradiction and working at cross-purposes. Furthermore, 'the state' does not embody merely one political group, one class of employees or even one unified ideology. It is a very human machine with all of the whims, quirks, prejudices and faults that typify the vast majority of everyday interaction. Given the above then, it can be seen how within departments, between hierarchies and across departments, particular groups of officials may not and do not approve of or embed the status quo and actively find ways to protest and rebel.

In the cases that are described in the next few sections, relatively less powerful officials within the state hierarchy protest against powerful politicians and political forces. In such cases, direct confrontation and open disobedience are simply not options, both because they are not sufficiently powerful to be paid attention to and also because many of the officials are life-time civil servants. As Von Holdt (2010) has pointed out in the South African context, becoming a civil servant is a potential road to social mobility and is a long-term commitment. Given the highly hierarchical nature of the South African bureaucracy and its close ties to party politics, open protest and confrontation could be a career limiting move. Thus, as Hull (2003), pointed to in other contexts, there is the need for 'the erasure game that is required: bureaucracies generate collective agency, but it is achieved paradoxically through the elaborately detailed individuation of action, and bureaucrats' professional survival relies on their careful and continual eschewal of authorship' (Hoag 2011: 82).

As such, officials need to find modes of protest that are at once covert, and untraceable but more effective than direct and open hostilities. The advantage of these means of resistance is that they 'require little or no coordination or planning; they often represent a form of individual self-help; and they typically avoid any direct symbolic confrontation with authority or with elite norms' (Scott 1985: 29). These are the tactics of the *other* within the state and, as will be seen, comprise a repertoire of action and inaction that is generally ascribed to non-state actors.

There is also an important point of convergence with Scott's (1985) work on poorer communities and De Certeau's (1984) on the subaltern, which is the response by the strong. In both framings, the 'strong' are neither idle nor unresponsive, they too find ways to adapt, respond and push back: varying from violence to the incorporation and adaptation of the counter-hegemonic ideas for coercion and securing agreement.

Provincial officials: Passive-aggressive behaviours

In Gauteng province, officials in one of the units of the Departments of Human Settlements, protested the planned mega projects but the politicians and senior officials were apparently not listening. Possibly driven by political ambitions, senior figures 'might have ... rallied behind the issue ... since government came in place they have not created any cities ... we've been in power for 20 odd years but ... we can't show a city that we have created ...' (Anonymous provincial official 5, 2016). As such, there was pressure that the public 'should see the fruits of this, in this current political term' (Anonymous provincial official 5, 2016).

These provincial officials had been working on spatial change in the province, looking to increase the number of units delivered but as one official put it 'our goal should be compacting cities' (Anonymous provincial official 2, 2016). The officials were also concerned about the feasibility of the mega projects policy direction. As the implementing agents, they wondered how such a project could ever be made a reality, noting concerns around scale and 'the challenge of giving massive numbers to one contractor is what if there happens to be hiccups in that, [...] on that site' (Anonymous provincial official 3, 2016). As well as the lack of sufficient funding 'policy implementation will have to shift, we should not be talking about USDG [Urban Settlements Development Grant] and HSDG [Human Settlements Development Grant] alone because that will not be sufficient in building the kind of ideology that you're looking for' (Anonymous provincial official 4, 2016).

Their fears were not addressed, so they came to Professor Philip Harrison's research chair in Spatial Analysis and City Planning (SA&CP) at the University of the Witwatersrand which has strong connections, personal and professional, to many of the officials. Although the provincial team had been asked to work on a mega projects document, which they duly did, the project was eventually handed over to a service provider who, together with the MEC, produced the final document and they had a number of anxieties over the new document. The requests were simple:

> Could we assist with the construction of a 'neutral' space in which to raise concerns and demonstrate that there were strong empirical arguments for why mega projects were a bad idea?

The team leader worried that 'there were so many things … which were basically cut and paste from somewhere else' (Anonymous provincial official 3, 2016). The new document raised concerns that, 'The modelling of the cities was based on some picture that was taken from China or somewhere' and had no basis in the actual infrastructure layout of the province and did not access the repository of information that the officials had access to and used in their work. Effectively, their expertise and their knowledge were sidelined. Furthermore, they were also left in a more awkward position: 'How do you critique what you initially conceptualised?' (Anonymous provincial official 4, 2016). The officials were also keenly aware that the process had been top-down and that 'for municipalities … not to be in [on it from] the beginning … was an oversight, especially, knowing, we [provincial government] are going to *their* spaces to build' (Anonymous provincial official 4, 2016).

It was being caught in this bind that also inspired the officials to approach Wits University to host an event, invite municipalities and metros so that they could also voice their concerns. The idea was to invite the relevant politicians and officials to ensure that they heard all the parties. We were also asked for any readings, research or materials that could be shared to help them with their internal briefs. These actions were motivated by trying to bring the status of the university to bear, to ask for an external voice, something driven by both research and 'science' to get through to those in power. Officials clearly recognised and had previous experience of engagement with academics and their so-called 'authority,' recalling an event where the MEC had had a conversation with Professor Harrison which had helped to shift some of the MEC's thinking: 'And he [the MEC] was keen on engaging on that because, cause remember how Phil [Harrison] gave him information, the information he could have gotten inside from us … [but] when he hears it outside he's like wow!' which does imply that coming to our specific unit also was no accident.

A workshop with a combination of leading 'experts' and officials was planned for engagement between the various units in the provincial department, a way to get the senior officials to listen and a channel to allow municipal officials to share their thoughts, since they had not been consulted. The workshop went ahead but at the eleventh hour, the senior politicians declined and did not attend, leaving the platform in some ways as a proverbial case of preaching to the choir. However, a conversation began where local authorities voiced their disenchantment: 'If Gauteng Province seeks to pursue a model which promotes dispersion, while underpinning metropolitan municipalities are pursuing compaction, there's a problem with this and we do have to align it.' And arguing that there is a need to continue to engage with the MEC, 'So I think it's more important to engage with him to kind of lower expectations around this agenda (CoJ official 2016).

Following the meeting, it was agreed that there could be a set of actions undertaken by Wits University, the Gauteng City Regional Observatory (GCRO) and provincial officials: (1) another colloquium organised by the Provincial Department of Human Settlements similar to the first one but this time more specifically focused on municipal engagement, (2) a city lab organised by the GCRO, as well as using a MEC-MMC forum (IGR), both technical and political meetings, as sites of engagement. The provincial officials also continued with what may be termed a low-level set of activities: writing memos, preparing research and asking the academy for opinion-editorials and material to support their protests against mega projects. Their tactic seemed to be one of utilising empirical findings, and fact-based analysis to contest rhetoric and political force.

However, most of these activities were halted when the key figure in the provincial department was mysteriously seconded to another province, officials noted 'since he left then it was, like, this dialogue just died' (Anonymous provincial official 4, 2016); a move that was apparently in the works for quite some time but was suspicious in its timing. It did mean that the unit leading the charge was left without a head. Almost simultaneously, other members of the project management team were moved to regional offices with new mandates. These transfers served to successfully intimidate some of the staff who were critical of the new policy direction. It was also at this point that officials became slightly more cautious and began to speak about how their engagement with the researchers, was really about 'looking at the core concept [mega projects] critically and ... trying to actually enhance it and make sure that it succeeds' (Anonymous provincial official 4, 2016).

Contesting and cattle-trading:
The City of Johannesburg (COJ)'s response

A key concern voiced by the provincial officials was the lack of consultation, and the 'top-down' nature of the new policy, which was also an area of frustration for the metros. The CoJ engaged in two courses of action. Both of which were relatively more confrontational: they continued to argue against mega projects within the internal and regular meetings that are a part of the normal cycle of engagement between the province and the metros. Also, instead of attempting to wrangle with the provincial department of human settlements, where they apparently were having no effect, they engaged with the provincial planning department with whom they shared a longstanding and collegial relationship. The stakes were high for the city and were both specific and principled: the specific stakes were around particular projects and sites that the CoJ objected to, amongst them were Syferfontein, and Lanseria, both of which are far outside of the areas designated for development. The related matter was the CoJ's principled stance on development: the promotion of densification and compaction along transit-orientated routes, and within specified nodes, to curtail sprawl and redevelop parts of the city. Mega projects as a directive contradicted all of these approaches.

The interaction with the provincial planning authorities was broader than just about mega projects and included ensuring coherence between the key planning documents such as the spatial development frameworks. The documents were duly aligned and, given that the Spatial Development Framework (SDF) is supposed to be the overarching framework of spatial development, the presumption was that most of the mega project ideas would be quashed. However, this was not to be.

Feigned compliance: Ekurhuleni

The Ekurhuleni Metropolitan Municipality (EMM) took a very different approach: that of feigned compliance. The geography of the municipality is highly dispersed, comprised of a number of old town centres that are separate and spread out. The idea of another new town or towns within this area was simply untenable. However, instead of directly confronting the province or national government, the officials apparently agreed to the policy by stating that there was 'a council resolution in support of mega projects.' But then they 're-packaged' a number of smaller, infill projects, into so-called mega projects, noting 'we didn't want to submit too many projects so we aggregated 16 projects into 3: northern cluster, eastern cluster and southern' (Anonymous EMM official 1, 2016).

Using some very ingenious political thinking, they noted, 'There is still no clear distinction between mega projects and catalytic and we are for both. We have clustered projects. We have 9 towns and 9 townships. Lots of buffer in between. If we keep on looking for land on the urban edges there (will be) no services or social facilities. So, we are looking inside. They are both mega and catalytic' (Anonymous EMM official 2, 2016). The EMM have cleverly adopted the language of national but continued with their own spatial plans.

Conclusion: The successes of the tactical deployment of weapons of the weak

The cases analysed in this chapter demonstrate three modes of contestation: provincial officials began with direct engagement but after its failure used the research unit at Wits SA&CP as mediator in order to mobilise the status of experts, scientific knowledge and empirical evidence to counter political rhetoric. However, the success of such a strategy seems very limited with most of the 'rebel leaders' being transferred and senior figures still determined to continue with the policy direction. The CoJ, which also began with direct confrontation ended with circumvention, found some success and some compromise: it would seem that the Departments of Human Settlements found ways to get round their objection to Syferfontein, by simply excluding Johannesburg from the decision-making cluster around projects in the province, despite the fact that it is Johannesburg's land. There is also speculation that there was some cattle trading and CoJ agreed to other projects if the province would support another version of urban renewal in Alexandria. Finally, EMM 'feigned compliance' which seems to have garnered the greatest success. At the time of writing, the mega projects list to be approved included all three of the projects that EMM proposed. Instead of engaging in confrontation, EMM officials chose their moments, found collaborators and mediators to act as their mouthpieces, used alternative paths, circumvented processes and feigned compliance to use the rules of the game against those in power. Taken together these demonstrate the weapons of the weak within the state. While their success was mixed, it is also clear that the national government responded. It removed people, transferred them and thus intimidated the rest of the teams, dragged its feet, utilised opaque processes and finally compromised.

There have been subsequent changes to the list of approved projects and mega projects are now referred to as Priority Human Settlements and Housing Development Areas or PHSHDAs. The latest list, revealed in May 2020, shows a number of projects that are neither mega nor new and seem to indicate there have been more backroom negotiations and debates since the original research was commissioned. However, these PHSHDAs are still seen as vitally important to the National Human Settlement's strategy and will receive a significant portion of national funding and attention over the next few years (Business Insider 2020). This very top-down approach, is also in direct contravention with the more 'bottom-up' approaches of *in situ* upgrading in informal settlements and other resident-led modes that have also been encouraged by national government and will no doubt lead to further contestation and conflict within the state and with its stakeholders over the next few years.

These narratives demonstrate how contested a terrain the state actually is. Although the national government's vision is powerful and is being pushed into the realms of the local it is not uncontested. Despite the power, violence and authority of national government elites, local actors push back, using the weapons at their disposal and the politics of the *other* to reshape policy tools and intents. As such, the city landscape becomes a compromise influenced as much by the powerful, obvious agendas of the strong as the subtle tactical deployment of the weapons of the weak.

References

Ballard R & Rubin M (2017) A 'Marshall Plan' for human settlements: How megaprojects became South African housing policy. *Transformation: Critical Perspectives on Southern Africa* 95(1): 1–31

Bénit-Gbaffou C (2007) Local councillors: Scapegoats for a dysfunctional participatory democratic system? Lessons from practices of local participation in Johannesburg. *Critical Dialogue: Public Participation in Review* 3(2): 26–33

Bénit-Gbaffou C (2008) Are practices of local participation sidelining the institutional participatory channels? Reflections from Johannesburg. *Transformation: Critical Perspectives on Southern Africa* 66/67(1): 1–33

Bernstein A & Mertz E (2011) Introduction: Bureaucracy: Ethnography of the state in everyday life. *PoLAR: Political and Legal Anthropology Review* 34(1): 6–10

Blauvelt A (ed.) (2003) *Strangely Familiar: Design and Everyday Life*. Minneapolis: Walker Art Center

Bratton M & Van de Walle N (1997) *Democratic Experiments in Africa: Regime Transitions in Comparative Perspective*. Cambridge: Cambridge University Press

Buitelaar E, Galle M & Sorel N (2011) Plan-led planning systems in development-led practices: An empirical analysis into the (lack of) institutionalisation of planning law. *Environment and Planning A* 43(4): 928–941

Business Insider SA (2020, 16 May) LIST: These are SA's new priority housing areas, due for a 'significant' portion of govt funding. https://www.businessinsider.co.za/priority-human-settlements-and-housing-development-areas-phshdas-now-declared-2020-5

Cameron R (1996) The democratisation of South African local government. *Local Government Studies* 22(1): 19–39

Cameron R (2005) Metropolitan restructuring (and more restructuring) in South Africa. *Public Administration and Development* 25(4): 329–339

Cameron R (2014) Vertical decentralisation and urban service delivery in South Africa: Does politics matter? *Development Policy Review* 32(s1): s81–s100

Chabal P & Daloz J (1999) *Africa Works: Disorder as Political Instrument.* Bloomington: Indiana University Press

Chatterjee E (2012) Dissipated energy: Indian electric power and the politics of blame. *Contemporary South Asia* 20(1): 91–103

Chatterjee P (2004) *The Politics of the Governed: Reflections on Popular Politics in Most of the World.* New York: Columbia University Press

Chipkin I (2011) Transcending bureaucracy: State transformation in the age of the manager. *Transformation: Critical Perspectives on Southern Africa* 77(1): 31–51

Chipkin I (2013) Whither the state? Corruption, institutions and state-building in South Africa. *Politikon* 40(2): 211–231

De Certeau M (1984) *The Practice of Everyday Life.* (tr. S Rendall). Berkeley: University of California Press

Gerth HH & Mills CW (eds) (1991) *From Max Weber: Essays in Sociology.* London: Routledge

Golden MA (2003) Electoral connections: The effects of the personal vote on political patronage, bureaucracy and legislation in postwar Italy. *British Journal of Political Science* 33(2): 189–212

Hannan S & Sutherland C (2015) Mega-projects and sustainability in Durban, South Africa: Convergent or divergent agendas? *Habitat International* 45: 205–212

Harrison P & Todes A (2017) Satellite settlement on the spatial periphery: Lessons from international and Gauteng experience. *Transformation: Critical Perspectives on Southern Africa* 95(1): 32–62

Herbert CW & Murray MJ (2015) Building from scratch: New cities, privatized urbanism and the spatial restructuring of Johannesburg after apartheid. *International Journal of Urban and Regional Research* 39(3): 471–494

Hoag C (2011) Assembling partial perspectives: Thoughts on the anthropology of bureaucracy. *PoLAR: Political and Legal Anthropology Review* 34(1): 81–94

Hornby D, Kingwill R, Royston L & Cousins B (eds) (2017) *Untitled: Securing Land Tenure in Urban and Rural South Africa.* Pietermaritzburg: University of KwaZulu-Natal Press

Hossain N (2010) Rude accountability: Informal pressures on frontline bureaucrats in Bangladesh. *Development and Change* 41(5): 907–928

Hull MS (2003) The File: Agency, authority, and autography in an Islamabad Bureaucracy. *Language and Communication* 23: 287–314

Jessop B (1997) The governance of complexity and the complexity of governance: Preliminary remarks on some problems and limits of economic guidance. In: A Amin & J Hausner (eds) *Beyond Markets and Hierarchy: Interactive Governance and Social Complexity.* Cheltenham: Edward Elgar. pp. 111–147

Kopecký P & Spirova M (2011) 'Jobs for the boys'? Patterns of party patronage in post-communist Europe. *West European Politics* 34(5): 897–921

Kroukamp H (2008) The single public service in South Africa: Recentralisation reinstalled? *Journal of Public Administration* 43(1): 145–155

Li TM (2007) *The Will to Improve: Governmentality, Development, and the Practice of Politics*. Durham, NC: Duke University Press

Mamabolo J (2015, 19 June) Gauteng Human Settlements Provincial Budget Vote 2015/16. Gauteng Provincial Legislature. https://www.gov.za/speeches/mec-jacob-mamabolo-human-settlements-budget-vote-201516-19-jun-2015-0000

Mehra D (2012) Protesting publics in Indian cities: The 2006 Sealing Drive and Delhi's traders. *Economic & Political Weekly* 47(30): 79–88

Merten M (2014, 16 July) Human Settlements mega project to address backlogs. *IOL*. http://www.iol.co.za/dailynews/news/human-settlements-mega-project-to-address-backlogs-1720469

Meyer-Sahling JH (2006) The rise of the partisan state? Parties, patronage and the ministerial bureaucracy in Hungary. *Journal of Communist Studies and Transition Politics* 22(3): 274–297

Mould O (2014) Tactical urbanism: The new vernacular of the creative city. *Geography Compass* 8(8): 529–539

Moya HN (2011) Examination of centralisation practices in South African local government. MA dissertation, University of Cape Town

Narsoom (2016) Personal communication, Johannesburg

Petterson D (2014, 16 July) Human settlements to build 1.5m houses. *Infrastructure News*. http://www.infrastructurene.ws/2014/07/16/human-settlements-to-build-1-5m-houses/

Resnick D (2014) Urban governance and service delivery in African cities: The role of politics and policies. *Development Policy Review* 32(s1): s3–s17

Rubin M (2018) At the borderlands of informal practices of the state: Negotiability, porosity and exceptionality. *The Journal of Development Studies* 54(12): 2227–2242

Scott JC (1985) *Weapons of the Weak: Everyday Forms of Resistance*. New Haven: Yale University Press

Steytler N (2005) The place and pole of local government in federal systems. Konrad-Adenauer-Stiftung Occasional Papers. Johannesburg: Konrad-Adenauer-Stiftung

Van de Walle N (2003) Presidentialism and clientelism in Africa's emerging party systems. *Journal of Modern African Studies* 41(2): 297–321

Van der Westhuizen J (2007) Glitz, glamour and the Gautrain: Mega-projects as political symbols. *Politikon* 34(3): 333–351

Veron R, Corbridge S, Williams G & Srivastava M (2003) The everyday state and political society in Eastern India: Structuring access to the employment assurance scheme. *The Journal of Development Studies* 39(5): 1–28

Von Holdt K (2010) Nationalism, bureaucracy and the developmental state: The South African case. *South African Review of Sociology* 41(1): 4–27

Watson V (2003) Conflicting rationalities: Implications for planning theory and ethics. *Planning Theory & Practice* 4(4): 395–407

Popular protests and the limits of civil society in the struggle for democracy in Zimbabwe, 2013 to 2016

Ngonidzashe Marongwe

Introduction

Using the cases of Itai Dzamara of the Occupy Africa Unity Square movement, #*Thisflag* by Pastor Evan Mawarire of the Baptist Church and *Tajamuka* (We have rebelled), this chapter discusses the impacts of the growth of popular protests on governance and struggles for democracy in Zimbabwe during the period 2013–2016. Earlier postcolonial protests were organised by and around formal civil society (CS) movements and organisations (CSOs). What sets the protests that took place between 2013 and 2016 apart is that they were centred around particular individuals and issues such as the dislodging of President Mugabe from power, the annulment of Statutory Instrument 64 of 2016 (SI 64/2016), which restricted imports and other issues of concern without necessarily containing the vision for long-term politics. Furthermore, compared to traditional CSOs, protesters did not use rule-bound methods of negotiating with the state but used tactical and informal methods such as violent and unsanctioned demonstrations as well as undiplomatic language.

This chapter utilises the work of the Indian scholar Partha Chatterjee on political society to analyse the characteristics of these popular politics. As opposed to the CS that Chatterjee considers as bourgeoisie, restricted and elitist, 'political society' is an arena where 'politics emerg[es] out of the developmental policies of government aimed at specific population groups. Many of these groups, organised into associations, transgress the strict lines of legality in struggling to live and work … [As such, state] agencies … deal with these associations not as bodies of citizens but as convenient instruments for administration of welfare to marginal and underprivileged population groups' (Chatterjee 2004: 41). Chatterjee's formulation contrasts sharply with the traditional liberal understanding of the CS that is conceptualised in the work of other scholars who value CS as a 'progressive [transformational] social force', which 'struggles against [the undemocratic and often authoritarian] modern state ... and against a pre-modern communitarian sociality ... often lodged in rural areas [in the third world]' (Helliker 2012: 42).

Drawing on this distinction, the central question for this chapter is: What was the role of popular politics in the democratisation of Zimbabwe in the period between 2013 and 2016? In order to tackle this profound question the chapter further asks as a sub-question: To what extent were the shortcomings of traditional CSOs and methods connected to the rise of the violent popular protests in Zimbabwe?

The use of tactical and informal methods and politics by protestors was not so much because they belonged to a population group that did not have access to bourgeois legality associated with CSOs. In fact, some leaders of organisations with international connections, such as Pastor Mawarire and Itai Dzamara, theoretically belonged to the CS. Instead, their *modus operandi* essentially emanated from the repressive state that stifled room for formal CS operations. Consequently, protesters ended up using measures and membership from the unemployed ranks, informal traders and cross-border traders that belong to Chatterjee's political society. In doing this, the chapter analyses the significance and limits of the mobilisational strategies of the Zimbabwean popular protests.

The chapter is divided into three sections. The first historicises the development of violent protests by the CS against the government in the 1990s and highlights connections with the recent popular protests. The second part discusses some of the leading popular protesters, including Itai Dzamara, arguably the pioneer of the post 2013 anti-Mugabe protests from Africa Unity Square (AUS). The third part traces the impacts of the popular protests on the democratisation struggle in Zimbabwe.

Civil society and the antecedents to the 2013–2016 popular protests

This section reflects on the development of militant protests by the CS in Zimbabwe, which offer a precursor to the 2013–2016 popular protests, especially in their deployment of non-rule bound styles of engagement. CS is considered in this chapter as 'a plurality of social enclaves which exist in contradistinction to the dominance of a particular monopolistic social system within the same social realm or territorial unity', like the state, church, market economy and political parties (Moyo 1993: 2), including non-governmental organisations, gender-based organisations, charities, trade unions, work associations, social movements, business associations and advocacy groups (Ncube 2010). However, the earlier CS postcolonial protests differed from the 2013–2016 popular protests in the sense that these were organised around more formal movements, and occurred before the large-scale informalisation of the country's economy that took root during Zimbabwe's crisis (Bond & Manyanya 2003). The development of CS in postcolonial Zimbabwe occurred in phases. In the first decade of independence in the 1980s, the CS sought to be on the side of the state for reasons such as continued economic prosperity which enabled the state to roll out massive social service programmes, and the continued domination of the mainstream economy by the minority whites which presented the state with the opportunity to present itself as the midwife for economic democratisation (Ncube 2010). Additionally, the ZANU-PF government, like its predecessor, the colonial state, and also in pursuance of its 'democratic centralism' under its targeted one-party state (Moyo 1993: 2), actively discouraged the growth of an independent CS in favour of one that it created, controlled and bank rolled (Helliker 2013).

However, from the end of the 1980s and the start of the 1990s the CS-state relations soured as the CS radicalised and asserted its independence and became more militant (Moyo 1993). This was based on the decline of economic prosperity and as the negative effects of the economic structural adjustment programme (ESAP) worsened the livelihoods of the majority (Moyo 1993; Ncube 2010). The CS also openly challenged the ZANU-PF state's preferred one-party state (Helliker 2013). As a result, there emerged a plethora of CS organisations including clubs in urban areas, political parties, burial societies, trade unions, industrial confederations, commercial organisations, student groups and fundamentalist religious cults in addition to 'white-dominated' CS such as the Confederation of Zimbabwe Industries (CZI), Commercial Farmers' Union (CFU), Zimbabwe National Chamber of Commerce (ZNCC) and the Employers' Confederation of Zimbabwe (EMCOZ) (Moyo 1993: 4). Out of this constellation emerged assertive CSOs such as the Zimbabwe Congress of Trade Unions (ZCTU) and the National Constitutional Assembly (NCA) and the Crisis in Zimbabwe Coalition, in addition to various other NGOs such as the Catholic Commission for Justice and Peace (CCJP) that also nagged the government for democratisation and societal transformation (Helliker 2013). Additionally, there also emerged protests from the Zimbabwe National Students Union (ZINASU), militant academics and women lobby organisations. Eventually and critically, the ZCTU and the NCA protests gave birth to, and provided most of the national leadership of, the opposition Movement for Democratic Change (MDC) in 1999 (Marongwe & Makaye 2016).

Below, the chapter turns to the discussion of the 2013–2016 popular protests with a view to evaluating their impact on the democratisation of post-Government of National Unity (GNU) Zimbabwe, as well as to exhibit how they were different from the CS demonstrations discussed above. As shall be demonstrated, these various individuals and groups were made up of marginalised and disgruntled citizens, including the unemployed youth, clergy, cross-border traders, civil servants, despondent ZANU-PF and MDC supporters and those in underpaying employment. What is important to note is that whilst these demonstrators articulated the need for economic and political reforms as well as the need for former President Mugabe to leave power, they were not led in the protests by opposition leaders nor were they openly supported by these leaders.

Itai Dzamara and the Occupy Africa Unity Square movement

Itai Dzamara, the forerunner of popular protests from AUS became famous following his abduction from a Harare township barbershop by five unidentified men on 9 March 2015 (Musewe 2015). The abduction helped to focalise attention not only on Dzamara, but on the growing wave of popular protests in Zimbabwe. He was a father of two, a journalist and the editor of the *News Leader* newspaper which he founded in 2008 having previously worked for various publications including *The*

Zimbabwe Independent, The Standard and *The Zimbabwean*. Dzamara also operated a Facebook page also known as News Leader (*Ifex News* 2015). Between October 2014 and 2015 Dzamara led the pro-democracy group Occupy Africa Unity Square (OAUS) (Zimbabwe Human Rights NGO Forum 2015), in demonstrations primarily targeting President Mugabe to resign because of his advanced age and for mismanaging the economy of Zimbabwe. At some point Dzamara delivered a petition at President Mugabe's Munhumutapa Offices imploring him to quit (Zimbabwe Human Rights NGO Forum 2015). He also addressed an MDC-T rally at Harare Grounds in Highfields on 7 March 2015 calling for mass protest action against the declining economic conditions in Zimbabwe (Amnesty USA 2015).

Prior to his abduction, Dzamara had, on various occasions, either been arbitrarily arrested or severely beaten by both state security agents and ZANU-PF members for his activism (Amnesty USA 2015). For example, on 6 November 2014, he was brutalised by the police and left for dead (Amnesty USA 2015). Also, on 26 November 2014, Dzamara together with four other members of the OAUS, was arrested after presenting a petition to the Speaker of Parliament and after staging a peaceful protest in Parliament's Speaker's Gallery (Amnesty USA 2015). Upon their arrest they were allegedly undressed, severely beaten and ordered to beat each other before being released (Amnesty USA 2015). In addition, at times, Dzamara and the OAUS members were denied legal representation; had their lawyers also beaten; and yet at other times the lawyers would be denied access to Dzamara and other OAUS members (Amnesty USA 2015).

Pastor Evan Mawarire and #*Thisflag* campaign

Pastor Evan Mawarire of the Baptist Church started the #*Thisflag* campaign after he had failed to raise school fees for his children in 2016. #*Thisflag* campaign started on 19 April 2016 when Mawarire, wearing a Zimbabwean flag around his neck, recorded a video titled *Thisflag*. In the video, the Pastor lamented that: 'When I look at the flag, it's not a reminder of my pride and inspiration, it feels as if I want to belong to another country' (Allison 2016). The video went viral, generating up to 115 000 views within a few days from Zimbabweans who also vented their anger against Mugabe and the ZANU-PF government (Chidza 2016a).

Among its well-known campaigns, #*Thisflag* ran a campaign of 25 'days of digital activism using #*ThisFlagday*' from the 1st to the 25th of May 2016 (*The Zimbabwean* 2016). Broadly, this was a call for the citizens to post comments of their stolen hopes, dreams, anger and disillusionments under the banner of #*Thisflag*. Among the issues that the campaign targeted included rampant unemployment, deteriorating social services, Mugabe's continued reign, corruption, and diminishing hope among the citizens (*The Zimbabwean* 2016).

What made #*Thisflag* profound was the symbolism of the appropriation of the central symbol to Zimbabwe's sovereignty, the national flag. As a column by the *Daily Maverick* in *The Zimbabwean* (2016) highlighted:

> #ThisFlag has appropriated the state's most potent symbol. They have seized the one icon that the state can't ban or suppress, and made it their own. The

flags that fly above government buildings, the flags that are pinned on the chests of government officials, the flags that fly on the bonnets of President Mugabe's motorcade, these are all now subversive acts that the regime cannot ignore – or does so at its peril.

Tajamuka/Sesijikile and a Zimbabwe 'shutdown' campaign

Protests under the banner #*Tajamuka/Sesijikile* were witnessed across the country on Wednesday, 6 July 2016. The prelude to the nationwide protests were the Monday, 4 July 2016 demonstrations of commuter omnibus taxi operators in most of Harare's high density suburbs who protested against police clampdowns and blatant police corruption at roadblocks that resulted in the arrest of up to 113 people (*NewZimbabwe* 2016b). The Wednesday, 6 July 2016 protests targeted the removal of former President Mugabe through a 'total shutdown of business and official administration countrywide' by staying away from work (Raath 2016). Indeed, the protest message was overwhelmingly received as home industries, industrial sites, schools and hospitals were closed for business. Central business districts across the country were deserted with most businesses shut down, except for a few outlets such as OK, Bon Marche, TM, Pick 'n Pay, Spar and Choppies that remained open (*The Financial Gazette* 2016a).

Despite managing a nationwide stayaway, *Tajamuka/Sesijikile* did not have a recognised leadership. Rather, it had a faceless leadership and its activities were coordinated via social media platforms, primarily WhatsApp, and others like Facebook and Twitter (Raath 2016). This is notwithstanding the fact that some 'leaders' eventually emerged or began to be associated with *Tajamuka/Sesijikile*, including Pastor Evan Mawarire, Stern Zvorwadza and Promise Mkwananzi. Most of these 'leaders' were intermittently arrested and released. The advantage of using the social media platform, especially WhatsApp, was that it was largely beyond the control of the state. It also meant that the majority of Zimbabweans with cellphones were able to access the message of the stayaway. Critically, it also demonstrated how, in the absence of viable mobilisational capacity by the groups, social media could undercut the hegemonic power of a repressive state that strictly controlled state media.

It, however, has to be said that there were some threats of violence made against those who would not heed the call to stayaway. To this extent, there were some messages on WhatsApp that called for violence against those who would attempt to go to work or the kombis that ferried people to work. There were also some reported cases of violence against those who were against the stayaway. These included the skirmishes in Mufakose suburb of Harare where some protestors attacked some commuter omnibuses that were ferrying people and in Makokoba suburb of Bulawayo, tyres were burnt to blockade roads which invited the police to fire tear gas canisters resulting in some running battles between the protestors and the police (Raath 2016). In Harare's Epworth suburb, the police engaged in running battles with some protestors (Kanambura 2016). As well, there was an ongoing civil service strike over salaries that was in motion (Raath 2016). However, the fact that most businesses closed shop was illustrative of the success of the protest action.

A follow up attempt on 13 July 2016 was, however, a spectacular flop as most businesses remained open and most of the remaining workers, in formal and informal employment, reported for work (Chidza et al. 2016). Nonetheless, the failure can also be attributed to the threats of state violence on protesters. The Ministers of Home Affairs, Defence, State Security and Information, gave chilling threats at a press conference held on 12 July to this effect (Chidza et al. 2016). The threat seemed real coming from a government that had periodically unleashed violence against its citizens to great cowing effect. Indeed, some personalities who were blamed for the successful 6 July protests were arrested on the eve of the 13 July protests, including Promise Mkwananzi of #Tajamuka/Sesjikile and Pastor Mawarire of #Thisflag. In total, between the 1 July Beitbridge protests and the 4 and 6 July protests and stayaways, some 200 people were arrested (*The Financial Gazette* 2016b). It also has to be mentioned that the call for a follow up stayaway within one week of the first one seemed too close for comfort to many potential protesters as they feared losing their jobs and livelihoods. The essence of this was neatly captured by an unidentified businessperson who pointed out that 'we need to work otherwise there would be no bread and butter on the table' (*The Financial Gazette* 2016b). In the end, the saving grace for the protestors was that there was a huge turnout at Pastor Mawarire's court hearing on the same day (*NewZimbabwe* 2016c).

From the foregoing, against the backdrop of heightened state intimidation and other coercive tactics aimed at thwarting the popular protests, including abductions, arrests, physical lynching of the protesters and media attacks, the protests continued. A host of measures were taken in sustaining the protests, incorporating shifting tactics, illegal demonstrations and increased resort to social media. Below we now turn to some of the central reasons behind the growth of the popular protests in the post-GNU period which indicate the failings of the CS.

Convulsions in ZANU-PF and the MDC-T and their failure to represent the people's interests

Between 2013 and 2016, the country's two main political movements, ZANU-PF and the MDC-T suffered tumultuous implosions and splits which not only weakened them, but which also divested from their political mandate of representing the interests of their supporters. To start off with, ZANU-PF was enfeebled by divisive, tumultuous and often violent Mugabe succession politics. This resulted in the purging of former Vice-President Joyce Mujuru and her alleged supporters from both ZANU-PF and government in 2014, including ministers (Magaisa 2017).

Added to the above, ZANU-PF failed to arrest the deteriorating socio-economic conditions in the country that were undergirded by rising de-industrialisation, unemployment that was spurred by a Supreme Court ruling of 2015 that allowed employers to dismiss workers on three months' notice (*The Herald* 2015), the rampant informalisation of the economy, rampant corruption and failure to access lines of foreign credit by the Zimbabwean government (Choruma 2016). Furthermore, the conditions were exacerbated by the indigenisation policy that required foreign owned companies to surrender 51% equities to locals. As well, ZANU-PF leadership exhibited unmitigated financial indiscipline as evidenced by former Vice-President Phelekezela Mphoko's close to two-year residency at the expensive four-star Rainbow Towers (Manayiti 2016). What made ZANU-PF's position worse was a crisis of legitimacy it suffered following its controversial victory in the 2013 elections. Notwithstanding the apparent peaceful nature of the 2013 harmonised elections, there were allegations that ZANU-PF had rigged the elections with the support of the Israeli-based Nikuv International Projects (Raftopoulos 2016). As a result, the election results were not widely accepted by the international community as representative of the wishes of Zimbabweans. In the end, based on the lack of sympathy from the international community, the ZANU-PF government perennially struggled for lines of credit to fund its operations (Raftopoulos 2016). On the whole, the deteriorating socio-economic conditions manufactured rampant poverty and widespread existential hardships.

On the other hand, the MDC-T also underwent major paroxysms. Troubled by incessant splits; reduced funding; waning support base; and the health woes of its leader, ideologue and face, Morgan Tsvangirai, the MDC-T increasingly struggled for continuity (Marongwe & Makaye 2016). Due to MDC-T's continued devolving into smaller factions, it lost the stamina to wrestle power from ZANU-PF as it was reduced from being a major movement into a pale shadow of its former self. Outside of the 2005 split of the parent MDC which resulted in the formation of MDC-T and the smaller MDC led by Arthur Mutambara, the MDC-T further split in 2014 into the main MDC-T that still remained under Morgan Tsvangirai and the smaller faction led by former Secretary General Tendai Biti known as the MDC-Renewal that went on to splinter further into the People's Democratic Party (PDP) led by Biti and the Renewal Democrats of Zimbabwe (RDZ) led by Elton Mangoma (Marongwe & Makaye 2016). The following is a pithy discussion of how the deteriorating economic crisis – one of the hallmarks of ZANU-PF's failures during the post-GNU era – facilitated the growth of popular demonstrations.

Deepening economic crisis

Following the end of the coalition government in 2013, Zimbabwe's economic situation took a turn for the worse. From the serious recovery path that the economy had witnessed since 2009, the period 2013 to 2016 saw significant economic downturns. To start with, the growth rates recorded since the GNU's foundation continued to decline significantly from 10.6, 4.5, 3.1, 2.7 to 1.7% in 2012, 2013, 2014, 2015 and 2016, respectively (Choruma 2016). This was largely due to many company closures. Additionally, many workers were laid off under the controversial Supreme Court ruling that allowed companies to lay off workers after giving them three months' notice without offering them retrenchment packages, which worsened levels of impoverishment. Following this ruling, up to 20 000 workers were retrenched in July 2015 alone (*The Chronicle* 2015). At another level, as already alluded to, the ZANU-PF government also failed to access lines of credit to ameliorate the situation based on legitimacy concerns, its failure to provide an acceptable repayment plan, lack of property security and the need for some reforms in governance (Raftopoulos 2016).

The government also worsened the economic difficulties by striving to curtail the growth of the informal sector, especially the cross-border trading business, by passing SI 64/2016, which imposed stringent import controls. Among others, SI 64/2016 precipitated the Beitbridge violent protests of 30 June 2016 that served as the harbinger of the 4 and 6 July 2016 demonstrations. The latter demonstrations saw the torching of some commuter omnibuses and some buildings, including some Choppies shops owned by Vice-President Phelekezela Mphoko who had spent many months staying at the Rainbow Towers. As Stern Zvorwadza, the Vendors Association of Zimbabwe leader, posited, SI 64/2016 was an instrument designed to drive the informal sector out of business because the Zimbabwean government was 'responsible for the poverty and pushing people into being vendors, yet the same government [was] coming up with policies to stop people from earning an honest living at a time when they [had] killed the economy and failed to create jobs' (Raftopoulos 2016). What gave further credence to Zvorwadza's argument was that Zimbabwe had a low industrial capacity utilisation of between 25 and 30%, which meant that there was very little manufacturing in the country and the increased informalisation of the economy that saw up to 95% of Zimbabweans eking out livelihoods in the informal sector mostly through selling or reselling imported wares (Choruma 2016).

What worsened the economic situation were the cash shortages experienced from April 2016 which resulted in winding bank queues as people struggled to withdraw their savings or salaries. The government tried to reduce the cash shortages by introducing a surrogate currency called bond notes, which officially were to work alongside the basket of foreign denominations. However, the introduction of the bond notes resulted in panic withdrawals and a black market for cash trading (Choruma 2016).

Democratic struggles enhanced?

One major goal of the protests was to open up the closed democratic space in Zimbabwe by calling for the resignation of President Mugabe. The demonstrations were, according to Evan Mawarire, a means to push the national leadership to be responsive to people's needs and 'restore order and cast [a new] vision' for the nation (Chidza 2016b). Traditionally, it had been inconceivable for one to openly discuss the failings of the state, including corruption and Mugabe's shortcomings, in particular his advanced age and long stay in power. Such actions were construed as undermining the authority of the president and usually brought the full wrath of state-sanctioned violence on the culprits, including being sent to prison or being tortured (Phiri 2015).

One of the profound effects of the protests was in tackling head on and undercutting the Mugabe and ZANU-PF fear factor. The essence of debunking the mythical standing of President Mugabe by the protesters was encapsulated in the words of a social media commentator Tom Gumede who posited that the protests 'represented the courage and new momentum [that was] building in Zimbabwe' (*NewZimbabwe* 2016c). Citizens were literally 'girding their loins, raring to take the government' (*The Financial Gazette* 2016a).

The essence of the protests undercutting Mugabe's standing came, first, from the fact that most of the protesters openly challenged Mugabe to step down. Second, discourses also began to emerge around some of the leaders of the protests as potential presidents of Zimbabwe. Pastor Mawarire, among others, was presented as potentially 'the new face of Zimbabwe's struggle for democracy,' a 'national hero' and one who 'suited the profile of a national leader and enjoyed [massive] support' (*NewZimbabwe* 2016c). In the end, what also emerged is that the protests inadvertently refocused attention to the succession issues both within and outside ZANU-PF, former President Mugabe's party. The common questions around which included: who could/would succeed Mugabe? And, what kind of a leader and politics would Zimbabwe desire in the post-Mugabe era? Regarding the former question on the possibility of change of leadership for Zimbabwe, the discussions occurred against the backdrop of the growing crisis to which the then current government seemed out of solutions to address and where the citizens were getting bolder and more fearless in their assertions for socio-economic reforms. The latter question emerged out of the need to move away from a generally suppressive authoritarianism that had dominated the last stages of colonialism and first four decades of postcolonial rule towards one that strengthened responsiveness from the state and entrenched strong pillars of participatory democracy. That desire sought to move the nation from its previous 50 years or so that had been dominated by two rulers, Ian Smith and Robert Mugabe, whose successive governments had, in Sachikonye's (2011) terminology, literally, turned against the citizens.

It is imperative to note, however, that the deepening economic crisis seemed to coalesce different sections into a galvanised opposition to Mugabe's continued reign. Among others, as the Zimbabwean political analyst Ricky Mukonza aptly noted: 'the youth cannot find employment, businesspeople cannot do business because of a disabling environment and civil servants cannot get paid at the end of the month (Chidza 2016b)'. To this the Zimbabwean academic Maxwell Saungweme added that 'the socio-economic problems Zimbabweans are going through are vast and people have naturally reached a level where they cannot take it anymore. People have been pushed to the wall and the only option is to question the system through action and words' (Chidza 2016b). In the end, as one western diplomat posited, 'Zimbabweans have never faced a future so devoid of hope, there is nothing this government can do to fix it. People know that and they want change' (Raath 2016).

Against the backdrop of a tightening and biting economic crunch, regarding which the Minister of Finance, Patrick Chinamasa, admitted that the state coffers were empty, leading to non-payment of salaries for state workers, President Mugabe had reportedly flown to eight countries between January and June 2016 and undertaken up to ten trips to Singapore. In addition, former Vice-President Mphoko had been staying in the expensive presidential suite at the Rainbow Towers for long periods even when the state had purchased a USD 3.5 million house for him (Raath 2016).

Because the protests were citizen driven, they were vital in bridging the political divide amongst Zimbabweans who had in the past been cast in the political polarity of ZANU-PF and MDC-T. In this fashion, the protests managed to draw support from across the ZANU-PF-MDC-T divide, especially from those who were disillusioned by the (already discussed) convulsions that had afflicted these two major political parties since 2013. By straddling the political polarity the protests grew in strength as they articulated, in non-partisan discourses, the everyday challenges that confronted many ordinary Zimbabweans such as the constitutional failure by the government to eradicate poverty, enduring corruption, unending and potentially fleecing police roadblocks, the desire to stop the government from printing bond notes, the annulment of SI 64/2016 and salary delays for civil servants (Raath 2016).

Following the protests, especially the nationwide 6 July 2016 stayaway, the government rescinded some of its policies. Among others, the government realigned the civil servants, pay days to fall within the calendar month, reduced the number of roadblocks (Kanambura 2016), and it revised SI 64/2016, allowing individuals to bring import limited quantities of basic commodities per month without penalties (*NewZimbabwe* 2016a; *NewZimbabwe* 2016b).

Catching on the wave of regime change and personal aggrandisement?

The converse side of the argument that popular protests kept the democratic struggle alive in Zimbabwe is the narrative that some of the leaders of the protests sought personal gain, including fame and fortune. This view was largely articulated by the ZANU-PF government which even went to the extent of linking some of the leading protesters to western-led regime change efforts. Constructed in this modality, the popular protesters were regarded as stooges of imperialists whose machinations were designed to remove the ZANU-PF from power. Former Home Affairs Minister, Ignatious Chombo, amplified this discourse by directly accusing the United States of America (USA) and France ambassadors of helping to 'engineer [the] civil disturbances' and for 'working through dodgy groups and leveraging on social media to foment civil disobedience and ultimately destabilise Zimbabwe' (Bwititi 2016). Even more telling was the insinuation by the state that when Mawarire left the country following his release on Wednesday, 13 July 2016, he had gone to the United States of America to 'debrief on his activities and possibly to secure more funding for his campaign' (Chitemba 2016).

It was also insinuated that some of the protesters acted in order to get recognition and political asylum in economically better rewarding countries. In this context, appearing to lead the protests was taken to be a new form of career in a search for better livelihoods based on the economic gains accrued from the donor community, especially from the western countries that were considered to be against President Mugabe and ZANU-PF's continued reign. Walking the streets of many cities of Zimbabwe, it was not uncommon to hear whispers intimating that Mawarire had, for example, made a fortune for himself and had secured sanctuary for his family in the USA. This was after his family had been granted asylum in the USA.

Elsewhere, some of the leaders of the protests were regarded as attention seekers. Among the most vocal in this camp was former Minister of Higher Education, Professor Jonathan Moyo, who characterised Pastor Mawarire's *#Thisflag* as simply a 'pastor's fart in the corridors of power' (*The Zimbabwean* 2016). In this fashion, the derision did not only dismiss *#Thisflag* as a fluke, but also categorised it as an attention seeking gimmick, targeted to get Pastor Mawarire some publicity or to grow congregants of his church. A more damaging attack on Mawarire came through the state controlled *The Herald* newspaper, which ran a headline story on 23 July 2016 titled 'Mawarire is no saint,' which, among other things, alleged that *#Thisflag* was Mawarire's 'money spinning venture' (*The Herald* 2016) In spite of such attempts at defamation, the demonstrators managed to influence the governance of the country by forcing the government into implementing some levels of reform and accountability (as highlighted in previous section). As events unravelled, however, it became evident that, apart from providing temporary platforms for disillusioned Zimbabweans against the country's leadership, popular protests were unable to sustain as potent forces beyond 2016. This was primarily due to lack of coordinated and consistent leadership and heightened state repression that was directed against the leaderships of these movements.

Conclusions

On the whole, the chapter has demonstrated how popular protests visualised a subversion of the grand narratives of the Zimbabwean nation that were formulated around unquestioned loyalty to President Mugabe and ZANU-PF, which ratcheted pressure on the ZANU-PF government for important pro-people reforms. The protests utilised a gap that the crises in ZANU-PF and in MDC-T, as well as a worsening socio-economic decline, presented. Besides contributing to the worsening livelihood conditions for the majority of Zimbabweans, these crises also demonstrated the weakening of the formal CS that had in the 1990s provided a rallying point for channelling grievances against the state's shortcomings and excesses. The enfeebling of the CS was based on the entrenched authoritarian rule and growing socio-economic hardships that generated massive unemployment and the informalisation of the economy. Notwithstanding the above, popular protests could not take full advantage in their attempts to democratise the country because they faced challenges related to state repression, long-term sustainability rooted in the absence of constant leadership, a lack of mobilisational capacity, inadequate management skills and also legal protection.

As such, the chapter has showcased the limits of the transgressional tactics of engagement of what Chatterjee has termed political society in the struggles for greater representation in postcolonial Zimbabwe. What became apparent was that the popular protests lacked the strengths of the older CS movements in postcolonial Zimbabwe that had been derived from the combination of trade union structures and mobilisational capacity interlinked with the leadership skills of middle-class intellectuals and professionals. The lack of such structures and the circa early 2000s weakening of a middle class not linked to the state in Zimbabwe greatly affected the sustainability of the popular protests. Nonetheless, and notwithstanding the above weaknesses, and the abuses by the state that the demonstrators suffered including physical harassment, torture, media condemnation and disappearances, popular politics kept the democratic struggles active besides nagging the state into implementing some levels of accountability. What needs to be noted, however, is that while the popular protests failed to dislodge Mugabe from power, this desire remained popular amongst Zimbabweans who supported a military-underwritten removal of Mugabe as state president in November 2017 through participating in urban demonstrations that, together with a parliamentary impeachment process, sanitised the controversial ascendancy to power of President Emmerson Mnangagwa.

References

Allison S (2016, 26 May) The man behind #*Thisflag*, Zimbabwe's accidental movement for change. *The Guardian.* https://www.theguardian.com/world/2016/may/26/this-flag-zimbabwe-evan-mawarire-accidental-movement-for-change

Amnesty USA (2015) Pro-democracy activist abducted. https://www.amnestyusa.org/sites/default/files/uaa05615.pdf.

Bond P & Manyanya M (2003) *Zimbabwe's Plunge: Exhausted Nationalism, Neoliberalism and the Search for Social Justice.* Harare: Weaver Press

Bwititi K (2016, 10 July) US and France behind violence. *The Sunday Mail*

Chatterjee P (2004) *Politics of the Governed: Reflections on Popular Politics in Most of the World.* New York: Columbia University Press

Chidza R (2016a, 7 May) Flag pastor speaks of threats, passion. *Newsday*

Chidza R (2016b, 3–9 July) Under siege Mugabe hangs on in the face of protests. *The Standard*

Chidza R, Chadenga S & Manayiti O (2016, 14 July) Brute force stifles shutdown. *Newsday*

Chitemba B (2016, 17 July) US, UK summon Evan Mawarire. *The Sunday Mail*

Choruma A (2016, 7–13 July) Zimbabwe in economic distress. *The Financial Gazette*

Daily News (2017, 15 November) Military takes over, says Mugabe safe

Helliker K (2013) Imagining civil society in Zimbabwe and "most of the world". In: E Obadare (ed.) *The Handbook of Civil Society in Africa.* New York: Springer Science and Business Media

Ifex News (2015, 20 March) Zimbabwe: Clarify fate of missing activist and former journalist Itai Dzamara. https://www.ifex.org/zimbabwe/2015/03/20/missing_activist/

Kanambura A (2016, 7–13 July) Whose victory was it-the state or demonstrators? *The Financial Gazette*

Magaisa A (2017, 7 October) The month of long knives? *Saturday Big Read.* https://www.bigsr.co.uk/single-post/2017/10/07/Big-Saturday-Read-The-month-of-long-knives

Manayiti O (2016, 30 June) Mphoko kicked out of hotel. *Newsday*

Marongwe N & Makaye P (2016) Violence and the politics of the Movement for Democratic Change – Tsvangirai's (MDC-T) mobilisation and continued survival, 1999–2014. In: M Munyaradzi & N Marongwe (eds) *Myths of Peace and Democracy? Towards Building Pillars of Hope, Unity and Transformation in Africa.* Bamenda: Langaa. pp. 167–194

Moyo JN (1993) Civil society in Zimbabwe. *Zambezia* 20(1): 1–13

Munyaradzi M & Marongwe N (eds) (2016) *Myths of Peace and Democracy? Towards Building Pillars of Hope, Unity and Transformation in Africa.* Bamenda: Langaa

Musewe V (2015) Opinion: I am Itai Dzamara. *Konrad-Adenauer-Stiftung Country Report.* www.kas.de/wf/doc/kas_40707-1522-2-30.pdf?150316170440

Ncube C (2010) Contesting hegemony: Civil society and the struggle for social change in Zimbabwe, 2000–2008. Doctoral thesis, University of Birmingham. https://etheses.bham.ac.uk/1086/

NewZimbabwe (2016a, 9 July) Uneasy calm prevails in Zimbabwe after violent clashes. http://www.newzimbabwe.com/news-30115-Uneasy+calm+after+anger+explosion/news.aspx.

NewZimbabwe (2016b, July 10) Protests and the growing risks for Mugabe. http://www.newzimbabwe.com/news-30128- Riots+and+the+growing+risks+for+Mugabe/news.aspx

NewZimbabwe (2016c, 13 July) Is Pastor Mawarire the new face of Zimbabwe's struggle for democracy? http://www.newzimbabwe.com/news-30188-Is+Mawarire+the+new+face+of+Zim+struggle/news.aspx

Phiri G (2015, October) Man charged with insulting Mugabe. *Daily News*

Pindula News (n.d.) Itai Dzamara. https://www.pindula.co.zw/Itai_Dzamara

Raath J (2016, 9 July) Shutdown: National show of defiance against Mugabe. *NewZimbabwe*. http://www.newzimbabwe.com/news-30114-Wed+National+defiance+against+Mugabe/news.aspx.

Raftopoulos B (2016, 16 July) This time the uprising is different – but will it bring regime change? *NewZimbabwe.com*. http://www.newzimbabwe.com/opinion-30234-Will+the+uprising+bring+regime+change/opinion.aspx

Sachikonye L (2011) *When a State Turns Against its Citizens: Institutionalized Violence and Political Culture*. Harare: Jacana

The Chronicle (2015, 18 August) Companies recall retrenched workers

The Financial Gazette (2016a, 7–13 July) Zim shuts down

The Financial Gazette (2016b, 14–20 July) Stayaway flops

The Herald (2015, 24 July) Supreme Court on termination with notice

The Standard (2016, 12 June) Police crush Occupy Africa Unity Square protest

The Zimbabwean (2016, 24 May) The simple genius of Zimbabwe's #ThisFlag protest, and the man who started it. http://www.thezimbabwean.co/2016/05/the-simple-genius-of-zimbabwes-thisflag-protest-and-the-man-who-started-it/.

Zimbabwe Human Rights NGO Forum (2015, 10 March) Alert: Abduction of Itai Dzamara. www.hrforumzim.org/wp-content/uploads/2015/03/Alert.pdf.

CHAPTER 8

'We will be back to the street!': Protest and the 'empires' of water in Nairobi

Wangui Kimari

You and water can never be close even a little bit, how many days have you not washed? – Michi, *The Real Househelps of Kawangware*

You ask yourself 'why do people have water and electricity and I don't?'
– Youth Leader, Mathare

Introduction

On 25 August 2016 there was a water protest in Mathare, and a resolution was prepared for prompt dissemination. Community members from the six wards of this poor settlement sent a message to all concerned through the mobile phone platform WhatsApp, which I set out unedited below:

> 25th August 2016 Mathare protest resolution. Let's petition government to remove Nairobi water company CEO for failing to supply adequate, clean and safe water. For several months now residents of Mathare and other informal settlements have lacked sufficient, clean and safe water to drink and for use on there day to day activity at there house, due to cartel surrounding the business and incompetency man power. For example residents of Mathare, Mashimoni, huruma and ngei in average are forced to purchase water for at least ksh 20 per 20ltr up from ksh 5 per 20ltrs on normal days. Today on 25th August 2016 resident of Mathare staged a protest along juja road to demand the reconnecting of water pipes that has led to water shortage for mathare for almost 2week resident blocked road with tires, rocks, mukokoteni, and human shield from as early as 8am to 3pm in a bid to attract the attention of the relevant authority. The bid by Pangani OCPD, Huruma AP commander

and deputy OCS to stop the angry protesters mostly comprised of women and children did not succeeded in return they opted to arrest Richard Bonke whom they later released unconditional after public opted to continue with the protest over night. Most of the protester claimed they have not bathed for 3days due to lack of water, other claim there haven't cleans there kids uniform keeping in mind school are opening next week, mzee onyango, and mutisia claimed there kids are now admitted hospital due to poor hygiene due to lack of water. The demo stopped at around 3:30pm after some area started receiving some traces of tap water and the release of Richard Bonke. Note: this 3rd protest in four months over inadequate water supply, result have been the safe the pipes are reconnected after several hours. This were some of the resolution. 1.We will be back to the street in case of water shortage and supply since is the only solution with immediate answer. 2. A bid to open a long time camp across Nairobi on right to clean and safe water. 3. To develop a petition to impeach Nairobi water company [CEO] for failing to execute his mandate to give clean safe and adequate water to Nairobi resident.

It is important to note that residents were not protesting the ongoing lack of water from taps in their *own* houses, but the absence of water in the few communal and 'illegal' water points that dot the landscape, infrastructures usually shared by hundreds if not thousands of people (Dafe 2009; MSJC 2019; Kimari 2019). The objective of this chapter is to attend to the histories that have enabled these now formalised drought conditions and elaborate on the methods that residents of Mathare take up to address this situation.

For almost a century Mathare has stubbornly existed within, but also seemingly without, Nairobi's city grids. Despite its endurance and the unusual distinction of being (against popularised narratives about 'recent' rural-urban migration causing slums in Nairobi) one of the city's oldest neighbourhoods, it remains unconnected to the formal water system and other basic services. As a consequence, the residents' actions for water noted above register the persistent and metamorphosising violence of uneven urban governance in Nairobi. This is spatial management that, through seemingly intentional omission, deprives many residents of basic rights guaranteed in the Kenyan Constitution. At the same time, however, the fact that this was the third water-related protest in four months and was accompanied by innovative solutions (including a call to impeach the CEO of the city water company), illustrates the many incremental ways that residents, long tired of pursuing the path of least resistance, stake enunciatory and material claims for their rights (Deleuze & Guattari 1987). They engage in imperfect 'messy-labours' (Simone 2015), comprised of both 'machinic assemblages and collective assemblages of enunciation' (Deleuze & Guattari 1987),[1] to ensure they have water, however temporarily, while also acting to counter narratives

---

1   Derived from Deleuze and Guattari (1987) I use 'machinic' assemblages to refer to the multidimensional physical work residents take up to improve their terrain, while collective assemblages of 'enunciation' are joined up to index the language residents use symbolically to alter the status quo. These assemblages come together to bring about the effects desired by their protagonists, although unanticipated consequences may also be produced.

that position them as undeserving of this resource. To these ends, they organise meetings and campaigns like the ones I describe within this chapter, which – in the absence of real political will to provide water to the poor – target access to this resource while also deploying local narratives that speak of imperial orders to explain the absence of, and demand, this service within their community.

I, therefore, centre 'the[ir] desperate, indignant, and defiant acts that duress' can produce (Stoler 2016: 35), in this case, the institutionalised lack of a basic service. What's more, I also make evident how Mathare residents narrativise their lives without this resource, and, in the context of hypermodern city developments for which the public purse always pays, highlight what they see as the continuation of empire in their poor region. In the following section, a brief history of Mathare is provided to contextualise the chronic lack of water that residents continue to endure. Thereafter, under the rubric of 'waterless scars,' I document the failures over the years of urban planning in Nairobi, before turning to some of the 'machinic' and 'enunciatory' community-led initiatives to ensure residents access to water, and show how they frame its scarcity as connected to the persistence of 'empire' – an imperial governance of the city. I conclude by reviewing my main arguments and suggesting directions for future research on water access in Nairobi.

Mathare

Both in public discourse and in the archival record, Mathare is imagined through a number of registers. On a socio-political index it is constructed, as a recent member of parliament for the area decreed, as a site of 'criminals and prostitutes' (Kimari 2016). Current and not so current alcohol raids have also firmly entrenched it as the headquarters of illegal brew in the city. And while it is also identified sympathetically as a 'slum' or 'unplanned settlement' (County of Nairobi & Japanese International Cooperation Agency 2014: 2–4; Médard 2010), there is an unspoken insistence that it is unworthy of basic services due to the amorality supposedly fixed in this setting.

While other local 'slums,' many of which are also located in the eastern part of Nairobi, are subject to similar representations,[2] Mathare is consistently constructed as a more extremely immoral geography. In this sense, there are definitely hierarchies of rectitude applied to this region that legitimise its exclusion vis-à-vis other poor urban settlements and Nairobi broadly, even though in geography and population it remains relatively small. It is only 3km² in size and has roughly 350 000 inhabitants – significantly less area and population than Kibera and even the Mukuru settlements (Muungano Support Trust 2012). Certainly, Mathare is depicted as a site where 'the real thugs live,' and the habitat of the city's detritus, casting a long shadow over the mainstream 'visions' of this East African metropolis.

Elsewhere (Kimari 2017) I have documented how these now normalised positionings of Mathare residents as amoral citizens, established over decades, influence urban planning discourse and practices, enabling what I argue is spatial governance not of inclusion but of neglect and force. This is since these negative framings are popularly anchored within the decaying 'slum' environment, engendering a space-subjectivity

---

2 In my experience, Dandora and Korogocho are framed in similar ways.

enterprise that, in a 'cognitive feedback loop' (Vargas 2006: 51, 63), maps this polluted ecology onto residents' bodies and subjectivities in a process that has been reified, formally and informally, across decades. As these monikers of home (and their residents) coincide and inform one other, they cascade into the many scales of urban spatial management, principally animating the omissions and exclusions within 'master-planning' for Mathare and the other poor settlements of Nairobi. Accordingly, such an imperial order reproduces a negative symbiosis between subjects and their space in the *longue durée* and is often called upon to explain shortages of water and other basic services.

Despite provisions for the right to water in Article 43 of the Constitution, nationally, 41% of the Kenyan population relies on 'unprotected wells, springs or informal water providers,' and another 69%, many of whom live in poor urban settlements, do not have 'access to safe and hygienic toilets or latrines' (Wekesa 2013). A study conducted in Mathare in 2015 found that, on average, about 315 people, and in some areas up to 1 500, relied on a single public water point (Corburn & Hildebrand 2015). A more recent study by a community organisation identified approximately 117 public water points in this settlement. Therefore, if everyone in Mathare needed to use them, it would amount to 2 560 residents for each water point (MSJC 2019). Furthermore, given both regular leakages and regular shortages, long waiting lines to access water are common (Corburn & Hildebrand 2015). In sum, residents of Nairobi's informal settlements are disadvantaged fourfold: they pay more for an inferior supply, inferior access and inferior quality (Ng'ethe 2018), even as the governor of the city continues to promise 'water for all' (*Capital News* 2019).

Against this background, residents' life stories highlight what they see as the continuation of empire, since the neglect of Mathare – part of the former 'native city' – began with the colonial administration and continues today, both formally and informally, under postcolonial urban governance regimes. As a consequence, the grounded discourses expressed by Mathare residents are intentional everyday ideological practices contesting an ongoing imperial city management, one that, in this case, provokes community members to threaten: 'we will be back to the street!'.

Waterless scars: The failure of urban planning

Since its early days, Nairobi's administration has not been immune to accusations of investing in inappropriate infrastructures as well as financial malfeasance. Anderson (2005) details how in the 1950s colonial city administrators used public monies to build swimming pools for their own residences and engaged in numerous nepotistic contracting ventures. More recently, in 2015 the governor of Nairobi, Evans Kidero, reportedly allocated KES 50 million (Kenyan Shilling) from the county purse in order to give the city a 'face lift' for former US President Obama's 'homecoming,' a significant portion of which went towards planting a few kilometres of what has come to be known as 'Kidero grass' (BBC 2015b). While these events contribute to an archive documenting the proliferating infrastructural irresponsibility and corruption in both local and national government operations, it is Mathare residents, and those from similar settlements, who know, intimately, the follies of an urban governance that refuses to provide equal and accessible basic services to the majority of Nairobi's residents.

Historically, municipal documents have often argued otherwise, that the city administration consistently invests in, as its current motto provides, a 'better city, better life.' Nairobi's first Master Plan, the 1948 *Nairobi, Master Plan for A Colonial Capital* (White, Silberman & Anderson 1948), for instance, purported to eschew the racial segregation established in the city since its beginnings as a railway town in 1899. Rather, the three South African planners who were its authors argued:

> The Master Plan however, is able to be completely neutral on the subject of racial segregation by being confined to the principles of planning which take their measure on the human and technical needs. It is concerned with the satisfaction of wants which all men require such as privacy, open space, education, protection from through-traffic, water supplies, etc. The more attention that can be devoted to what is common to man the more likely are we to concentrate on what can to-day be planned in the light of reason while leaving to political and educational action and to the individual to sort out the rest. If the plan has a bias it is this humanistic one. (White, Silberman & Anderson 1948: 49)

Of these humanistic claims to universal 'privacy, open space, education, protection from through-traffic [and] water supplies,' few were made available to all: little urban infrastructure was provided for the majority of Nairobi's residents (Médard 2010; Slaughter 2004).

Scholars such as Hake (1977) and White (1991) document the negative impacts of infrastructural distinctions drawn and implemented between the east of the city and other more prosperous parts of Nairobi, both before and after this 1948 plan. In this context, Londsdale (2001: 220) is able to argue that the colonial metropolis 'was a perfect Apartheid city without trying.' Postcolonial urban governance efforts unfortunately cannot be said to have improved on these segregatory practices, in particular in areas like Mathare – the former 'native city.' Accordingly, Hake (1977: 248, 99) comments that formal post-independence spatial management practices remained 'ambiguous, half-hearted, confused and self-contradictory' with little change 'since 1922, when the Municipal Council discussed native squatters on Kikuyu Road.'

Thirty years after Hake's (1977) evaluation, Owuor and Mbatia (2008) do not see any definitive change between the first post-independence urban plan, the 1973 *Nairobi Metropolitan Growth Strategy*, and earlier colonial spatial designs. In their paper they show how the first postcolonial planning proposal emerged from within the embryonic Nairobi Urban Study Group, which sought to chart the development of Nairobi until the year 2000. However, despite some of the more progressive interventions proposed in this vision, Owuor and Mbatia (2008) contend that this 1973 submission 'supported the interests of the hegemonic class alliance of the local bourgeoisie and the multinational corporations.' And, as a result, 'the urban majority were marginalised further and informalisation thrived since the late 1970s to date.'

Subsequent efforts such as the 1988 Nairobi City Commission Development Plan and the 'Nairobi We Want' forum of 1993, also failed to bring about any substantive changes for the majority of poor areas in the city (Owuor & Mbatia 2008: 4). And while more recent interventions pursue 'world-class city' status, such as the *Integrated*

Urban Development Masterplan for the City of Nairobi (NIUPLAN) (County of Nairobi & Japanese International Cooperation Agency 2014) and *Nairobi Metro 2030: A World Class African Metropolis* (2008), when it comes to providing basic services for the large number of disconnected city residents, they only inspire what Myers (2015) calls a 'jaundiced optimism.' As a consequence, many Nairobi dwellers, like those in Mathare, have to continue to find ways to sustain their own neighbourhoods themselves. In terms of access to water, these residents have to bear a quadruple penalty: they are exposed to higher costs for a less dependable, accessible and safe water supply (Médard 2010; Rodriguez-Torres 2010; Corburn & Makau 2016; MSJC 2019).

Waterless scars: Local mobilisation

Beyond protests like that of 25 August 2016 highlighted in the introduction to this chapter, there have been many fervent collective attempts to change the grave water situation in this settlement. For example, Hake (1977) describes an instance in the early 1970s when some Mathare residents and their sympathetic MP collaborated to take up the cost of laying pipes within a yard of the city's water arteries, in a bid to get formal access to this network for Mathare. This was in the same decade that an average of 870 residents shared the same water tap and there were roughly 136 people to each latrine (Corburn & Makau 2016: 164). In spite of these collective efforts, the city declined to include Mathare in the water network and their inflexibility prompted a question that was widely asked in response: 'Who, then, was responsible if they drank impure water?' (Hake 1977: 161). No one has claimed responsibility yet.

Four decades later, in a series of community meetings held in 2018 and organised by local activists, a cross-section of residents of all ages and genders – fathers, students, carwash operators, mothers, young workers – continued to lament the absence of this basic service. It was noted that even in the formal building where these water campaign meetings were being held, the last time anyone had seen 'even a drop of' water was in November 2016, almost two years earlier.[3]

Attendees spoke of the increased costs of water when they purchased it from unregulated local providers, expenses far beyond what those connected to formal water grids paid, and how this impacted what were already very tiny family economies. Speaking to these costs, one participant shared that:

> It is expensive to buy because of cartels. In a week people can even pay 900 shillings [USD 9] if they have kids, when they do not even have 200 shillings [USD 2] extra for water.

What's more, the water that came was 'so-so' water, a resource whose providence and purity was heavily suspect. Claims were made that it brought typhoid and cholera and even caused the death of a brother of one of the water campaign activists, who said of his kin: 'He just fetched water to drink from a jerrican that my mother had bought, and the next day he was sick and died.'

---

3   See Anand (2012) and Graham et al. (2013) for similar examples of this in Mumbai.

For those who came to these community meetings from other peri-urban informal locations, such as Kayole and Ruai, complaints of paying for water meter connections even when these instruments did not work, and water never appeared, were raised. In addition, they lamented that their piping was of poor quality, held together by rubber bands, and, especially during the rainy season, had seepage from sewage and sanitation systems, making many local residents sick. The extent of illness was so bad that, and as one female participant from Kayole shared, 'in 2017 we had the highest cases of cholera in Nairobi.' The 'slum' equivalent of these meters are the neoliberal-era automated 'ATMs' for water that were established with much fanfare in 2015 (BBC 2015a), but that have since stopped working, and have never been repaired by county authorities.

Besides the costs to purse, health and time, participants also discussed the 'stigmatisation by people if you are dirty' that leads to a lack of self-esteem. In a country where ethnic identity can have shifting and tragic salience, the lack of water at times contributed to an ethnicised spatial divide in Mathare. For example, one interlocutor shared that:

> It brings ethnic conflict because, for example, in August 2017 [during the elections] there was no water in Mathare except in the 4A and 4B [Luo] area, and then people here had to go and buy 20 litres for 50 shillings and even 100 shillings across the river – this caused conflict.

There were, indeed, many 'waterless scars' in Mathare.

Undoubtedly, water rationing occurs in other neighbourhoods in the city, including in wealthy areas, and is scheduled to continue for a few years until adequate dam infrastructure is built. Notwithstanding these shortages across Nairobi, what participants in these Mathare campaign meetings were contesting was not rationing, but a systematic absence, what Graham et al. (2013) term 'systemic dehydration,' or a lack of 'hydraulic citizenship' (Anand 2012). This systemic absence is anchored in long-term colonial neglect and divestments from populous city areas, providing fertile ground for a wide array of actors to build water 'empires.'

The empires of water

'Empires' of water in Nairobi, established by local water operators – usually city elites with strong connections to the main water regulator – were regularly identified during the 2018 community meetings. That they were seemingly above the law and had consistent access to water to sell to various consumers even when most of the city was 'dry,' illustrated the reach of their business kingdoms.

In one area close to Mathare, it was reported that despite frequent house fires, 'cartels had stopped a fire hydrant from being constructed because they were afraid people would get free water.' At the same time, notwithstanding the criminality inherent to these operations, the generous profits produced by these businesses proved alluring even to those who suffered from a chronic lack of this resource. So much so that one young participant shared how some of his peers were 'think[ing] about getting or stealing water to sell.'

Unlicensed 'booster' pumps that were paid for among neighbours in Mathare, and used to tap into the water network, are prohibited and oftentimes confiscated violently by the police and Nairobi City Water and Sewerage Company (NCWSC) officials who accuse residents of 'dragging water from the main pipes.' Though these officials complain of the 'waste' of what they term 'non-revenue' water in poor urban settlements – water 'illegally' tapped from main lines and that could not be costed – it was in fact in the more prosperous city areas where more blatant abuse of this network was and remains in play (see Kimari 2019; MSJC 2019).

Ultimately, however, it is long-term exclusionary spatial conditions, based upon clear 'biopolitical' choices (Graham et al. 2013: 123), that have created conditions for the development of these mini empires. One respondent at a community meeting stated:

> I think the people responsible for Mathare are the British because they are the ones who took land away from the communities. They forced them to establish a slum in Mathare. I also think the leaders who came immediately after independence are responsible because they did not return the land back to the original owners. And politicians to date, they keep promising people that they will change issues, but they don't, so I think they are also responsible.

It is the persistent *longue durée* neglect in this part of the city by subsequent county administrations that is held responsible for the dearth of water in Mathare and in similar communities. As is apparent in the interview excerpt below, it is the commodification of water in an unequal urban environment that ought to bear the blame:

> Water is life! It is becoming a normalised thing that you can sell water. It did not used to be this normal in the 1990s, and now people are accepting this and there is even rationing. Ten years ago it was not such a big problem, but now it is increasingly a commodity when WATER IS A RIGHT! Kwani we don't pay taxes ama? It is our right!

While residents within elite neighbourhoods such as Runda can dig their own boreholes and create their own water company that provides water exclusively to this wealthy area, Mathare residents are left at the whim of empires, both recent and not so recent, that deprive and exploit. At the same time, their incremental actions — going to the streets, trying to impeach water CEOs, 'illegally' tapping into the water system and consistent demands for basic services — appear to be bearing some fruit: the governor of Nairobi, who campaigned on the promise of bringing water to poor settlements in 2016, had, during our 2018 community meetings, further commited himself to this intention, and was to begin with Mathare and a few other spaces. I was informed of these governmental promises a few weeks after I had participated in a water meeting where the participants were seeking to sue the government for not providing water. Okocha (not his real name), a resident and activist, asked me whether I had heard of the governor's new water intentions. And when I replied that I hadn't, he said:

It [is] as if he has heard all of the work we have been doing and what we have been saying. Let us see if he will bring water like he said in the campaign, at the same time we will still continue with our campaign.

Conclusion

Nairobi, named after the Maasai term *Enkare Nyrobi,* the 'place of cool waters,' has, despite its original name, never been able to provide adequate water for its growing population. Certainly, for those who live in the 'slum' settlements that persist in what was formerly the native city, provision has always been a dream. While Article 23 of the 2010 Constitution states that all citizens are legally required to have access to 'clean and safe water in adequate quantities,' those confined to what is considered 'informal' and 'impermanent'[4] regions and infrastructures, have never been privy to any formal inclusion in the water network. Their own community efforts, 'machinic' initiatives – that produce 'non-revenue' water – are often criminalised. And their voices on the streets of Nairobi – 'enunciatory' community-led initiatives – have not to date succeeded in enabling long-term access to this resource. As a consequence, they continue to pay more for irregular and unsafe water brought to them by various 'empires.'

Yet, undoubtedly, there will continue to be many more resident-led efforts directed towards finding alternative sources of water, and towards achieving a more just urban environment. These are not perfect, and constitute the 'illegal' improvisation and 'development from below' that have become the daily enterprise of many of those confined to poor neighbourhoods in the Global South (Hake 1977; Bayat 1997, 2000; Simone 2004). Future research on 'systemic dehydration' in Nairobi should continue to document and historicise the long-term denial of 'hydrological citizenship' for the majority, and how residents narrate the absence of water through a tale that speaks of colonial and postcolonial empires, against which they are always ready to protest, to come 'back to the streets.'

References

Anand N (2012) Municipal disconnect: On abject water and its urban infrastructures. *Ethnography* 13(4): 487–509

Anderson D (2005) *Histories of the Hanged: The Dirty War in Kenya and the End of Empire.* New York: WW Norton

Bayat A (1997) Uncivil society: The politics of the 'informal' people. *Third World Quarterly* 18(1): 53–72

Bayat A (2000) From dangerous classes to quiet rebels: Politics of the urban subaltern in the Global South. *International Sociology* 15(3): 533–557

---

4   I use impermanence within quotation marks since, given the longevity of these structures, and the fact that they are built and rebuilt over decades, it is highly contradictory that literature on 'slums' reinforces the alleged informality of this and other poor urban settlements.

BBC (2015a, 22 June) Kenya slum Mathare gets cheap water through ATMs. https://www.bbc.com/news/world-africa-33223922

BBC (2015b, 30 July) Kenyan Governor Kidero denies grass removed after Obama. http://www.bbc.com/news/world-africa-33719845

Capital News (2019, 2 May) Sonko launches 'Water For All' initiative in Nairobi County. https://www.capitalfm.co.ke/news/2019/05/sonko-launches-water-for-all-initiative-in-nairobi-county/

Corburn J & Hildebrand C (2015) Slum sanitation and the social determinants of women's health in Nairobi, Kenya. *Journal of Environmental and Public Health*. doi: 10.1155/2015/209505. http://downloads.hindawi.com/journals/jeph/2015/209505.pdf

Corburn J & Makau J (2016) Coproducing slum health in Nairobi, Kenya. In: J Corburn & L Riley (eds) *Slum Health: From the Cell to the Street*. Berkeley: University of California Press. pp. 153–189

County of Nairobi & Japanese International Cooperation Agency (2014) *NIUPLAN/ The Project on Integrated Urban Development: Master Plan for the City of Nairobi in the Republic of Kenya (Final Report)*. Nairobi: County of Nairobi & Japanese International Cooperation Agency

Dafe F (2009) *No Business Like Slum Business? The Political Economy of the Continued Existence of Slums: A Case Study of Nairobi*. London: London School of Economics Development Studies Institute Working Paper Series

Deleuze G & Guattari F (1987) *A Thousand Plateaus: Capitalism and Schizophrenia*. Minneapolis: University of Minnesota Press

Government of Kenya (2007) *Kenya Vision 2030*. Nairobi: Government of the Republic of Kenya

Government of Kenya (2008) *Nairobi Metro 2030: A World Class African Metropolis*. Nairobi: Ministry of Nairobi Metropolitan Development

Government of Kenya (2010) *Constitution of Kenya*. Nairobi: National Council for Law Reporting with the Authority of the Attorney General

Graham S, Desai R & McFarlane C (2013) Water wars in Mumbai. *Public Culture* 25(1): 115–141

Hake A (1977) *African Metropolis: Nairobi's Self-Help City*. New York: St. Martin's Press

Kimari W (2016) Humble living and hustling: Youth struggles in Mathare Constituency, Nairobi. In: P Ugor & L Mawuko-Yevugah (eds) *African Youth Cultures in a Globalized World*. London: Routledge. pp. 129–144

Kimari W (2017) Nai-rob-me Nai-beg-me Nai-shanty: Historicizing space-subjectivity connections in Nairobi from its ruins. Doctoral dissertation, York University

Kimari W (2019) The story of a pump: Life, death and afterlives within an urban planning of 'divide and rule' in Nairobi, Kenya. *Urban Geography*. DOI: 10.1080/02723638.2019.1706938

Lonsdale J (2001) Town life in colonial Kenya. *Azania: Archaeological Research in Africa* 36–37(1): 206–222

Mathare Social Justice Centre (MSJC) (2019) *Maji ni Uhai Maji ni Haki: Eastlands Residents Demand Their Right to Water – A Participatory Report*. Nairobi: Mathare Social Justice Centre

Médard C (2010) City planning in Nairobi: The stakes, the people, the sidetracking. In: H Charton-Bigot & D Rodriguez-Torres (eds) *Nairobi Today: The Paradox of a Fragmented City*. Dar es Salaam: Mkuki na Nyota Publishers and Institute for French Research in Africa (IFRA). pp. 25–60

Muungano Support Trust (2012) *Mathare Zonal Plan. Nairobi/Kenya: Collaborative Plan for Informal Settlement Upgrading*. Nairobi & Berkeley: University of Nairobi & University of California

Myers G (2015) A world-class city-region? Envisioning the Nairobi of 2030. *American Behavioural Scientist* 59(3): 328–346

Ng'ethe V (2018, 12 February) Nairobi's water supply: 2 claims about losses & high prices in slums evaluated. *AfricaCheck*. https://africacheck.org/reports/nairobis-water-2-claims-losses-high-cost-slums-evaluated/

Owuor S & Mbatia T (2008) Post-independence development of Nairobi City, Kenya. Paper presented at Workshop on African Capital Cities, Dakar, Senegal, September 22–23

Rodriguez-Torres D (2010) Public authorities and urban upgrading policies in Eastlands: The example of 'Mathare 4A Slum Upgrading Project.' In: H Charton-Bigot & D Rodriguez-Torres (eds) *Nairobi Today: The Paradox of a Fragmented City*. Dar es Salaam: Mkuki na Nyota Publishers and Institute for French Research in Africa (IFRA). pp. 61–97

Simone AM (2004) People as infrastructure: Intersecting fragments in Johannesburg. *Public Culture* 16(3): 407–429

Simone AM (2015) It's just the city after all! *International Journal of Urban and Regional Research* 40(1): 210–218

Slaughter J (2004) Master plans: Designing (national) allegories of urban space and metropolitan subjects for postcolonial Kenya. *Research in African Literatures* 35(1): 30–51

Stoler A (2016) *Duress: Imperial Durabilities in Our Times*. Durham, NC: Duke University Press

Vargas J (2006) When a favela dared to become a gated condominium: The politics of race and urban pace in Rio de Janeiro. *Latin American Perspectives* 33(4): 49–81

Wekesa S (2013) Right to clean and safe water under the Kenyan Constitution 2010. *ESR Review: Economic and Social Rights in South Africa* 14(1): 3–6

White L (1990) *The Comforts of Home: Prostitution in Colonial Nairobi*. Chicago: University of Chicago Press

White L, Silberman L & Anderson P (1948) *Nairobi, Master Plan for a Colonial Capital: A Report Prepared For the Municipal Council of Nairobi*. Nairobi: HM Stationery Office

PART III

The global in urban Africa

Edgar Pieterse

This section brings together three chapters on three cities that are amongst the most rapidly growing on the continent. With over 20 million inhabitants, Lagos surpasses that of other major metropolises on the continent, such as Cairo, and is expected to be amongst the world's largest cities in the next few decades. With an estimated 4 and 7 million inhabitants, the cities of Addis Ababa and Luanda, respectively, represent a different scale, but with rapid growth rates, they face similar urbanisation challenges.

The chapters show that the ways in which city governments deal with rapid urbanisation are not only determined by colonial legacies, local histories, politics and geographies, but also by the circulation of global knowledge circuits and imaginaries, plans, policies that represent the ideal city as 'world-class', as well as by global finance. The interplay between both domestic and external forces is manifested in different ways in each city, but results in similar governance challenges.

All three countries are democratic in name, but federal (in the case of Nigeria and Ethiopia) or national (in the case of Angola) governments continue to exercise power over cities, limiting the ability of local governments to effectively manage their cities. Lagos is different since the state government is a decisive actor but, given the size of the state population, still at considerable distance from local communities. In all three cities, there is little space for bottom-up civic engagement.

In Lagos, after decades of military rule and urban neglect, the state government of Lagos managed to take a proactive approach to urban management. A series of flagship projects demonstrate how urban reform has been inspired by examples from Dubai and Singapore and framed around the notion of smart cities, but with different outcomes.

In Addis Ababa, in spite of the relative autonomy of the city government, the flagship Light Rail Transit project was driven by the prime minister's office as a way to mark 'Ethiopia's renaissance,' leading to a record time implementation but at a significant financial cost and with unintended negative socio-economic impacts.

The redevelopment of the war-torn Bay of Luanda equally shows how political drivers and top-down decision-making translate into flagship projects that project political power. Whereas, as in Lagos, Dubai also represents an important source of inspiration, the case of Luanda shows that colonial models and legacies continue to influence aesthetical preferences in seemingly contradictory ways.

CHAPTER 9

Africa's new Dubai? Intersections between the global and the local in the redevelopment of the Bay of Luanda[1]

Sylvia Croese

Introduction

Ten years after the end of nearly three decades of civil war, in 2012 then Angolan President José Eduardo dos Santos inaugurated the first phase of the redevelopment of the Bay of Luanda. Hailed internationally as a successful waterfront redevelopment project (*PR Newswire* 2013) and widely promoted as the 'new face' of Luanda (Lopes 2011),[2] critics see in the redevelopment proof of the capital city's increasing 'Dubaification' through the emulation of an architecture that is marked by the construction of skyscrapers (towers), but also ultra-modern and distinctive airports, trade centres, office blocks and retail centres (Elsheshtawy 2013).

Indeed, according to Power (2012: 15), 'Dubai has become both a critical reference point and a model of the city's future.' Vanin (2015: 166) in turn speaks of 'Dubai-like aesthetics' as a driving paradigm behind most new constructions in Luanda, while Blanes (2015) refers to the 'botox real estate' that underpins the becoming of 'Dubanda'.

Such voices echo a growing critique of the increasing emulation across the African continent of new models of urbanism represented by cities such as Dubai. Previously

1   This chapter draws on research conducted with financial support from the UK Government's Department for International Development (DfID) as part of the research project 'Urban Governance and Turning African Cities Around', managed by the Partnership for African Social and Governance Research (PASGR). Parts of this chapter were previously published by the author in Croese (2018).

2   For promotional videos see the YouTube channel of the Bay of Luanda: https://www.youtube.com/user/baiadeluanda

seen as part of the 'Third World,' Dubai, and cities such as Singapore and Shanghai, have now joined the world city hierarchy in which, for decades, cities have been ranked according to their place in global capital, service and knowledge production (Hall 1966; Friedmann 1986; Beaverstock et al. 1999; Sassen 2001; Taylor 2004). In doing so, they have become models of global cities in their own right and examples for (plans for) the redevelopment of African cities ranging from Khartoum and Nouakchott (Choplin & Franck 2010) to Kinshasa (de Boeck 2011), Kigali (Goodfellow & Smith 2013) and Nairobi (Myers 2015). In these cities, urban redevelopment is characterised by iconic high-modernist architecture, as well as large-scale urban renewal or restructuring through the construction of new satellite cities and close links to global circuits of finance and property construction (Watson 2014; Murray 2017).

While post-war urban redevelopment in Luanda mirrors global world-class city-making elsewhere, efforts to revive modernist colonial architecture as part of the redevelopment of the Bay of Luanda show that alongside Dubai-like futuristic aesthetics, internal and historical considerations equally play an important role in shaping the city's built environment. Based on the case of Luanda, the chapter seeks to provide a better understanding of the variegated and inherently local drivers and dynamics involved in world-class city-making in Africa or the ways in which global plans, models and visions of the urban are shaped and adapted at the local level.

Research for this paper was conducted from 2015–2016 as part of a comparative research project on urban governance in African cities and involved the review of relevant historical and academic literature, as well as grey literature such as government policy and research reports, legislation, online media records and archived newspaper articles. In addition, interviews and informal conversations were conducted with government representatives (central, provincial, municipal/district government level), representatives of the private sector and civil society, as well as ordinary residents of Luanda.

The chapter will start by outlining the main tenets of the quest for world-class city-ness as it has unfolded in Luanda over the first decade after the end of the war. It then offers a brief overview of the history of the Bay of Luanda and its post-war redevelopment, before turning to the elaboration of the central argument. It concludes by reflecting on the usefulness of the case of Luanda for thinking about world-class city-making in other African cities and the Global South more generally.

World-class city-making in Luanda: Africa's new Dubai?

The city of Luanda offers an interesting case study of world-class city-making in Africa as, unlike places such as Kinshasa or Nairobi, many urban development plans have actually been translated to reality (see Cain 2014 in response to Watson 2014).

In the decade that followed the end of the war in 2002, Angola became known as the posterchild of the 'Africa rising' narrative. From a war-torn and failed state, it rose up to being Africa's second largest oil producer, one of Africa's fastest growing economies and an Eldorado for foreign investors (Soares de Oliveira 2015).

Central to Angola's rise have been the government's post-war reconstruction efforts, which have been largely financed through oil-backed loans from China. While the construction and rehabilitation of basic infrastructures and services have covered the entire country, they have been concentrated in the capital of Luanda, turning the city into a permanent construction site. As such, Luanda has been at the centre stage of the post-war economic boom, with the city accounting for two-thirds of the national GDP which grew at double digit rates in the period between 2002 and 2007. At the height of the boom in 2007, 55% of all companies were established in the capital, generating 77% of jobs in the private sector and 27% of jobs in the public sector (Alves da Rocha 2010).

Yet, more than simply rebuilding the city's infrastructures and services, such as roads, schools, hospitals, water and energy networks, reconstruction efforts have been underpinned by the desire to transform Luanda into a modern 'world-class city' (Croese 2016). Perhaps the most (in)famous illustration of this desire is the construction of the new city of Kilamba, a USD 3.5 billion project financed with an oil-backed loan from China and contracted out to the Chinese state-owned company CITIC. Other mega projects include the construction of a new port and international airport, the latter (still under construction) promoted as 'Africa's largest airport,' a Special Economic Zone, (plans for) the creation of a Bus Rapid Transit system and major real estate, office and commercial development. All of this changed the city's landscape and skyline, sparking numerous references and comparisons by critics as well as admirers to the city as 'Africa's Dubai' (e.g. *Sonangol Universo Magazine* 2008).

As in other aspiring world-class cities, world-class city-making in Luanda has also been accompanied by its fair share of urban boosterism or city branding: 'strategies intended to distinguish cities as part of interurban competition which include advertising, sloganeering, and marketing tactics' that construct aspiring world-class cities as a commodity to be marketed (McCann 2013: 6). This includes extensive media campaigns to advertise the governments' investments and efforts which are broadcast on public television, radio, newspapers and billboards, as well as on international channels such as CNN. In addition, government documentaries such as *Made in Angola*[3] and promotional videos by the Angolan National Investment Agency (ANIP) contribute to an effort to rebrand and promote the country, all with a particular focus on Luanda. Over the course of the first post-war decade, Luanda also hosted a number of mega sporting events, such as the Africa Cup of Nations in 2010, as well as international and regional events and summits, all of which have been accompanied by the construction of stadiums and hotels to host visitors.

These campaigns and events have been implemented against the backdrop of the adoption of a number of development plans which, like city development plans adopted elsewhere on the continent (Myers 2015), position Luanda as a future regional and global hub that is 'open for business.' The first one, dating from 2007, is the country's long-term development plan, *Angola 2025: Angola a Country with a Future: Sustainability, Equity and Modernity*, which outlines the country's vision for the future and in this regard speaks of the aim of turning Luanda into a 'modern, efficient, creative and unified metropolis' that connects the country to the outside world (GoA 2007 – part III: X-46). The National Development Plan adopted in 2012 for the years of 2013–2017 in turn refers to the metropolitan region of Luanda as a

---

3   See the Made in Angola channel on YouTube: https://www.youtube.com/user/MadeInAngolaTV/

'platform of internationalization' (GoA 2012: 86). This idea similarly formed the basis for the Provincial Development Plan for Luanda for the years 2013–2017, which refers to Luanda as already 'one of the most dynamic and diversified cities of the African continent and a leader of great initiatives in its community' (GPL 2014: 22).

The new master plan for Luanda launched in December 2015, which was to be implemented over the following 15 years, in turn identifies three pillars of change which are to transform Luanda into a 'liveable', 'beautiful' and 'international' city. This last pillar foresees the establishment of Luanda as 'a future economic, touristic and service pole in Southern Africa' by 'keeping its international profile' and 'creating world standard infrastructure'. More specifically, Luanda's new port and airport hubs are set to 'bolster Luanda's regional and global profile, as a centre for services and logistics, manufacturing and as a market for agricultural produce to diversify Angola's economic base in a world-class capital city environment' (GPL 2015: 10). This aim was reiterated in Angola's most recent National Development Plan for 2018–2022 (GoA 2018).

In this context, the redevelopment of the Bay of Luanda represents the epitome of efforts towards the positioning of Luanda as a world-class city and a typical illustration of the type of imaginary and development usually associated with global world-class city-making. Before challenging this initial impression, the next section provides a brief overview of the history and redevelopment of the Bay of Luanda.

Redevelopment of the Bay of Luanda

Until independence the Bay of Luanda was known as *Avenida de Paulo Dias de Novais*, after the Portuguese explorer who founded the city of Luanda in 1576. Like waterfronts elsewhere in the world, the Bay of Luanda has traditionally been a place of 'flow', connecting the city/state to the world (Dovey 2005). For centuries, the Bay represented the heart of the city, where goods such as rum, food, clothes, sugar and tobacco, as well as hardware came into the country from across the Atlantic in exchange for slaves, ivory, wax and seeds (do Amaral 1968: 43).

Until the first half of the 20th century, boats would dock at the entry of the bay, along a strip of sand referred to as the *Ilha* or Island of Luanda (see Figure 1), with the connection to the shore made by smaller boats. The construction of a new port, with its own wharf, under the urbanisation plan for the waterfront of Luanda (*Plano de Urbanização da parte Marginal de Luanda*) of 1943 and subsequent construction works under the Colonial Urbanisation Department, created in 1944 for the design and execution of architecture and urbanisation projects in the Portuguese colonies (Vaz Milheiro & Dias 2009), shifted the main focus of the city's movements from the centre of the bay to 2km north of the city (do Amaral 1968: 27).

In a context of rapid economic growth, fueled by a coffee boom, and increasing investments in and growth of the city, during the 1950s and 1960s the Bay of Luanda became a place of leisure, the symbol of the city's transformation to modernity and the postcard of the jewel of the Portuguese colonial empire (Fonte 2007: 184). According to Rossa (2016: 109–110), city-ports like Luanda served to concentrate the political, military, and administrative importance of Portugal's colonial territories and boost their economic activities and cultural development, thereby becoming important centres of cosmopolitanism.

Figure 1: Bay of Luanda

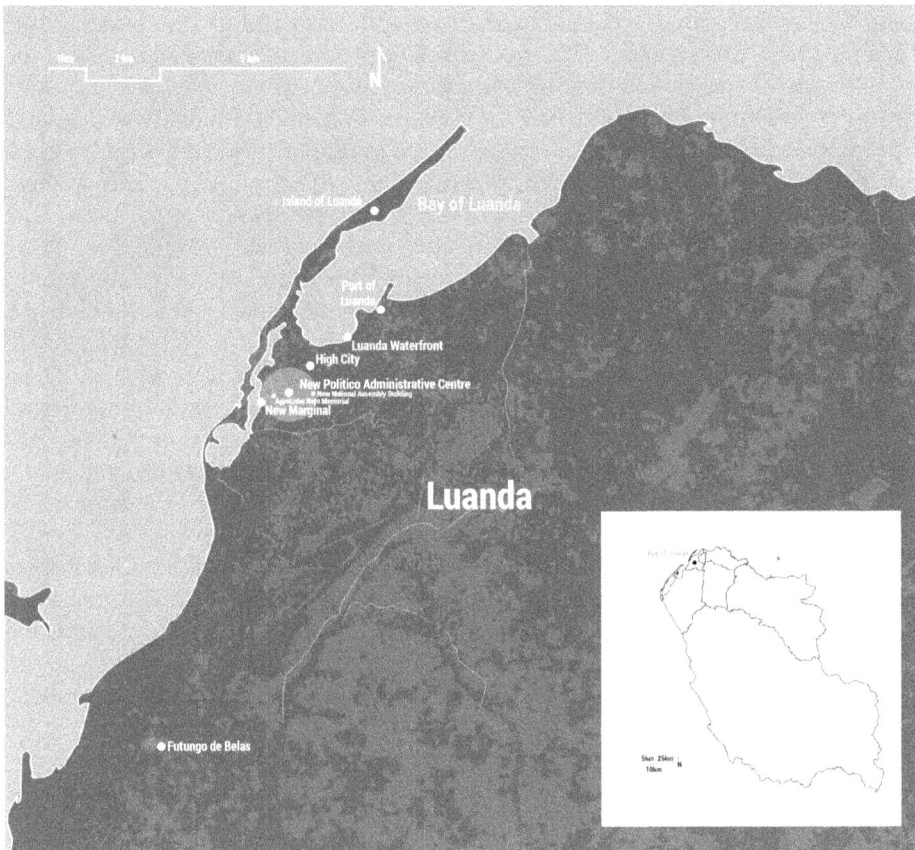

Source: Produced for author by Jhono Bennett

After Angola achieved independence in 1975, the name of the waterfront was changed to *Avenida 4 de Fevereiro*, which refers to the date of the start of the armed struggle against Portuguese colonial rule in 1961. During the years of war that followed independence, the waters of the bay started to become polluted as sewerage and drainage systems stopped working as a result of a virtual standstill of public investment in urban infrastructures. By the end of the war, raw sewerage continued to flow into the bay, roads and buildings were frequently flooded and a substantial volume of contaminated sludge was built up in the bay along most of the waterfront and traffic on the waterfront was increasingly congested (Booyens 2013).

In 2003 plans were commissioned by the Ministry of Public Works for the redevelopment of the bay. A Portuguese businessman, José Carlos Moreira Récio, who had been working in Angola since the late 1980s, in collaboration with his Angolan partner, António Mosquito, a business man with ties to the ruling party, presented a proposal for the redevelopment of the Bay to the government in October of the same year in a ceremony assisted by President dos Santos (Nexus 2003).

The proposal included, amongst others, plans for the dredging and cleaning of the bay, the extension of the waterfront road and the construction of parking lots and green spaces. According to the proposal, these works would be financed with private funding to the cost of about USD 76 million. In return, the promotors asked the government to compensate this investment with land, which would be reclaimed using dredged sand of the ocean, in order to create two artificial islands with an area of 900m² in the bay of Luanda parallel to the Island of Luanda to be used for private real estate development with a projected investment of USD 462 million. The proposal was subsequently scheduled to be discussed at the next Session of the Council of Ministers, which took place on 30 October 2003 (Nexus 2003).

However, concerns soon arose regarding this plan (Mukuna 2003). A group of prominent citizens, including the first prime minister of Angola, Lopo do Nascimento, a number of famous Angolan writers and intellectuals, but also professionals such as doctors, businessmen, teachers and university students, sent a series of signed petitions to President dos Santos expressing their concern with 'a private project of this nature and size' which went 'against the traditions and identity of the people of Luanda' and threatened to destruct 'the soul and mirror of the city of Luanda and its ex-libris, its Bay, considered to be one of the most beautiful of the world'. The letters furthermore expressed a fear that the project had not sufficiently taken certain essential issues into account, such as the environmental, ecological, cultural, geo-physical and socio-cultural impact of the project. Finally, they stated that, for a project such as the redevelopment of the Bay of Luanda to be approved, prior consultation and a wide and public debate was required.[4]

Notably, decisions regarding the project were delayed while an 'awareness raising campaign' was launched by the Luanda Waterfront Corporation, the company set up to implement the project, reportedly upon the request of the minister of public works at the time, Higino Carneiro (*Semanário Angolense* 2003). This involved the organisation of special meetings aimed at journalists and 'opinion makers' (Guerreiro 2004), as well as the publication of a number of advertisements in the daily state newspaper *Jornal de Angola*.

Eventually, the initial plan was reformulated and the creation of the two artificial islands scrapped and substituted by the reclaiming of land along the waterfront and Island of Luanda. After its approval by the Council of Ministers in 2005, followed by further studies, the completion of the final design and the licensing process, construction works under the first phase of the project eventually began mid-2008 (*Angop* 2005).

The works under this first phase were largely completed in August 2012 and inaugurated on the 70th birthday of President dos Santos on 28 August, three days before the country's second post-war elections. With a total investment of USD 376 million (almost triple the amount initially projected), the new bay of Luanda now had a 3km upgraded promenade with over 2 000 newly planted palm trees, 147 000m² pedestrian spaces, about 3km of cycle lanes, ten new open spaces along the beachfront, three playgrounds, three sport fields, five basketball courts and five spaces for cultural

---

4   Letters signed and dated 28 October 2003, 26 November 2003 and 19 January 2004. Copies kindly made available by Associação Kalu and in possession of author.

events, in addition to a new waste water system, a six-lane road (three-ways each), a fuel station and a fly-over connecting the waterfront to the Island of Luanda (*Expresso* 2012; SBL 2015).

In return for the investment made, Sociedade Baía de Luanda (SBL), the holding company set up to finance the project, received a 30-year concession for all publicity outdoors along the waterfront; a 30-year concession for all retail spaces along the waterfront; and a 30-year concession for access to all newly built 3 100 parking spaces along the waterfront, in addition to 60 years' land development rights of three plots of land of 38 hectares that had been reclaimed during the process (Resolution 51/05 of 26 October).

Office and residential development on the three plots of reclaimed land on 'prime locations' along the waterfront and Island of Luanda started in 2013 as part of the second phase of the project (Interview SBL, 9 July 2015). In addition, this phase included the installation of kiosks at strategic points along the promenade to function as restaurants, snack bars and shops, introducing the concept of 'open air shopping' and turning the waterfront into a 'point of reference within the capital for internal and foreign tourism' (*Angola Today* 2016).

Retrospective city-making: Backward into the future[5]

As outlined in the previous section, references to modernity and the future are rife in the numerous plans that underpin Luanda's post-war redevelopment. These reflect an overall desire to do away with the past and the poverty, informality and disorder associated with it, a common feature of urban planning in the Global South (Watson 2009). Similar references can be found in the promotion material produced in the planning phase of the redevelopment of the Bay. Advertisements refer to the project with the slogan: 'the future starts now', while the start of construction works was marked by a billboard which alerted those passing that 'the future is arriving to our Bay'. In various magazines and publications promoting the project, the redeveloped Bay has been referred to as the face of the 'new Angola' and the symbol of Angola's efforts to construct 'a bold new country'. Promotional material published for the occasion of the 440th anniversary of the city in January 2016, in turn celebrates Luanda as 'a city turned towards the future' (see Figure 1). According to Vaz Contreiras (2013: 126), this is part of a process of starting anew: by 'giving the postcard image of the City of Luanda – its Bay – a new face it claims a new post-colonial originality and can therefore claim a new history'.

However, more seems to be at play as the image accompanying the promotional material of 2016 includes an image of the Bay of Luanda taken in the early 1950s. This illustrates a recurring pattern in which references that portray the Bay as a symbol of modernity and the future are almost systematically accompanied by references to the past and the need to restore the Bay to its 'original' state.

---

5   I draw here on the title of the conclusion to John Friedmann's (2005) book *China's Urban Transition.*

Figure 2: Luanda: a city turned towards the future

Uma cidade
virada para o futuro.
Parabéns Mãe Luanda.

Source: Sociedade Baía de Luanda, 2016

Other examples include promotional material on the project published in the daily state newspaper *Jornal de Angola* when the redevelopment was still in its conceptual stages, explaining that:

> This project was conceived to meet the need to give back to the bay its natural splendour, upgrading *Avenida 4 de Fevereiro – Marginal*, turning it into the unequivocal signifier of the city of Luanda. [...] This is our dream, the dream of revitalizing the image of our capital, the dream that will celebrate its unequalled beauty and energy.

According to an architect from the Portuguese firm that was involved in the design of the project, conscious efforts were made to ensure the continuity of the new design of the Bay with its original state.

> The design was based on the idea of the city as a place of encounter. The *Marginal* is not a new place, it was already heritage of the city, what was attempted was to turn it into something closer to current times, something

more contemporary, allowing for a more universal use. [...] The strategy was to create a spatial structure of continuity, not of rupture (Interview architect Costa Lopes, Luanda, 4 December 2015)

With reference to the completion of the first phase, SBL's business development manager in turn highlights the way in which the project has achieved the almost impossible task of reviving the historical image of the Bay as it was known in the heyday of colonialism:

> There is the environmental aspect, because the project cleaned the bay of Luanda, which is, [...] a symbolic area of the city. In all the pictures of the city, even the old ones, the bay of Luanda appears as a postcard of the city. It was a shame that this postcard had become polluted, its image had become worn out. So, this image was cleaned, the waters were cleaned, and today we can for instance see dolphins in the bay, something once unthinkable (Interview SBL, Luanda, 9 July 2015)

References to history and heritage in contemporary urban development projects are not new and especially common in projects involving urban waterfront regeneration. Projects across the world, ranging from the redevelopment of Zanzibar's Stone Town (Hoyle 2002), to the Victoria and Alfred Waterfront Development in Cape Town (Ferreira & Visser 2007), or waterfront development in Singapore (Chang & Huang 2011) mobilise history and heritage in different ways. However, these references usually function to attract outside heritage tourism or investment or serve as a way to pay lip service to local heritage lobbies or global sustainability agendas and sources of funding.

These motives may not entirely be disregarded for the case of Luanda, as we have seen that initial plans for the creation of artificial islands in the bay were reformulated in response to resistance from a group of prominent residents of the city. However, the way in which the redeveloped waterfront subsequently was planned to mirror its original colonial design goes beyond paying lip service to these demands, but rather is reflective of a more deep-seated and structural way in which post-war urban policies and planning are informed by the country's colonial past rather than a clear vision of the future. This kind of retrospective city-making in turn extends beyond the revival of a certain historical aesthetics to the mobilisation of associated notions of grandeur, allowing for the creation of 'spaces of power' (Mabin 2015).

Indeed, the redevelopment of the bay of Luanda does not stand on its own but forms part of a wider project of urban redevelopment and renewal of the city's politico-administrative centre and associated public buildings and infrastructures that surround the bay, with the aim of allowing for the return of the country's President and political power to the city centre after years of absence.

Ever since proclaiming the country's independence in 1975, the ruling Popular Movement for the Liberation of Angola (MPLA) party has been based in the capital of Luanda, from where it waged a war with the forces of the National Union for the Total Independence of Angola (UNITA) in the countryside. However, during most of the war, President dos Santos (in power from 1979 to 2017) operated from a presidential compound located outside the city centre in an area called *Futungo de Belas* (see Map 1). According to the Angolan anthropologist António Tomás (2012: 97), in colonial times *Futungo de Belas* was the summerhouse of the governor, while the *Cidade Alta* (High City) was his official residence. In 1975, Agostinho Neto, the first Angolan president, transformed the governor's palace into his presidential palace, but a few years later he established his official residence in Futungo de Belas. His successor, dos Santos, in the context of cold and civil wars, transformed the entire area of Futungo de Belas into a military compound. During these years, the state and people became increasingly disconnected, with the state failing to fulfil even basic state functions.

When the war was seen to be coming to an end in the mid-1990s, preparations started to move the seat of the president back to the *Cidade Alta*, the part of the city which overlooks the Bay and Island of Luanda and the traditional headquarters of political power ever since the foundation of Luanda. In the following years, works developed under this project consisted of the rehabilitation of some of the main buildings in the politico-administrative centre, such as the presidential palace, and the completion of a memorial centre around the mausoleum containing the remains of President Neto. Works also included the expansion of the area with road works, laying a new main road southward called the New Marginal or *Nova Marginal*, as well as the construction of a new High Court and a new National Assembly. In line with the colonial continuity sought in the design of the redeveloped waterfront, the new building of the National Assembly, inaugurated in 2015, is modelled after the National Bank of Angola, another symbol of the neoclassical architecture of the Portuguese *Estado Novo* which was concluded in 1956 and which has since been a landmark of Luanda's skyline.

Moreover, since the conclusion of the initial works in the politico-administrative centre and the first phase of the redevelopment of the Bay of Luanda, the area has served as the primary location for the realisation of key events such as President dos Santos' inauguration after his first official election as President in 2012 and military marches which display the state's power on the day that marks the anniversary of the start of the country's armed struggle for independence. More recently, plans were presented to extend the site with the construction of a new neighbourhood, called the *Bairro dos Ministérios* or Neighborhood of Ministries, which would link the new National Assembly to the Presidential Palace in the *Cidade Alta* and house 28 ministerial buildings, including a building for the Council of Ministers, a convention centre and an exhibition space (*Jornal de Angola* 2019).

Hence, while in cities such as Dubai the 'technology of symbolic power' or the development of world-class infrastructures and the construction of iconic buildings primarily serves to 'seduce a global audience' (Acuto 2010: 276), the redevelopment of the Bay of Luanda forms an important part of a wider project that serves to convey a political message about the nation-state, not just to an international but also to a domestic audience. From this perspective, the redevelopment of the bay – while incorporating some elements of global plans and models of 'word-class' urban development – forms part of an effort to project political power onto the physical landscape, a common feature of capital cities in postcolonial Africa, especially in the early years of independence (Bekker & Therborn 2011). In doing so, the city becomes a vehicle for the national government to convey messages about the state and invoke global imaginaries of modernity and development, even in the face of pervasive levels of widespread urban poverty and deprivation.

Indeed, while the waterfront is widely used as a public space for leisure, it is largely disconnected from the rest of the city and inaccessible for most of Luanda's nearly 7 million residents who inhabit the vast informal settlements spread out in the city's periphery. The costs of products sold in the waterfront shops also mean that most of its patrons are among Luanda's most well-off residents. Hence, while branded as a landmark to attract foreign investors and tourists, the bay is mainly visited by locals. Similarly, the main investors in both the first and second phase of the redevelopment have been Angolan. Following the drop in oil prices and the ensuing economic crisis of 2014, during which much real estate construction and development ground to a halt, the Angolan government intervened and nationalised the bay by assuming all rights to the exploitation and development of the waterfront and surrounding areas, leaving no doubt as to who was in charge all along.

Conclusion

Luanda represents an example of increasing attempts across the African continent towards world-class city-making in the image of new global city models represented by cities such as Dubai. Futuristic and iconic architecture and aesthetics mark (plans for) the construction and redevelopment of waterfronts, shopping centres and entire new cities across Africa.

However, the case of Luanda also shows that alongside these global and futuristic imaginaries, historical models and legacies continue to influence aesthetic preferences in seemingly contradictory ways. Numerous other plans have emerged in Luanda's post-war years which involve the revival or restoration of unfinished ambitions dating from late colonial times, such as plans for the development of the Island of Luanda and the area of Futungo de Belas and architects, contractors and companies involved are often from Portugal (Fonte 2007). At the same time, such efforts go hand in hand with the demolition of icons of colonial modernist architecture, such as the Kinaxixe market, and their replacement with new and shiny shopping centres.

Projects such as the redevelopment of the bay are then indicative of the ways in which utopia and nostalgia intersect in the remaking of a postcolonial city such as Luanda (Siegert 2014). While problematic in terms of the selective mobilisation and appropriation of colonial memories of grandeur and modernity for political purposes and the uncritical reproduction of a misplaced sense of colonial nostalgia, such tendencies do not necessarily have to be seen as oppositional. Instead, they should be seen as a reflection of the ways in which global models of urban planning are provincialised through local histories, interests, politics and laws (Datta 2015).

Hence, the case of Luanda contributes to an understanding of the variegated local drivers and dynamics that may be involved in practices of world-class city-making in postcolonial as well as post-conflict contexts. The study of the different dynamics of city planning, development and renewal as they are currently arising and developing across the African continent may in turn prove useful for re-thinking notions and practices of world-class city-making across the wider Global South.

References

Acuto M (2010) High-rise Dubai urban entrepreneurialism and the technology of symbolic power. *Cities* 27(4): 272–284

Alves da Rocha MJ (2010) *Desigualdades e Assimetrias Regionais em Angola: Os Factores de Competitividade Territorial.* Luanda: Universidade Católica de Angola, Centro de Estudos e Investigação Científica

Angola Today (2016, 26 January) Bay of Luanda develops outdoor shopping centre. http://www.angola-today.com/news/bay-luanda/

Angop (2005, 1 September) Aprovado Projecto Baía de Luanda. http://www.portalangop. co.ao/angola/pt_pt/noticias/sociedade/2005/8/35/Aprovado-Projecto-Baia-Luanda,5b4ee059-2f9c-43de-b7b2-96b290e6dd6a.html

Beaverstock JV, Taylor PJ & Smith RG (1999) A roster of world cities. *Cities* 16(6): 444–458

Bekker S & Therborn G (eds) (2011) *Capital Cities in Africa: Power and Powerlessness.* Cape Town: HSRC Press

Blanes R (2015) O estereoscópio de Luanda: visão, política e memória no espaço urbano. Paper presented at the International Conference Studies of Angola, CEIC, Catholic University of Angola, Luanda, 7–8 December

Booyens Y (2013, 15 February) Firm assists in changing the face of Angola's capital. *Engineering News.* http://www.engineeringnews.co.za/print-version/firm-assists-in-changing-the-face-of-angola-2013-02-15

Cain A (2014) African urban fantasies: Past lessons and emerging realities. *Environment and Urbanization* 26(2): 1–7

Chang TC & Huang S (2011) Reclaiming the city: Waterfront development in Singapore. *Urban Studies* 48(10) 2085–2100

Choplin A & Franck A (2010) A glimpse of Dubai in Khartoum and Nouakchott: Prestige urban projects on the margins of the Arab World. *Built Environment* 36(2): 192–205

Croese S (2016) Urban governance and turning cities around: Luanda case study. *Partnership for African Social and Governance Research Working Paper* No. 018. Nairobi, Kenya

Croese S (2018) Global urban policymaking in Africa: A view from Angola through the redevelopment of the Bay of Luanda. *International Journal of Urban and Regional Research* 42(2): 198–209

Datta A (2015) New urban utopias of postcolonial India: 'Entrepreneurial urbanization' in Dholera smart city, Gujarat. *Dialogues in Human Geography* 5(1): 3–22

de Boeck F (2011) Inhabiting ocular ground: Kinshasa's future in the light of Congo's spectral urban politics. *Cultural Anthropology* 26(2): 263–286

do Amaral I (1968) *Luanda. Estudo de geografia urbana.* n° 53, 2° série 152. Lisbon: Memórias da Junta de Investigação do Ultramar

Dovey K (2005) *Fluid City: Transforming Melbourne's Urban Waterfront.* Sydney & New York: University of New South Wales Press & Routledge

Elsheshtawy Y (2013) *Dubai: Behind an Urban Spectacle.* New York: Routledge

Expresso (2012, 29 August) Inaugurada nova marginal da baía de Luanda. http://expresso.sapo.pt/economia/inaugurada-nova-marginal-da-baia-de-luanda=f749660

Ferreira S & Visser G (2007) Creating an African riviera: Revisiting the impact of the Victoria and Alfred Waterfront development in Cape Town. *Urban Forum* 18(3): 227–246

Fonte Afonso MM (2007) Urbanismo e arquitectura em Angola. De Norton de Matos à Revolução. Doctoral dissertation, Technical University of Lisbon

Friedmann J (1986) The world city hypothesis. *Development and Change* 17(1): 69–83

Friedmann J (2005) *China's Urban Transition.* Minneapolis: University of Minnesota Press

Goodfellow T & Smith A (2013) From urban catastrophe to 'model' city? Politics, security and development in post-conflict Kigali. *Urban studies* 50(15): 3185–3202

Government of Angola (GoA) (2007) *Angola 2025. Angola um País com Futuro: Sustentabilidade, Equidade, Modernidade.* Luanda: Ministry of Planning

Government of Angola (GoA) (2012) *Plano Nacional de Desenvolvimento 2013–2017.* Luanda: Ministry of Planning and Territorial Development

Government of Angola (GoA) (2013) *Plano de Acção. Actividades integradas para a melhoria da mobilidade urbana em Luanda.* Luanda: Ministério dos Transportes

Government of Angola (GoA) (2018) Plano de Desenvolvimento Nacional 2018–2022 Vol. I. Luanda: Ministry of Economy and Planning

Guerreiro J (2004, 29 January) A Baía e a Demagogia. *Jornal Angola*

Hall P (1966) *The World Cities.* London: Weidenfeld and Nicolson

Hoyle B (2002) Urban revitalization in developing countries: The example of Zanzibar's Stone Town. *The Geographical Journal* 168(2): 141–162

Jornal de Angola (2019, 23 July) Executivo constrói bairro dos Ministérios na Praia do Bispo. http://jornaldeangola.sapo.ao/politica/executivo-constroi-bairro-dos-ministerios-na-praia-do-bispo

Lopes LF (2011, December) Os milhões que estão a mudar Luanda [The millions that are changing Luanda]. *Rumo* 1, 29–36

Mabin A (2015) Tshwane and spaces of power in South Africa. *International Journal of Urban Sciences* 19(1): 29–39

McCann E (2013) Policy boosterism, policy mobilities, and the extrospective city. *Urban Geography* 34(1): 5–29

Mukuna P (2003, 1 November) Luandenses prestigiados querem travar mega-projecto da Baía de Luanda [Prominent Luandans want to stop mega-project of Bay of Luanda]. *Agora*

Murray M (2017) Frictionless utopias for the contemporary urban age: Large-scale, master-planned redevelopment projects in urbanizing Africa. In: A Datta & A Shaban (eds) *Mega-urbanization in the Global South: Fast Cities and New Urban Utopias of the Postcolonial State.* London: Routledge. pp. 31–53

Myers G (2015) A world-class city-region? Envisioning the Nairobi of 2013. *American Behavioral Scientist* 59(3): 328–346

Nexus (2003, 12 November) Requalificação da Baía de Luanda estimada em USD 76 milhões. Also undated powerpoint presentation on the Bay of Luanda project with images of the proposed plan available at http://www.slideshare.net/Jals/projectos-para-a-baia-de-luanda-1178921

Power M (2012) Angola 2025: The future of the 'world's richest poor country' as seen through a Chinese rear-view mirror. *Antipode* 44(3): 993–1014

PR Newswire (2013, 10 December) Sociedade Baía de Luanda presents an outstanding real estate project at the seafront of Angola's capital. http://www.prnewswire.com/news-releases/sociedade-baia-de-luanda-presents-an-outstanding-real-estate-project-at-the-seafront-of-angolas-capital-235214331.html

Provincial Government of Luanda (GPL) (2014) *Plano de Desenvolvimento Provincial 2013/2017 – Luanda*. Luanda: Provincial Government of Luanda

Provincial Government of Luanda (GPL) (2015) *Plano Luanda. Viva a nossa Cidade*. Luanda: Provincial Government of Luanda

Rossa W (2016) Luanda and Maputo: Accounts of the two capitals in urban heritage discourse. *Journal of Lusophone Studies* 1(1): 107–116

Sassen S (2001) *The Global City: New York, London, Tokyo*. Princeton, NJ: Princeton University Press

Semanário Angolense (2003, 8–15 November) Altos & baixos [Highs and lows]

Siegert N (2014) Luanda Lab – Nostalgia and utopia in aesthetic practice. *Critical Interventions* 8(2): 176–200

Soares de Oliveira R (2015) *Magnificent and Beggar Land: Angola since the Civil War*. London: Hurst

Sociedade Baía de Luanda (SBL) (2015) Unpublished presentation of the redevelopment of the Bay of Luanda, Luanda, September

Sonangol Universo Magazine (2008) Future city: Why Luanda is the New Dubai. Available on request at http://universo-magazine.com/

Taylor PJ (2004) *World City Network: A Global Urban Analysis*. London: Routledge

Tomás AA (2012) Refracted governmentality: Space, politics and social structure in contemporary Luanda. Doctoral dissertation, Columbia University

Vanin F (2015) Questioning the urban form: Maputo and Luanda. In: C Nunes Silva (ed.) *Urban Planning in Lusophone African Countries*. London: Ashgate

Vaz Contreiras B (2013) Luanda: Running on the wrong track towards global acceptance. In: T Brabazon (ed.) *City Imaging: Regeneration, Renewal and Decay*. New York, London: Springer. pp. 125–130. doi: 10.1007/978-94-007-7235-9_10

Vaz Milheiro A & Costa Dias E (2009) Arquitectura em Bissau e os Gabinetes de Urbanização Colonial (1944–1974). *arq.Urb* (2): 80–114

Watson V (2009) The planned city sweeps the poor away ...: Urban planning and 21st century urbanisation. *Progress in Planning* 72(3): 151–193

Watson V (2014) African urban fantasies: Dreams or nightmares? *Environment and Urbanization* 26(1): 215–231

Urban governance and smart future cities in Nigeria: Lagos flagship projects as springboard?

Muyiwa Elijah Agunbiade, Oluwafemi Olajide & Hakeem Bishi

Introduction

Lagos colony emerged from the creation of a geographical entity known as Nigeria, through the amalgamation of the southern and the northern protectorates by the British in 1914. This, supposedly, set the stage for the building of a prosperous and egalitarian society. Agunbiade and Olajide (2016: 1), note that the 'quality of physical form, socio-economic structure and governance outlook of what later became of Nigerian cities are products of many interacting forces over time and space'. The historical and political development of Nigeria can be generally categorised into three eras – pre-colonial (years before 1861), colonial (1861–1960) and postcolonial (1960 – present). Agunbiade and Olajide (2016) further discuss the political dimension of governance in Lagos, in time and space, as well as the implications on urban development and service delivery.

In the early years of Nigeria, there was less need for infrastructure development. In addition, the governance arrangement remained effective in meeting the needs of the indigenous society. The period of colonial administration, particularly from 1900, has been described as a period of rapid urban growth and metropolitan expansion. Major cities like Lagos, Port Harcourt and Kano experienced dramatic changes in population. For example, the population of Lagos increased marginally from 25 518 in 1871 to about 40 000 in 1901, and subsequently to 267 407 in 1953 and was projected to have risen to 662 246 by 1963 (Mabogunje 1961). As noted by Decker (2010), this, however, led to several social problems and corresponding poor urban management. The consequences of these included inadequate social infrastructure, poverty and massive rural-to-urban migration that could not be effectively managed or contained within the regulatory capacity of the government.

The structure of government since Nigeria's independence in 1960 has been that of three distinct administrative levels – national, state and local government areas – each with defined spheres of jurisdiction and constitutional functions. Lagos region emerged as one of the federating states in 1967 and has since dominated the country's socio-political landscape despite its relatively small land area, the smallest in the country.

The country's political trajectory, shortly after independence in 1960, ended in jagged governance systems. Since independence in 1960, Nigeria has witnessed political and economic instability occasioned by continuous military interference in the political and governance system. As noted by Gandy (2006), the successive military governments reinforced the earlier colonial forms of social, economic, political and spatial inequality. The military interrupted the political structure in 1966 and ruled from 1966 to 1979 and once again between 1983 and 1993. Thereafter was a mix of military and civilian rule until 1999. In all, the military had ruled Nigeria for a total of 34 years. The military ruled without respect for the rule of law and no specific political will to pursue any meaningful development agenda (Agunbiade & Olajide 2016).

At the close of military rule in 1999, Nigeria had declined politically and economically. While most other countries in transition and with similar economic prospects and a natural resource base were advancing and aiming at developing productive cities, this was stymied by vandalism, lawlessness, and grossly inadequate infrastructures in many cities in Nigeria. However, in a relatively short period of time, commencing precisely from year 1999, Lagos went from a basket case to one of the examples of a well-run African city with promising prospects. The potential of Lagos was always framed in terms of its potential and capacity to become 'world-class'.

From this perspective, reformers have been heavily influenced by specific examples of urban efficiency and prosperity, for example, Dubai, Singapore, etc. There is a desire to become Africa's main financial services and economic hub, a key node in the locational dynamics of economic globalisation. To achieve this, determined political leaders have embarked on ambitious policy reforms and flagship projects. In the more recent years this modernisation agenda has been framed by the smart cities discourse, manifest most acutely in fashioning the character of Dubai. In order to explicate one aspect of how the global manifests in the local, the chapter focuses on the relevance and impact of smart city discourses on governance and policy priorities of Lagos, using the transition from neglect to proactive urban management as context.

Transition from neglect to proactive urban management

At the turn of the millennium, owing to the long period of infrastructure and services neglect, Lagos already demonstrated signs of urban decay and inefficiency in all its sectors. This resulted in a chaotic mixture of socio-economic and environmental problems, manifested in high incidence of slum formation, inequality, poverty, unemployment, overcrowding, crime, violence, pollution and urban disorder. Evidently, these are contrary to the ideology of a smart city, which seeks to improve the efficiency of infrastructure and services and, in turn, the quality of life of the citizens. The emerging nuanced discourse of smart cities in Lagos is a combination of many factors including political stability and a steady development policy framework backed by visionary leadership, political will and strategic spatial planning mechanisms. Also important to recognise is the tremendous improvement in the city's economy and government revenue base. The improvement of the revenue base stemmed from effective reform of taxation systems which brought considerably more resources into the public purse.

From the available data, Lagos currently generates about 75% of its income from internally generated revenue (IGR) and is unarguably the most financially viable state in Nigeria today. The increase in the state government's revenues resulted in huge investment in urban development plans (model city plans, regional master plans and integrated transportation master plans), transportation facilities, new housing schemes, new industrial and commercial districts (Lekki Free Trade Zone and Eko Atlantic City), healthcare facilities, city beatification and slum regeneration efforts. These are tagged as flagship projects (Table 1 on p. 136). Several of these projects have attracted global acclaim and interest while serving as potential platforms for advancing smart city initiatives. Taken together, they are expected to provide an opportunity to examine the intersection of ICT, digital Spatial Data Infrastructure (SDI) and sustainable good urban governance in the smart city aspirations of Lagos.

Conceptualising urban governance, smart city and flagship project

There seems to be some commonalities or overlaps between good urban governance and smart city debates as presented by some scholars, such as Dirks and Keeling (2009), Hatzelhoffer et al. (2012), Komninos, Pallot and Schaffers (2013). From the views presented by these scholars, it could, however, be argued that every city with good urban governance is not necessarily smart, but every smart city has good urban governance components. To advance this argument, it will be necessary to put in proper perspective what urban governance is and how it relates to the smart city.

Urban governance

There is extant literature relating to the definitions of governance (World Bank 1989; McCarney, Halfani & Rodriguez 1995). The World Bank (1989: 60) defines governance, at the national scale, as the exercise of power in the management of a nation's affairs. Within the context of this paper, focusing on the urban scale, governance is described as the relationship between civil society and the state; between rulers and the ruled; and between the government and the governed (McCarney, Halfani & Rodriguez 1995). Governance involves a variety of actors – formal and informal/traditional, local and international – who share responsibility to govern and exercise power through a multiplicity of instruments. Central to this exercise of power are the people: the government and the governed. This is usually shaped through continuous interactions. In this regard, the quality of relationships amongst the various stakeholders (rulers and the ruled) and the instruments involved are critical.

The outputs of governance within the urban systems is a product of many interacting forces resulting from diverse decisions taken by city administrators (state) and a spectrum of people (agency). These decisions are informed by the desire to satisfy certain motives. Depending on what these motives are, the society is continuously shaped and modified by the outcomes. Some scholars (Beall & Fox 2009; Harvey 1989, 2007; Vliet 2002), have commented on the political economy implications of injecting neoliberal ideology into spatial planning and development to support corporate capital accumulation and foreign investments in most developing countries, especially in Africa. These days, urban administrators are being guided by the contemporary events and fashionable policy discourses circulating around the world. Some of the significant ones being issues, discussions and conventions around: climate change, sustainable development, smart city initiatives, city deals, and the internet of things.

It is not unusual for thinkers to suggest that developing countries can jumpstart their socio-economic development by aligning local policies to leverage contemporary global thinking and development trends, for instance, green economy (UNEP 2011); and ICT for development (Pieterse 2010). However, beyond the rhetoric and buzzwords, as Watson (2004) termed some of them, there are some fundamental issues that need to be considered when discussing these trending issues. The focus of this chapter centres on smart city initiatives and good urban governance. Governance in this respect is considered to be an *institutional* factor in the smart city initiative. In other words, the motive of city administrators will determine the depth and perception of smart city initiatives and how these are translated to policies, especially with regards to flagship projects being embarked upon by government.

Smart city

The smart city is conceptually defined as 'an urban space that is surrounded by or is embedded with smart systems or a city with ideas and people that provide clever insights' (Anthopoulos 2017: 7). Eremia et al. (2017: 14) noted that 'the term incorporates elements of sustainability and social inclusion, at the same time being suited to the evolutions of the new internet technologies.' However, Albino, Berardi, and Dangelico (2015) observed that it remains a fuzzy concept. Clearly, there are conceptual variants of the term as some scholars have replaced smart with alternative adjectives like: digital (Shin & Kim 2012), intelligent (Komninos 2008), knowledge (Yigitcanlar, O'Connor & Westerman 2008), ubiquitous (Leem & Kim 2012). Albino et al. (2015) observe that, in the urban planning field, the term is treated as a normative claim and has an ideological dimension, that is, being smarter entails having strategic direction. Governments and public agencies now use 'smart city' as one of the contemporary master signifiers for urban development programmes and policies which aim to achieve sustainable development, sound economic growth, and better quality of life (Gunder & Hillier 2009).

Since the emergence of the sustainable development principles in the *Brundtland Commission Report of 1987*, the concept and practice have witnessed several transitions. The evolution and application of the concept has also been expanded to accommodate the digital and development realities of the last three decades. From the theoretical grounding and applications of the concept in the 1990s; to the Millennium Development Goals (MDGs) experience of the 2000's, and now the Sustainable Development Goals (SDGs), the core principles have not only survived, but they have also shaped most global development discourses since their emergence. During the same period, the smart cities movement was also developing and the digital realities of today have fuelled the sustained relevance and nexus of both concepts.

While precursors to the smart city concept first appeared in development discourse during the early to late 1990s, the conceptual evolution is traced to different terms ranging from digital city to future city and more. Although the article by Graham and Aurigi (1997) on *web or virtual city* is widely cited as one of the pioneer literature related to the present-day smart city concept, Anthopoulos (2017) showed that different cities around the world were gradually transitioning into future and digitally smart city approaches as early as 1994 but all took different pathways in their evolution. The different individual baby steps of those days (including basic efforts such as map digitisation, geographic information systems, e-commerce, e-government, e-library, e-books, computerisation of work processes, wireless broadband and databases etc.) have now collectively crystallised to drive the current ICT-focused smart city agenda.

Today, smart city considerations are increasingly becoming integrated into sustainable development discourse in many cities around the world, including Lagos. For instance, since 2016 the Lagos State Government has been vigorously promoting a comprehensive Smart City Programme that seeks to provide a 24-hour driven economy with recent announcements to install 10 000 high definition CCTV cameras around the state among other future interrelated projects (Onwuaso 2018). This will be expected to build on the reported 'installation of free wifi infrastructure across the city' in 2017 (Raji 2018). While information technology is elevated as the central tool to achieve the smart city objective, it seems the ultimate target is socio-economic development of Lagos and its people.

However, a closer look at different stakeholders confirms that this is being viewed from divergent perspectives and thus, it means different thing to different people. For instance, Nigeria's National Information Technology Development Agency (NITDA) adopts what it calls a 'multi-stakeholder approach' to help drive the smart city project in Lagos[1] while establishing the Nigeria Smart City Initiative (NSCI) in February 2016. The agency's primary vision is to champion e-governance in Nigeria but the trick is to align and balance social goals with private business opportunities for the ultimate public good.[2] With Lagos' reputation as Nigeria's centre of innovation and business excellence, it is only to be expected for the agency to view the Lagos smart city project as requiring public-private collaboration. Some urban development professionals, on the other hand, think there is a 'missing link' between the future smart city aspirations and the core infrastructure required for Lagos to survive.[3]

Ekwealor (2016) contends that while a smart city 'has digital technology embedded across all of its functions', Lagos is currently facing a deluge of debilitating infrastructural challenges including energy shortage, and the absence of basic databases required to run a smart city. Similarly, Raji (2018) noted that despite problematic infrastructure

---

1   http://tmclonline.com.ng/cyberafrica/2015/10/22/our-multi-stakeholder-approach-will-make-lagos-smart-city-project-world-class-nitda/
2   https://sunnewsonline.com/smart-cities-stakeholders-advocate-public-private-sectors-synergy/
3   https://www.tribuneonlineng.com/148140/

and unpredictable tax systems in Lagos, the smart city aspirations are not misplaced, but cautioned that it may be better to pursue Lagos as a smart ecosystem of which the government smart city initiative is only a component. Abiodun (2016) noted that Dubai had laid the foundations for essential infrastructure of a smart city starting in the 1990s. Therefore, promoters of the Lagos smart city project must understand that there is no shortcut around it. Rather it is an incremental development process, gradually evolving out of a strategic plan with specific elements of achievable targets.

Some scholars, like Bakıcı, Almirall and Wareham (2012); Marsal-Llacuna, Colomer-Llinàs, & Meléndez- Frigola (2015) and Zygiaris (2013), consider a smart city as a city that *innovatively* and *creatively* builds on its *resources* and *assets*, with a view to achieving a healthy environment, better living conditions, retain and enhance local economy, efficiently use city resources. Others, such as Caragliu, Del Bo and Nijkamp (2011) and Giffinger et al. (2007), argue that a smart city should not be limited to the integration of various ICT systems and solutions to manage the city resources, but that due consideration should be given to the people; hence, its human and social capital.

Caragliu et al. (2011: 50) observed that a city can be defined as 'smart when investments in human and social capital and traditional (transport) and modern (ICT) communication infrastructure fuel sustainable economic growth and a high quality of life, with a wise management of natural resources, through participatory action and engagement'. Put differently, a smart city not only possesses ICT, but also deploys it in a manner that impacts the local community and the environment positively. Furthermore, it should positively enhance regional competitiveness, transport, and information and communication technologies, economics, natural resources, human and social capital, quality of life, and participation of citizens in the governance of cities (Giffenger et al. 2007). In this regard, Albino et al. (2015: 4) argued that consideration should be given to strategies that enhance and 'enable transportation linkages, mixed land uses, and high-quality urban services with long-term positive effects on the economy'.

In spatial planning and development discipline, smart city is often considered as an ideology which prioritises and integrates investment in critical infrastructure and human capital through institutional strategic policy directions (Nam & Pardo 2011; Albino et al. 2015). Drawing on this understanding and to allow for a better structuring of thoughts, this chapter considers flagship projects within the context of smart city plans based on three pillars: smart policy, smart investment, and smart technology. These are further expanded into six dimensions: *smart economy, smart mobility, a smart environment, smart people, smart living, and smart governance* and how each of these are related to different aspects of urban life and urban living as presented by Giffinger and Gudrun (2010) and Lombardi et al. (2012).

Shapiro (2006) argues that smart cities start from the human capital dimension: governance and policy, rather than assuming that ICT can automatically create smart cities. From this perspective, Giffenger et al. (2007) conceptualises a smart city as one with positive outcomes in the aspects of *governance*, economy, mobility, environment and patterns of living. With this view, it could be argued that for a city to be smart, the governance structure and policy thrust should equally be smart. In other words, a smart city should have a strong governance-orientated underpinning that emphasises the role of social and human capital as well as good interactions to facilitate urban development. In addition, it must be able to deliver city deals of a shared vision for the city's productivity and livability. This will be achieved through coordinated investment and a collective plan for growth in the given city underpinned by suitable regulatory reforms and policies.

From an investment and economic perspective, smart city is expected to be structured to deliver long-term economic returns to all stakeholders. This, according to the Government of Australia (2016), involves: prioritising projects that meet broader economic objectives; treating infrastructure funding as an investment wherever possible; getting involved early to ensure rigorous planning and business cases; and increasing investment. This is, however, a contested issue in highly unequal societies, like many sub-Saharan African cities, where the majority struggle to cope with basic needs. From this perspective, there is limited general public support for investment in the smart city (Downs 2005), despite its normative ideology that it will promote social equity and inclusionary governance (Scott 2007). The implementation often shifts development benefits away from the majority through the exploitation of market mechanisms of capital accumulation (Scott 2007; Gunder & Hillier 2009). Therefore, arguably, contrary to its normative ideology, smart cities often promote social inequality and exclusionary governance through predominant market forces (Scott 2007). Paradoxically, while the market mechanisms of capital accumulation are enhancing the development of smart cities, they are also becoming barriers for socio-economic sustainability and inclusive development owing to higher cost of living (Anthony 2006; Scott 2007).

The third pillar is *smart technology*. Thinking about technology has been the interest of most governments and investors with regards to smart city initiatives. As cities evolve and new technologies emerge at a very high rate, cities are expected to leverage these technologies. For example, this means that cities should take advantage of open and real time data to drive the use of energy efficient technologies, especially with regard to investing in smart intermodal public transport systems. Considering these, therefore, the role of spatial data infrastructure in smart future cities is very fundamental. Harrison et al. (2010: 1) observe that the term denotes an 'instrumented, interconnected and intelligent' city. As described further by Harrison et al. (2010), *instrumented* is the capability of acquiring and integrating real time data through the use of sensors and devices. While *interconnected* refers to the integration of these data into a computing platform for better utilisation through various city services. To be *intelligent*, however, denotes there will be complex analytics, modelling, optimisation, and visualisation services to make better operational and policy decisions. These are the technical underpinnings of an evidence-based approach to urban governance which is something the smart city promises to achieve.

Urban governance, technology and smart city: The intersect

As illustrated by Nam and Pardo (2011), the three main dimensions of a smart city are: technology, people, and institutions (Figure 1). Significant in this equation are data that assist city administrators to make informed decisions about human settlements. Examining the connections between these factors, a city will be considered smart when investments in human/social capital and IT infrastructure stimulate sufficient

Figure 1: Fundamental components of a smart city

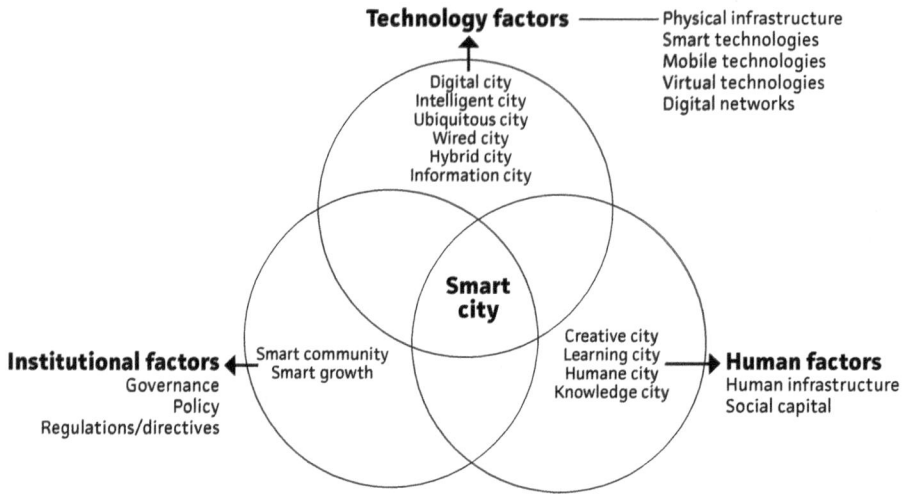

Technology factors ———— Physical infrastructure
Smart technologies
Mobile technologies
Virtual technologies
Digital networks

Digital city
Intelligent city
Ubiquitous city
Wired city
Hybrid city
Information city

Smart city

Institutional factors ← Smart community
Smart growth
Governance
Policy
Regulations/directives

Creative city
Learning city → Human factors
Humane city
Knowledge city
Human infrastructure
Social capital

Source: Nam & Pardo (2011)

sustainable growth and enhance better quality of life, through participatory governance (Caragliu et al. 2011). This intersect could potentially find expression in flagship projects.

Flagship projects

For a better understanding, it is important to contextualise flagship projects within the smart city initiatives. In this regard, it will be reasonable to know what constitutes a flagship project and how this is connected to smart city initiative. Most importantly, how significant are these projects within an urban setting? What role do they play in shaping the future growth and development of our cities? How are they helping to improve the quality of life of residents?

The first approach is to see this from the lens of *new urbanity*. As argued by Harvey (1989), new urbanity is achieved through recreating the urban space by relying on large-scale and symbolic projects, largely describing the evolution of the neoliberal city in which the state relinquishes its service provision role and assumes that of a collaborator in an entrepreneurial activity. The twin approaches of globalisation and liberalisation, as described by Swyngedouw et al. (2002), influence the production of new forms and scales of governance and the relationship between flagship projects and political, social, economic power relations in the city.

While Lagos may still lack the advanced institutional systems and structural capacities of similar megacities of the global North, the conception, design, financing and implementation of the selected flagship projects are modern, ambitious and global in outlook. As the next sections will show, proponents of these projects mostly envisaged them as iconic and, in some cases, uncommon on the African continent. Financed through public-private partnerships, the political leadership in Lagos has attracted local and foreign private investors to participate in urban redevelopment activities while guaranteeing returns on their investment. To achieve this, the local power relations rely on a delicate balance of political compromise and patronage. De Gramont (2015: 1) summarised these unique processes thus: 'governance transformation in Lagos was driven by a technocratic vision of a modern megacity but relied on creative policy proposals that also served multiple political interests'. The next section discusses the methodology for analysing the Lagos case study.

Methodology for Lagos case study

There are many approaches and schools of thought for developing knowledge. As described by Kitchin and Tate (2000) these include: empiricism, positivism, behaviouralism, idealism, realism, postmodernism and feminism. The realist approach is considered consistent with the central issues discussed in this paper. This involves the investigation of underlying mechanisms and structure of the social relations while still using a scientific approach. This is in addition to content analysis of available documents; newspaper articles, to understand the space in which discourse has emerged and in which it acquires meaning. Hollands (2008) identified three different discourses in the definitions and criteria that are selected to describe *smart cities* in African cities: infrastructure-based services; business-led urban development; and social inclusion, learning and development. It is believed that these different views will assist in understanding different assumptions about cities and their inhabitants.

The empirical analysis presented in this paper is underpinned by 'smart city' definition as presented in the earlier section. In other words, the broad considerations are: investments in human and social capital; the use of modern (ICT) communication infrastructure; a wise management of natural resources; participatory action and engagement. This approach is also consistent with the categorisation of Hollands (2008), as highlighted above. The focus is to bring out smart city initiatives within the flagship projects, emphasising the institutional dimension of participatory governance. It is apprehended through an analytical focus on: institutional capacity, inclusiveness, accountability, and contestation. This builds on the assessment of the context of flagship projects to know whether they reflect being smart investments, embodying smart technology and smart policy.

Findings and discussion

The shortage of basic infrastructure and the need to bridge the widening gap have remained a common urban management challenge for many African cities. Hence, recent reforms and the onset of a seeming Africa urban renaissance are the focus of attention. Lagos is one of the African cities with several flagship projects, as summarised in Table 1.

Table 1: Selected Lagos Flagship Projects and Initiatives

Description of Flagship Project	Urban Sector	Timelines	Status
Eko Atlantic City	Planned City Development	2003–2005 (Feasibility Study Conducted)	Currently under construction
Lagos Strategic Transport Master Plan – Lagos Bus Rapid Transit – Lagos Rail Mass Transit Network – Lagos Cable Car Project	Urban mobility/ transport	March 2008 (Phase 1) 2008 (Blue Line) 2013 (Terminus Sites)	Implementation ongoing Under construction Sites secured
Lagos Home Ownership Mortgage Scheme	Housing	February 2014 (Project launch)	Under construction / delivery ongoing
Lagos Tax System Reform	Revenue/finance	November 2005 (Commenced structural change of the LIRS)	Implementation ongoing
Lekki Free Trade Zone	Industrial Growth Pole	2006 (Master Plan initiated and document developed)	Under construction
Badagry Port and Free Zone	Industrial Growth Pole	Early 2018 (Planned soft start)	Pending construction
Some Major Road Infrastructure – Lagos-Epe Expressway Rehabilitation – Lekki-Ikoyi Link Bridge Construction – Lagos-Badagry Expressway Upgrade – Ikorodu Road Expansion Project	Urban mobility / transport	May 2008 (Contract) May 2013 (Launch) April 2009 (Launch) August 2012 (Launch)	Almost completed Completed Under construction Almost completed
Some Commercial Development Projects – Tejuosho Market Redevelopment – The Palms Shopping Mall, Lekki – Actis Shopping Mall, Ikeja – Expansion of the Palms Mall, Lagos	Modern market Retail shopping Retail shopping Retail shopping	August 2014 December 2005 December 2011 December 2016	Completed Operational Operational Under construction
Lagos City Beautification Project	Environment/ landscape		Continuous Project
Lagos Waste Management Reform	Environment/ sanitation		Continuous Project
Lagos-Dubai Smart City Project	Infrastructure and technology	June 2016	In progress

Motivation for the design and conceptualisation of flagship projects

It was noted that the main motivation was the commitment to transform cities and *invest beyond* the *conventional budgetary allocation* thereby responding to the noticeable signs of urban decay in all sectors. The question then is: are these configured to adopt smart city initiatives?

It could be argued that most of the projects were motivated by *infrastructure-based service provisions*. These have significantly altered the pace of development and are observed to be 'turning Lagos around', but there is still much more to be done in the journey to a 'smart' destination. So, if the concept of a smart city is viewed from an *infrastructure perspective*, it could be asserted that though many of these projects are not originally structured to satisfy smart city initiatives, they certainly have the potential to key into the broad policy direction.

Other significant drivers of change that have contributed immensely to smart city initiatives in the present political dispensation – the fourth republic – in Lagos, include: a clear vision and determination by the government; high improvement in the city's economy within a relatively short period, with potential for further improvements. Most importantly, there is apparent political stability and a functional policy direction backed by political will, conscious urban planning and management mechanisms. All these variables set the scene for a smarter city. These have been underpinned by the financial transformation triggered by a significant change in the taxation system. This motivated major urban development initiatives by the government and bolstered the confidence of private investors to participate in the process.

Analysis of specific flagship projects in Lagos

As initially noted, the understanding of flagship projects in Lagos is framed through the lens of participatory governance to establish the connections between the institutional, technological and human factors; being the three key dimensions of smart cities. The analysis is also based on the ways in which these projects have been promoted, how they link up with national or global smart city plans or policies and how they have been implemented on the ground; the perception of local people regarding the understanding of the flagship projects, limits and possibilities of smart cities in Lagos, in particular, Nigeria and Africa in general.

Lagos was once described as a 'self-service city' by Gandy (2006), where the residents had substantially given up any expectation of services being provided by the government. Gandy noted that the residents had developed several alternative means to provide necessary physical and social infrastructures. It is common knowledge that provision of physical and social infrastructures had degenerated to an unprecedented level in most cities in Nigeria, including Lagos. The concerns of city administrators to address this critical shortage led to deliberate efforts at developing large-scale projects as solutions to the problems facing Lagos. The next sections provide a more detailed assessment of these projects from the perspective of smart city initiatives.

Eko Atlantic City Project

The Eko Atlantic city project was conceived first as a mitigation measure to the perennial ocean surge along the bar beach area of Victoria Island, Lagos. Today, it is considered one of the most ambitious new city development projects, in terms of technology, cost and innovation, in the sub-Saharan Africa region. Substantial work had been carried out with regards to retaining walls and the land filling of the site. At the moment, a city is gradually rising from the depths of the Atlantic Ocean, as one of the strategic flagship projects in Lagos. This is one of the initiatives aimed at creating technology-enabled modern living and working spaces. Lagos State Government is collaborating with the private sector to build Eko Atlantic city on the southern tip of Lagos, abutting the Atlantic Ocean, as a massive futuristic living and business complex which is intended to become the financial centre of Nigeria.

Eko Atlantic city is structured to leverage the use of modern technology solutions to better manage traffic and coordinate emergency services in the city (Harrison et al. 2010). Lagos also participated in the IBM Smarter Cities Challenge where the use of technology was emphasised and reinforced to validate the philosophy of the initiators of Eko Atlantic. However, with regards to the way the project has been promoted, some have argued that it is elitist, with limited participation from the public. At the initial launch of the project, there were several negative comments from the residents and experts. Some of the comments regarding the draft EIA report suggest that the project lacks transparency, participation and does not always adhere to the rule of law (Njoku 2012).

The majority of Lagos residents consider the project to be grandiose and driven by profit-making capitalist motives under the hegemony of neoliberalism. The planning and implementation are considered too exclusive. There are no conscious efforts by either the government or project developers to address these concerns but instead construction continued unabated. The negative public perception of the development processes did not pose enough of a threat to affect neither the progress on site nor its global marketability. Ironically, the project website claims that Eko Atlantic City intends 'to solve the chronic shortage of real estate in the world's fastest-growing megacity'. The reality is, rather, that the project will only provide opportunity for investment and wealth creation for corporations and corporate elites, which some scholars regarded as unadulterated capital accumulation (Harvey 2007; Peck, Theodore & Brenner 2009).

However, with the level of development now, it appears the skepticism is gradually fading away, with many people getting excited at the prospect of this global city becoming the hub of activities in Lagos. The statement below describes the feelings of a few online commentators:

> I was dumbfounded such huge project is fast developing [and] becoming a reality. The visit to the city was a real push, I have been inspired, motivated, enlightened, educated and exposed beyond dots and lines ... At the completion of the project I see a city that will change the face of Africa and probably transform Lagos to a successful mega-city. It's going to be the source of great national pride for our country (Nigeria) ... Kudos to the city planners and developers for this great vision ... Looking forward to its completion. (Mustapha Holasunkanmi Yusuf, Eko Atlantic, 28 March)

> I think Lagos State has always produced thinking governors who are innovative, who believe in the impossible, who have gone beyond culture, tradition, religious and tribal politics, and instead are focused in transforming the state into a place where everybody will be welcome and be proud to call their home. (Esene Prayer Henry, Eko Atlantic, 3 May)

In total, out of 603 reviewers, as on 14 July 2017, 425 rated the project five out of five, and another 98 rated it four out of five.[4]

However, to sustain the good rating, Eko Atlantic will need a city manager, a mayor-type position, who is capable of running a city-within-a-city. In other words, there will be a need for a bespoke governance structure that will recognise the importance of effectively conducting the day to day running of the city. This would mean that

---

4   https://www.facebook.com/pg/EkoAtlantic/reviews/?ref=page_internal

Eko Atlantic city should operate under high standards of transparency and good governance consistent with similar cities around the globe.

Municipal waste management and urban greenery

Municipal waste management and urban greenery gained momentum in the last decade. Waste management that was initially the greatest nightmare of city administration has been turned into money-making ventures. Waste is now being recycled from the source. Viewed from the perspective of environment, one can argue that Lagos is becoming smart. As presented by Banire (2008), the Lagos beautification process commenced with the 'direct sponsorship, landscaping and beautification of open spaces, roundabouts, recreation parks, road medians and verges'. This effort saw the reclamation of encroached road right of ways for use as planting areas.

Several of the beautified public spaces were previously black spots or 'area boys' territories known for crime. Converting these spaces into recreational land uses not only served an aesthetic function, it also provides a solution to some of the city's safety and security challenges. One innovative approach, using a combination of reward and cohesive power, was to redirect the energies of the 'area boys' towards constructive activities including employment opportunities in gardening, traffic control and environmental policing (De Gramont 2015).

Specifically, prior to 2007, Oshodi was a notorious commercial hub in the heart of Lagos, avoided by residents and visitors alike after 6pm and before dawn. It was a permanent site of intense trading activities, as well as pedestrian and vehicular traffic. Daylight robberies were endemic; pickpockets and various other criminals held sway. Government interventions took different forms. First, the traders were cleared from the roads. A task force providing 24-hour security ensured that the place remained free for movement. Also, Oshodi was lit up with halogen streetlights that ensured that felons could no longer hide under cover of darkness to perpetrate their evil.[5] To ensure this intervention succeeded, there was a delicate balance of politics involving negotiations, concessions and patronage among key stakeholders; major market unions, opinion leaders, as well as local and state government actors. Many displaced traders from the roads and railway lines in Oshodi were resettled in an ultra-modern market constructed close by while the road and railway setbacks were beautified.[6]

Currently, Lagos boasts over 200 landscaped sites and 'over five million trees have been planted across the metropolis which is now wearing a new look as the trees planted some years back have enhanced the aesthetics of the environment' (Ugbodaga 2014). With high quality public spaces that bring people together to exchange ideas and build a sense of community, it could be argued that the environment is more sustainable and liveable. As it is the case in most advanced cities, amenities such as community gardens, public artwork and playing fields, as provided in Lagos, can give people a range of lifestyle options. Also, improved tree coverage and green spaces now provide significant benefits to Lagos residents. These will significantly improve

---

5   https://www.vanguardngr.com/2015/02/babatunde-raji-fashola-success-tackling-challenges-head-2/

6   http://www.tundefashola.com/archives/news/2014/01/07/20140107No1.html

the quality of air and reduce the heat island effect, while enhancing general amenity. They also give people greater connection with nature and provide important places for recreation and healthy lifestyles.

The Lagos State Home Ownership Mortgage Scheme (Lagos HOMS)

The Lagos State Home Ownership Mortgage Scheme (Lagos HOMS) is an initiative to address the problem of providing 'affordable' housing. It was aimed at developing a mortgage culture and institution in Lagos. It was also aimed at urban redevelopment through densification and infill of residential development across the metropolis on lands hitherto underutilised and otherwise prone to slum growth. The Lagos HOMS initiative was an outcome of a process of housing problem identification. Considering the structure for implementation, one of the requirements involves the digital registration of potential beneficiary as residents of Lagos state. This is considered as one of the ways to develop data infrastructure that is needed to facilitate efficient city governance. With regard to inclusiveness, the low-income groups and those who work in the informal sector, who are disproportionately affected by housing deficit, are excluded because of eligibility criteria. Thus, the initiative is largely considered as neither inclusive nor affordable. It could also be argued further that the Lagos HOMS specifically targets a particular economic group – the middle class who are working in the formal sector or those who have traceable income in the informal sector.

However, the process of allocation, through a public draw which goes through various stages, reasonably ensures transparency and accountability. Notwithstanding that homeownership through mortgage finance is a good approach to empower people, there are tensions and contradictions regarding the cost and economic capability of the majority of the targeted group. This makes the initiative fail the inclusiveness test. In response to these criticisms, the government recently introduced a rent-to-own option in the programme and is about to initiate incremental-development as another option. There are two big challenges that can potentially limit the sustainability of this programme. One is the capacity to sustain the programme's achievement and improve on the transparent processes. Also, the prospect of replicating this programme in other Nigerian cities and on an even larger scale will be critical to a lasting success. The first issue speaks to the need for building strong institutions in Lagos while the other will depend largely on how successful and popular the programme can become to attract interests from other cities in Nigeria. However, Lagos is no stranger to setting the pace of development as well as exporting successful ideas around the country.

The Bus Rapid Transit (BRT)

In the last decade and a half, Lagos has witnessed a significant improvement in urban transport development. This includes the development of major road infrastructure and improvement projects such as the expansion and modernisation of major roads like the Lekki-Epe Expressway. The estimated value of this project was about USD 450 million and was conceived as a Public-Private Partnership (LSPPP 2010a), in what could be described as smart investment.

More recently, Lagos state government has involved private organisations to develop the Bus Rapid Transit (BRT), as an important element of the city's changing public urban transport system. The vision of the Lagos public transport, as described by the state governor, is to develop 'the Strategic Transport Master Plan (STMP), which is already being implemented, a 30-year plan. Ultimately, the plan is expected to deliver to Lagos a truly world-class integrated public transport system with 6 rail lines, 1 mono-rail, 14 BRT corridors, 3 cable car corridors and 26 developed water routes' (Ambode 2015).

The goal of the BRT, as part of this integrated transport plan, is to provide 'significant socioeconomic benefits, especially for the low-income population' of Lagos. Therefore, the project is considered inclusive in conceptualisation. The successful engagement of the transport unions as well as other local stakeholders in the planning and implementation of the BRT project is a powerful example of the project's inclusiveness. The BRT project planning stage benefitted from inclusive measures of local and foreign consultations that eventually improved the final product.

The ongoing expansion of the BRT project to other districts as well as the parallel deployment of the Bus Franchise Scheme (BFS) allows a larger portion of the metropolitan population access to better public transport. When viewed through the lens of smart city, the BRT project is founded on sound technical and intellectual grounds, considering the composition of key technical experts in Lagos Metropolitan Area Transport Authority (LAMATA). In terms of strategic direction, it qualifies as a smart transportation vision for Lagos. LAMATA is manned by qualified personnel and the agency has an institutional structure that allows it to carry out its statutory responsibilities. The operating environment of LAMATA was acknowledged as productive and world-class while importance of local and foreign technical partners was emphasised as crucial to the agencies' capacity to deliver the BRT project.

With regards to accountability, its revenue collection system promotes financial accountability and provides comfort for local banks while introduction of electronic ticketing is expected to further improve the system. From the governance and institutional perspective, separation of power among government agencies involved in transport-related functions promote democratic relations with LAMATA while minimising the risk of conflict. However, the perception of local people regarding the understanding of the concept was put to the test, with the idea having been initially resisted. The informal transport union represents a major stakeholder identified as a potential impediment to the BRT project and was, therefore, engaged from the planning through implementation stages. LAMATA later made substantial efforts in the area of producing precautionary documentation and interaction with the project stakeholders to address contested issues

In terms of value addition, the BRT project has delivered a range of benefits for Lagos. These include: improved connections to employment and services, reduced congestion and increased productivity. Overall, it combines smart investment with smart policy and smart technology seamlessly.

The Lekki Free Trade Zone (LFTZ)

The Lekki Free Trade Zone (LFTZ), located 65km east of Lagos metropolis, is part of the overall multi-use development plan for a new city on the Lekki peninsula. The development objective of the LFTZ project is to 'establish a free economic zone and an international city with multi-functions of industry, commerce, trade, tourism, recreation and residence to attract foreign investment, create employment and expedite economic growth' (CCECC-Beyond International Investment and Development 2009).

From the investment perspective, the LFTZ is a major public-private economic investment and industrial development project, which targets different types of activities. This industrial zone encompasses hubs for oil and gas, logistics, light and medium scale industries, hospitality and resort, engineering and infrastructure support services, commerce, retail, real estate development for urban services, finance, trade, hotel, recreational, business and residential facilities, and information and communication technology (LFTZ 2014; LSPPP 2010b). The project is based on smart investment that enables partnerships between governments and the private sector. The global lesson is that cities collaborate to compete. Success requires all tiers of government, the private sector, and community, to work together towards shared goals.

However, the major challenges with the LFTZ included the legal and institutional framework, as well as land resettlement issues and infrastructure. The legal framework is a hurdle to all development zones in Nigeria; therefore, it needs to be tackled with great urgency. There are strong policy and infrastructure rationales behind establishing a Special Economic Zone like the Lekki Free Trade Zone. International experience has shown that successful SEZs have compelling business cases, enabling legal/regulatory frameworks, effective management arrangements and enjoy strong political support at all levels of government. In addition, they are well integrated with the local economy and have clear ownership and accountability arrangements.

The World Bank (2010) specified some of the more specific attributes of SEZs to include: the articulation of physical planning and development of infrastructure to allow for integrated, multi-use development and effective IT systems and networks. From an investment perspective, it also encourages a demand-driven, as opposed to policy-driven, approach. However, from the policy consideration, it encourages imposition of neoliberal ideals and expectations, but promotes national economic growth strategy through public-private partnerships or the private developer builds/owns/operates on a cost-recovery basis. Another good intent of SEZ is the support for reform and efficiency. Best practice regulatory frameworks and stable business environments are targeted at multi-markets and not just for exports. Therefore, a wide range of activities are permitted, which ensures environmental compliance. Most often, SEZs are promoted by emphasising an institutional framework that is based on the establishment of a single administration for efficient regulation, while MOUs with stakeholders govern relationships and public-private partnership arrangements. This often aligns with the smart investment consideration of a smart city.

However, contrary to these putative benefits, this study shows that the implementation of the Lekki Free Trade Zone has largely not delivered the socio-economic benefits assumed to be associated with this kind of development for the local communities. At the core of this development paradox is the issue of land governance which permitted local resource grabbing through large-scale land acquisitions. The project became a tool for displacement, exclusion, conflicts, dispossession of livelihoods capital, corruption and loss of livelihoods. Essentially, in its implementation benefits were significantly shifted in favour of corporate and elite investors.

Lagos-Dubai Smart City project

Lagos-Dubai Smart City project was conceived in 2016 through a partnership between Lagos state government and Smart City Dubai, to develop sustainable, smart, globally connected knowledge-based communities that drive the knowledge economy. According to Raji (2018), to achieve this objective, a memorandum of understanding was signed between the Lagos state government and Dubai Holdings LLC, owners of Smart City Dubai LLC, in June 2016.

The proponents have argued that the motive for establishing the Lagos Smart City initiative, like other similar projects, is to bring multi-billion dollar investments to the State to create jobs and transform the Ibeju-Lekki axis in particular. Governor Ambode added that the motive of the Lagos state government 'is a deliberate attempt to establish a strong convergence between technology, economic development and governance' (Ambode 2016). The governor added that Lagos 'will become an important centre for innovation in smart technologies, wellness and destination for green tourism.' By the time the Lagos Smart City is completed, it will have, among other features: 'a 12-lane road, hotel resorts, world-class technological education facilities, and a rail metro line' (Ambode 2016).

The question, however, is how these will be possible when electricity generation is actually falling in the face of geometrical higher demand for energy? In May 2016, the Ministry of Power released figures that showed national power output reduced significantly from a peak 4 500MW to 2 500MW; which is nearly half of the original capacity being generated (Ogundipe 2016). There is a huge electricity supply deficit in the state, as it only gets about 20% of the 5 000MW it currently requires to attain stable power supply.

Conclusion

Prior to the inception of the current political dispensation, the notion of smart cities in Lagos State, as conceived in this paper, was significantly constrained by inadequate infrastructure, lack of integrated transport plans, inadequate knowledge of investment strategies, inadequate technology and poor urban governance and the corresponding poor government policies.

This brief overview of a number of dynamic flagship initiatives in Lagos during the past decade, supported by technologies and governance structure, has laid a strong foundation for future smart city initiatives. Furthermore, the flagship projects arguably provide a *platform* to start sustainable inclusion of spatial data infrastructure in the urban agenda. This is very significant in a context where arbitrary policy-making was the norm. We also observe an opportunity to build and develop digital data infrastructure to improve the operation and maintenance of the flagship projects, creating a precedent for other developmental projects.

However, it is imperative that Lagos State must, as a matter of necessity, come up with its own unique smart city approach. In this regard, Lagos cannot afford to copy themes from other countries. It must evolve its own because of its uniqueness. Thus, its aspiration should be different. However, the obsession with Dubai is probably not a good sign that this is indeed happening.

Beyond the rhetoric of developing a smart city, as is being presented by the government, substantial challenges are noted that urgently need attention as these projects are being implemented. The major ones are electricity supply and mobility. Notwithstanding that most of these projects propose to have built-in power supply systems, the more fundamental imperative is that the entire city of Lagos should be well integrated and connected, drawing from a constant power supply across the state (i.e. outside the targeted enclaves such as Eko Atlantic).

It is logical to argue that a smart city cannot be a reality when over half of the city residents do not have access to basic social and physical infrastructures like electricity, reticulated water, good roads and drainages. Adequate availability of these infrastructures is meant to be a pre-requisite for smart city development. As it stands now and as it will be in the near future, the initiation and sustainability of smart city initiatives should be closely linked with the residents' ability to have access to the basic necessities of life, in an environment that promotes civil engagement and smart solutions.

References

Abiodun Y (2016, 30 June) Smart city Lagos: Necessity of the time. *EnviroNews Nigeria*. https://www.environewsnigeria.com/smart-city-lagos-necessity-of-the-time-2/

Agunbiade ME & Olajide OA (2016) Urban governance and turning African cities around: Lagos case study. *Partnership for African Social and Governance Research Working Paper* No. 019. http://www.pasgr.org/wp- content/uploads/2016/12/Urban-Governance-and-Turning-African-Cities- Around_Lagos-Case-StudyF.pdf

Albino V, Berardi U & Dangelico RM (2015) Smart cities: Definitions, dimensions, performance, and initiatives. *Journal of Urban Technology* 22(1): 3–21. doi: 10.1080/10 630732.2014.942092

Ambode A (2015) Speech delivered at the Launch of the Mile 12 Ikorodu BRT Extension Project on November 12, 2015. Lagos

Ambode A (2016) Lagos State Government signs historic smart city deal with Dubai. *The Guardian*. https://guardian.ng/news/lagos-state-signs-smart-city-deal- with-dubai/

Anthony J (2006) State growth management and housing prices. *Social Science Quarterly* 87(1): 122–141

Anthopoulos LG (2017) *Understanding Smart Cities: A Tool for Smart Government or an Industrial Trick?* Switzerland AG: Springer

Bakıcı T, Almirall E & Wareham J (2012) A smart city initiative: The case of Barcelona. *Journal of the Knowledge Economy* 2(1): 1–14

Banire M (2008) *Greening, Beautification Programme Boosts Investment in Lagos, 2015*. Lagos State Governor Office. http://www.tundefashola.com/archives/news/2008/04/11/20080411N01.html

Beall J & Fox S (2009) *Cities and Development*. New York: Routledge

Brundtland Commission (1987) *Report of the World Commission on Environment and Development*. United Nations

Caragliu A, Del Bo C & Nijkamp P (2011) Smart cities in Europe. *Journal of Urban Technology* 18(2): 65–82

Carli R, Dotoli M, Pellegrino R & Ranieri L (2013) Measuring and managing the smartness of cities: A framework for classifying performance indicators. Paper presented at the Proceedings of the 2013 IEEE International Conference on Systems, Man, and Cybernetics, Manchester, UK, 13–16 October

CCECC-Beyond International Investment and Development (2009) Lekki Free Trade Zone: China Nigeria Economic and Trade Cooperation Zone (Phase 1). *Feasibility Study Report, March 2009*

De Gramont D (2015) *Governing Lagos: Unlocking the Politics of Reform.* Washington, DC: Carnegie Endowment for International Peace

Decker T (2010) Social welfare strategies in colonial Lagos. *African Nebula* 1(1): 56–64

Dirks S & Keeling M (2009) *A Vision of Smarter Cities: How Cities Can Lead the Way into a Prosperous and Sustainable Future.* Somers, NY: IBM Global Business Services

Downs A (2005) Smart growth: Why we discuss it more than we do it. *Journal of American Planning Association* 71(4): 367–378

Ekwealor V (2016) The challenges to Lagos becoming a smart city. *Techpoint.* https://techpoint.africa/2016/06/28/lagos-smart-city/

Eremia M, Toma L & Sanduleac M (2017) The smart city concept in the 21st century. *Procedia Engineering* 181: 12–19

Fashola B (2009) Inauguration of the Lagos State Market Board. http://www.tundefashola.com/archives/news/2009/12/17/20091217N21.html

Gandy M (2006) Planning, anti-planning and the infrastructure crisis facing metropolitan Lagos. *Urban Studies* 43(2): 371–396

Giffinger R & Gudrun H (2010) Smart cities ranking: An effective instrument for the positioning of cities? *ACE Architecture City and Environment* 4(12): 7–25

Giffinger R, Fertner C, Kramar H, Kalasek R, Pichler-Milanović N & Meijers E (2007) *Smart Cities: Ranking of European Medium-sized Cities.* Vienna: Centre of Regional Science. http://www.smart-cities.eu/download/smart_cities_final_report.pdf

Government of Australia (2016) *Smart Cities Plan.* Canberra: Commonwealth of Australia

Graham S & Aurigi A (1997) Urbanising cyberspace? *City* 2(7): 18–39

Gunder M & Hillier J (2009) *Planning in Ten Words or Less: A Lacanian Entanglement with Spatial Planning.* Surrey: Ashgate

Harrison C, Eckman B, Hamilton R, Hartswick P, Kalagnanam J, Paraszczak J & Williams P (2010) Foundations for smarter cities. *IBM Journal of Research and Development* 54(4): 1–16

Harvey D (1989) From managerialism to entrepreneurialism: The transformation in urban governance in late capitalism. *Geografiska Annaler. Series B. Human Geography* 71(1): 3–17

Harvey D (2007) Neoliberalism as creative destruction. *Annals of the American Academy of Political and Social Science* 610: 22–44

Hatzelhoffer L, Humboldt K, Lobeck M & Wiegandt C (2012) *Smart City in Practice: Converting Innovative Ideas into Reality.* Berlin: Jovis

Hollands RG (2008) Will the real smart city please stand up? Intelligent, progressive or entrepreneurial? *City* 12(3): 303–320

Kitchin T & Tate N (2000) *Conducting Research into Human Geography.* Harlow: Pearson

Komninos N (2008) *Intelligent Cities and Globalization of Innovation Networks*. London: Taylor and Francis

Komninos N, Pallot M & Schaffers H (2013) Smart cities and the future internet in Europe. *Journal of the Knowledge Economy* 4(2): 119–134

Leem CS & Kim BG (2012) Taxonomy of ubiquitous computing service for city development. *Personal and Ubiquitous Computing* 17(7): 1475–1483

LFTZ (2014) Lagos Free Trade Zone. http://lagosftz.com/#timeline

Lombardi P, Giordano S, Farouh H & Yousef W (2012) Modelling the smart city performance. *Innovation: The European Journal of Social Science Research* 25(5): 137–149

LSPPP (2010a) Projects in construction – Lagos Infrastructure Project (LIP) Concession. http://lagosstateppp.gov.ng/projects/project_portfolio/project_in_construction.asp

LSPPP (2010b) Projects: Investment opportunities – Lekki Trade Zone. http://lagosstateppp.gov.ng/projects/investment_opportunities/LTZ/LTZ.asp

Mabogunje AL (1961) Some comments on land tenure in Egba Division, Western Nigeria. *Africa* 31(3): 258–269

Marsal-Llacuna ML, Colomer-Llinàs J & Meléndez-Frigola J (2015) Lessons in urban monitoring taken from sustainable and livable cities to better address the smart cities initiative. *Technological Forecasting and Social Change* 90(B): 611–622

McCarney P, Halfani M & Rodriguez A (1995) Towards an understanding of governance. In: R Stren (ed.) *Perspectives on the City*. Toronto: Centre for Urban and Community Studies, University of Toronto. pp. 95–98

Nam T & Pardo TA (2011) Conceptualizing smart city with dimensions of technology, people, and institutions. Paper presented at the 12th Annual International Conference on Digital Government Research, College Park, MD, USA, 12–15 June

Narula S (2003) Globalisation: India's experience for the African continent. *DPMF Occasional Paper* No. 7. Development Policy Management Forum

Njoku J (2012) Fresh concerns over multi-billion dollar Eko Atlantic City project. *Vanguard*. http://www.vanguardngr.com/2012/09/fresh-concerns-over-multi- billion-dollar-eko-atlantic-city-project/

Ogundipe T (2016) Smart City Project: Connecting Lagos to global knowledge economy. *The Guardian*. https://guardian.ng/news/smart-city-project-connecting-lagos-to-global-knowledge-economy/

Onwuaso U (2018, 14 May) Smart City Initiative: Lagos plans to deploy 10 000 CCTV cameras. *Nigeria Communications Week*. https://nigeriacommunicationsweek.com.ng/smart-city-initiative-lagos-plans-to-deploy-10000-cctv-cameras/

Peck J, Theodore N & Brenner N (2009) Neoliberal urbanism: Models, moments, mutations. *SAIS Review* 29(1): 49–66

Pieterse JN (2010) *Development Theory*. London: Sage

Raji R (2018, 27 April) Smart Lagos: Status, prospects and opportunities. *Premium Times*. https://opinion.premiumtimesng.com/2018/04/27/smart-lagos-status-prospects-and-opportunities-by-rafiq-raji/

Scott J (2007) Smart growth as urban reform: A pragmatic recording of the new regionalism. *Urban Studies* 44(1): 15–35

Shapiro JM (2006) Smart cities: Quality of life, productivity, and the growth effects of human capital. *Review of Economics & Statistics* 88(2): 324–335

Shin DH & Kim T (2012) Enabling the smart city: The progress of U-City in Korea. Paper presented at the 6th International Conference on Ubiquitous Information Management and Communication (ICUIMC), Kuala Lumpur, Malaysia, February

Swyngedouw E, Moulaert F & Rodriguez A (2002) Neoliberal urbanization in Europe: Large-scale urban development projects and the new urban policy. *Antipode* 34(3): 542–577

Ugbodaga K (2014, 21 July) Six years of greening Lagos. *PM News*. http://www. pmnewsnigeria.com/2014/07/21/six-years-of-greening-lagos/

United Nations Environment Programme (UNEP) (2011) *Why a Green Economy Matters for the Least Developed Countries*. https://unctad.org/en/docs/ ditcbcc2011greeneconomy_en.pdf

Watson D (2004) *Watson's Dictionary of Weasel Words, Contemporary Cliches and Management Jargon*. Sydney: Vintage

Vliet V (2002) Cities in a globalizing world: From engines of growth to agents of change. *Environment and Urbanization* 14(1): 31– 40

World Bank (1989) *Sub-Saharan Africa: From Crisis to Sustainable Growth*. Washington DC: World Bank

World Bank (2010) *Chinese Investments in Special Economic Zones in Africa: Progress, Challenges and Lessons Learned*. Washington, DC: World Bank

Yigitcanlar T, O'Connor K & Westerman C (2008) The making of knowledge cities: Melbourne's knowledge-based urban development experience. *Cities* 25(2): 63–72

Zygiaris S (2013) Smart City Reference Model: Assisting planners to conceptualize the building of smart city innovation ecosystems. *Journal of the Knowledge Economy* 4(2): 217–231

CHAPTER 11

The governance of Addis Ababa Light Rail Transit

Meseret Kassahun

Introduction

Improving urban governance is top of Ethiopia's urban development policy agenda (Ministry of Finance and Economic Development [MOFED] 2006, 2010; National Planning Commission [NPC] 2015). Specifically, Ethiopia adopts an urban governance model that follows a decentralised structure, in which urban centres are governed by 'an elected council, elected mayor, Mayor's Committee, and city manager' (Ministry of Urban Development, Housing, and Construction [MOUDHC] 2014). Principles of good urban governance are emphasised to guide overall urban development policy process. The good urban development principles are: (1) subsidiary administrative and fiscal decentralisation; (2) efficiency and effective service delivery; (3) sustainability equity and participation; (4) transparency and accountability; and (5) rule of law and security (Ministry of Works and Urban Development [MOWUD] 2007: 40). Urban governance has been widely promoted in developing countries as a means to increase accountability, better government responsiveness, and improved public services (Jones, Clench & Harris 2014; Speer 2012). This is partly explained in terms of the Ethiopian government's ambitious plan to ensure structural transformation in its economy through a shift from a rural-based subsistence production system to urban-based, high technology-driven economic activities (NPC 2015). In this regard, the government of Ethiopia has been convinced that transition from an agrarian to an industrial society cannot happen without the existence of a network of effective and 'competitive' cities (NPC 2015). The ambition to make Addis Ababa a global city is reflected in the City of Addis Ababa mission statement. It reads:

> By 2023, Addis Ababa and the surrounding Oromia will provide a safe and liveable environment for their people and become Ethiopia's hub to ensure

the national vision of becoming a middle income country, Africa's diplomatic capital and international competitive city. (Addis Ababa and Special Zone Development Planning Project Office 2013: 4)

Furthermore, evidence from recent studies shows that the implementation of mega city projects was part of the government's conviction in making Ethiopian cities global cities (Terrefe 2020; Kloosterboer 2019). In arguing how Ethiopian cities would be a hub for industrialisation, diversification and structural transformation, a chapter prepared to guide Ethiopia's structural transformation shows 'building both "hard" and "soft" infrastructure' would be instrumental to improve Ethiopian cities' competitiveness in the global economies (UN-Habitat 2014). Thus Ethiopia's commitment to urban governance is closely related to its perceived and tangible benefits in facilitating rapid growth and transformation. Within this background, this chapter aims to explore how one of the mega urban projects implemented in the city of Addis Ababa, that is, the Addis Ababa Light Rail transit (AA-LRT) has evolved; the government's discursive rationale in choosing AA-LRT as an urban transport option through elucidating whether or not the AA-LRT was developed out of a felt need or the pressure to be global. In addition, the study discusses the politics around the investment in AA-LRT and how it is governed through highlighting the governance structures and institutional setups.

Urban governance under a revolutionary developmental state

Urban governance refers to processes and mechanisms through which diverse actors in a given urban centre/city organise their actions and resources for the common urban good through utilisation of economic, social, political and environmental resources (Harpham & Boateng 1997). Multiple actors include formal and informal, governmental and non-governmental, public and private. For these actors to function effectively and achieve collective goals, institutionalised arrangements establishing structures and systems have to be put in place, and these will emerge out of the stakeholders' diverse interests through consensus building and/or contestation (Hendriks 2013; Lindell 2008; Melo & Baiocchi 2006). Under normal circumstances urban governance is robust enough to accommodate contestation, as relevant actors promote their own vested interests on what they want to be done and how. Ideally, urban governance as a process facilitates persuasion, contestation, bargaining and, finally, consensus building among actors during urban policy development. Lindell (2008: 1880) further suggests that urban governance consists of 'multiple sites where practices of governance are exercised and contested, a variety of actors, various layers of relations and a broad range of practices of governance that may involve various modes of power, as well as different scales'. Lindell's characterisation of urban governance as made up of multiple, contested sites highlights how any given urban policy is supported or opposed at different levels, and its fate will depend on the efficiency and effectiveness of formal institutions and the relative power between policy actors.

Hence, the effectiveness of urban governance is dependent upon how these multiple actors engage with different levels of governance structures and with each other, shaping the exercise of governance. The relationship of relevant actors as well as their active participation in the process of planning and implementation of urban policy and strategy vary by context. Ethiopia is one of the countries that endorsed the global campaign on 'urban governance,' which openly advocates for a participatory democratic process between citizens, public and private actors in urban agenda setting and decision-making processes (see UN-Habitat 2002). The globally promoted notion of urban governance includes planning and governing a city's common affairs through an ongoing process that accommodates conflicting or diverse interests, leading to cooperative action. In reality, however, Ethiopia's political landscape limits the applicability of many of the attributes of commonly accepted definitions of governance. This relates mainly to Ethiopia's ruling party's adherence to 'revolutionary democracy' as its guiding philosophy and political economic strategy. Ethiopia's 'revolutionary democracy' is an ideology that draws its inspiration from Marxism, Leninism, Maoism, and liberal ideologies in defining the socio-economic and political structures of the country (Bach 2011). The ideology is promoted as the only doctrine that would help defeat Ethiopia's major social, economic, and political challenges based on one vanguard political party system. It thus grants discretionary power to party leaders and bureaucrats at all levels, effectively eliminating other voices. In other words, a decision taken by the party can override a decision arrived at within state institutions following the normal conventions. Vaughan (2011) analysed the state party and the Ethiopian People's Revolutionary Democratic Front's (EPRDF) revolutionary democratic nation building process and highlights 'democratic centralism' as a fundamental tenet of EPRDF's ideology. Hence, Ethiopia's revolutionary democracy is an ideological tool legitimatising the way central committee members of the EPRDF leadership interact with local level structures to guide and lead the socio-economic development processes. According to Fantu Cheru (2016: 606), Ethiopia blends different ideologies together in 'a cleaver meshing of selected development experiences from East Asia (China, Taiwan, Vietnam, South Korea, Singapore and Japan) with 'soft neoliberalism' from the West under the guidance of a strong developmental state.' Thus, understanding Ethiopia's urban governance requires situating it within its historical, social, economic, and political history. Against this backdrop, this study looks at the governance of the Addis Ababa Light Rail Transit (AA-LRT) project as the country's major attempt to provide mass urban transport for a rapidly expanding city using a political economy approach.

Analytical approach and research questions

As discussed above, Ethiopia's political and economic strategy based on 'democratic centralism' empowers party leaders to make policy decisions and inhibits the application of globally promoted urban governance models that assume contestation and bargaining between interest groups with competing interests. This chapter applies a political economy lens in analysing the governance of AA-LRT. Mcloughlin (2014) describes the aim of political economy analysis as locating development interventions within an understanding of the prevailing political and economic processes in a given society. Applying a political economy approach offers a means to situate the structure and processes of Ethiopian urban affairs within the ruling party's overarching political ideology and how it dictates policy agenda setting and the interaction between the state and its citizens. According to Drake (2001), political ideologies are clusters of values espousing the underlying philosophies and principles of the government through which socio-economic and political systems and structures are operated. Drake further argues that political ideologies generally are determined by state views of how a society should be organised/governed, and the extent to which a state may interact with its citizens and intervene in their daily lives.

Specifically, this study draws on a 'state centred approach' to political economy in studying the governance of AA-LRT. In their seminal work on diverse strands within political economy, Caporaso and Levine (1992) show that different approaches vary by their assumptions about the primacy of economics or politics in decision-making processes. A state centered approach to political economy focuses on situations where states systematically exclude non-state actors from the policy process and generate policy initiatives on their own. This accurately describes how the political regime in Ethiopia has instituted a developmental state governance structure and allocates major decision-making power to party leaders in guiding urban development priorities. Thus, this chapter critically analyses AA-LRT's institutional and governance arrangements including its structures and capacities. Specifically, this chapter focuses on the following interrelated research questions:

1. Where did the idea for the AA-LRT originate?
2. What was the discursive rationale and strategy for the government of Ethiopia choosing AA-LRT as an urban transport option?
3. What are some of the politics surrounding the investments in AA-LRT and were there external influences?
4. How is AA-LRT governed? What are the structures and institutional setups?

Methodology: Design, data collection methods and data analysis

In order to address the aforementioned research questions, this study used a qualitative research design. Creswell (2007: 17) defines qualitative research as 'an inquiry process of understanding based on distinct methodological traditions of inquiry that explore a social or human problem. The researcher builds a complex, holistic picture, analyses words, reports the detailed views of informants, and conducts the study in a natural setting.' There were two reasons for choosing a qualitative study design. First, qualitative research is appropriate when not much is known about the topic under inquiry (Creswell 2007; Padgett 1998). As the AA-LRT was launched in 2015, there is no literature that studied the AA-LRT from a policy and urban governance perspective. Second, a qualitative design provides the most appropriate methodology to obtain in-depth information on the process through which AA-LRT received prominence and emerged as a major urban transport option in Ethiopia by generating explanations embedded within empirical observations. Hence, qualitative data were collected using in-depth interviews and focus group discussions[1] conducted with AA-LRT users in

---

[1] Focus group discussion (FGD) participants were selected based on their age and sex categories. Accordingly, 8 FGDs with female and male LRT users were conducted. 39 AA-LRT service users and 8 women's association leaders (i.e. 20 women, 14 male youths, and 13 older men) participated in the FGDs.

two stations (i.e. CMC station and Meskel Square). A total of 17 in-depth interviews with key government officials relevant to the AA-LRT project, research institutes, and civil society members were conducted (see Annex I: Summary of study participants). Specific attention was given to government officials who were involved at the initiation phase of the AA-LRT and were on the board of directors. Data were analysed using Padgett's (1998) multiple interrelated steps. Transcripts of interviews and discussions were reviewed and frequently emerging themes relevant to the study questions were identified. Once relevant themes were organised based on the research questions, interpretation of themes was conducted. To ensure the credibility, transferability and dependability of the data (Lincoln & Guba 1985), triangulation of emerged data by data source was used.

In presenting findings, this chapter is structured into three parts. First, a description of the overall status of public transport in the city of Addis Ababa is presented to contextualise the LRT's emergence as an important mass transit service in Addis Ababa City. In this section, the process that led to prioritisation of the AA-LRT in the public policy arena is discussed vis-à-vis the politics around financing the infrastructure, operation and maintenance costs of AA-LRT. The question of finance and delivery of the infrastructure goes to the core of external influences in the process. Second, the governance of AA-LRT is described, including the governance structure, institutional capacity, and relationship between national and city governments. Finally, the chapter discusses implications of the findings for urban governance policy and practice in the Ethiopian context.

Public transport in Addis Ababa: Current status and the quest for mass transit

Literature that provides a comprehensive understanding about the status of public transport in Ethiopia, in general, and the city of Addis Ababa, in particular, is sparse. The few available materials on public transportation do not have up-to-date data. Existing literature and government documents show that public transport in Addis Ababa has been dominated by city bus services provided by the public enterprise Anbessa City Bus Enterprise and taxis operated by private sector actors (Gebeyehu & Tekano 2007). Fenta (2014) conducted a study on public transport demand in Addis Ababa and estimated that there were nearly 10 000 taxis with a capacity of 12 persons, 460 buses that seat 22 to 27 persons, and 6 500 sedan taxis that seat four persons. Three-wheeler taxis (*bajaj*) and animal carts are also used in the peripheral areas of the city.

Qualitative findings for this study also indicate that public buses make up the bulk of public transport in the city, in addition to privately owned taxis (mini-buses and sedan taxis). According to key informants, different bus systems exist. For instance, the oldest bus service is Anbessa City Bus Enterprise, which is publicly owned and has 814 buses and currently transports nearly 500 000 passengers daily. After the city administration issued its transport policy in 2011, the city administration has been making efforts to improve the mass transport service in the city. For instance, the city administration introduced a Public Service Employees Transport Service Enterprise, which has provided free transport to civil servants, running during rush hours in the morning and after office hours since 2015. There are 410 of these buses transporting 98 000 persons per day. Furthermore, in May 2016, the Addis Ababa City Administration Transport Programs Coordination Office introduced a 'Sheger Express' bus system and deployed 150 buses. Sheger Buses are equipped with modern features such as automated ticketing and are accessible for the elderly and people with physical disabilities, which enhances the city's ambition to provide inclusive transport service for nearly 25 000 individuals. In addition to the newly introduced buses, the city administration planned to bring in 1000 metered taxis, of which 150 are already functioning. After critically examining the inadequacy of existing public transport systems, the city administration granted permission for 300 privately owned cross-country buses to serve citizens before and after office hours; these serve 65 000 individuals. Private cars only transport 20% of city residents[2] (see Table 1).

Table 1: Total public transport service users in Addis Ababa

Mode of transport	# of vehicles	Total # of service users/day
Addis Ababa City Bus Enterprise (publicly owned)	815	500 000
Sheger Express Bus (publicly owned)	300	25 000
Blue Public Buses (publicly owned)	410	98 000
Cross-country buses	300	65 000
Higer buses	640	17 280
Mini-bus taxis	10 000	120 000
Total public transport users		800 280
Private cars		646 200*
Total		1 446 480

Currently the city of Addis Ababa has an estimated 3.2 million residents (projected from CSA, 2014) of which 20% have private cars.
Source: Compiled from data obtained for this study from key informants and Fenta (2014)

Despite the City Administration's efforts, the existing motorised transport system does not meet Addis Ababa transport demands. Motorised transport (i.e. city buses, taxis, private cars) only provide for about 50% of Addis Ababa's residents. A significant majority of Addis Ababa residents do not have access to motorised transport. Available data estimates 40–60% of Addis Ababa residents use walking as their primary mode of transport. For instance, a 2012 report by Addis Ababa City Planning Office and Lyon Town Planning Agency shows that walking accounted for 45% of the trips made by residents in 2006 (Addis Ababa City Government & Lyon Planning 2012). Similarly, a recent report by the Addis Ababa City Road and Transport Authority (2014) estimates that pedestrians make up 55% of daily journeys but do not have appropriate walking facilities and confront a transport network characterised as 'non-pedestrian friendly'.

The inadequacy of public transport coupled with a lack of planning and integration of motorised transport systems makes mobility in Addis Ababa chaotic, unreliable,

---

2   Interview with representatives of Addis Ababa City Administration Mayor's Office (23 August 2016). Interview with representatives of Addis Ababa City Administration Transport Authority (27 July 2016)

unsafe, unaffordable and inefficient for an expanding city (Fenta 2014). A recent study by UN-Habitat (2017) confirms that public transport in Addis Ababa is inaccessible and unaffordable for the majority of city residents. As a result, the Addis Ababa City Government has been searching for an alternative mass transit system. The federal government eventually embarked on a massive project and introduced the AA-LRT service as the first modern mass transit system in the country (Ministry of Transport 2011a, 2011b). It has been promoted as a major breakthrough in the transport industry, not only for Ethiopia, but also in the history of sub-Saharan African countries (Jemere 2012; CNN 2015; *The Economist* 2015). The AA-LRT development took three years with a total infrastructure investment cost of USD 475 million and the project was inaugurated on 21 September 2015. The AA-LRT consists of two lines: the East-West axis from Ayat to Tor-Hailoch and the North-South axis from Minilik II square to Akaki/Kality. The LRT covers a total length of 34.25km (North-South line 16.9km and East-West line 17.35km) (see Figure 1).

Figure 1: Addis Ababa LRT North-South and East-West routes

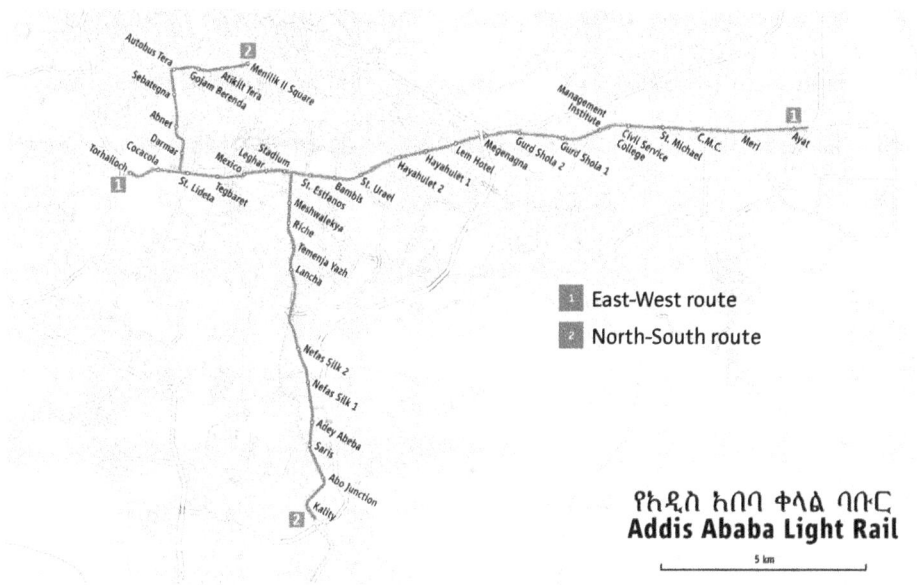

Source: Maximilian Dörrbecker

Light Rail Transit: Its origin, discursive rationale and the politics around financing the project

Over the past 15 years, several initiatives were considered and tested as the Addis Ababa city government searched for an afforfable and efficient mass transit system to reduce traffic congestion and urban pollution. A Bus Rapid Transit (BRT) system similar to successful bus transit systems in several Brazilian and Colombian cities was the first seriously considered initiative. The city government in collaboration with the French Development Aid agency commissioned a French consulting company to undertake a feasibility study for a Bus Rapid Transit (BRT) system for Addis Ababa in 2004.[3] The study recommended rapid bus corridors along the North-South and East-West direction of the city. In 2005, the city contracted and commissioned an Indian consulting firm to draw up a transport master plan (Lyon Town Planning Agency 2011).[4]

Based on its suggestions, several initiatives were taken to translate the BRT idea into practice on the ground. For instance, the current two LRT route (i.e. north–south, and east–west) corridors were initially planned for the implementation of BRT.[5]

Long before the Light Rail came to the fore, a BRT demonstration corridor was built in the north–south direction, starting from the centre of the city (i.e La Gare) to northern Kality. The current La Gare to Kality LRT route was a full-fledged asphalt road, which was designated as a BRT route. Buses with a carrying capacity of 23 and above started providing a rapid bus service along the proposed corridor. While the city of Addis Ababa was undertaking the BRT pilot project as a preferred mass transport option, a swift discussion on the idea of Light Rail Transit (LRT) emerged, seemingly out of the blue and without warning. As one key informant succinctly put it:

> BRT was initially considered as a solution to the city's mass/public transport need and the two lines; one from La Gare to Kality and Megenagna to Ayat round about was left as BRT corridors. Without any further consultation to relevant stakeholders. No justification was given on abandoning the BRT and embarking on LRT. The current LRT routes (North-South and East West lines) were originally planned to be BRT routes.[6]

Moreover, a key informant reported that the rise of LRT, while abandoning BRT, had been a public transaport idea imposed on the Addis Ababa City administration by the federal government:

> The city undertook various studies in search of mass transportation means and Bus Rapid Transit (BRT) was initially considered as solution. The city administration constructed one BRT corridor from La-Gahar to Kality, which now serves as LRT south-north route in due time though, LRT got momentum, and the focus shifted from BRT.[7]

Another key informant noted:

> BRT was the first choice of the city Administration and much was done from allocating a BRT corridor and running pilot rapid bus service in the city. The

---

3 Interview with Bureau of Addis Ababa City Administration
4 A report by Lyon Town Planning Agency reported that the pre-feasibility study and the development of Addis Ababa city transport master plan were part of the Ethio-French project from 2002–2010.
5 Interview with Addis Ababa City Road Authority
6 Interview with AACRA
7 Interview with Ethiopian Railway Corporation

BRT corridors were now serving as LRT routes. The LRT idea won and the city dropped the BRT idea. However, after the completion of the LRT, BRT is rising. The city has completed a study to introduce BRT so that it can be integrated with the LRT service. (Interview with Addis Ababa City Transport Authority)

The qualitative findings strongly suggest that Addis Ababa City's transport planners and the mandated city administrators developed the BRT strategy to curb the ever growing city residents's transport need. However, the swift decision to focus on the more expensive AA-LRT project poses a practical question: What was the rationale behind choosing AA-LRT over BRT?

The rise of LRT: Issue emergence and discursive rationale

'The late prime minister, Meles Zenawi, first suggested LRT as a quick solution to the city's growing transport problem.'[8] Almost all key informants who participated in this study unequivocally confirmed that the late Prime Minister Meles Zenawi was the person responsible for singlehandedly promoting the LRT as the best mass transit option. A key informant from the Addis Ababa City Road Authority stated:

> Once LRT was introduced as his 'Ethiopia renaissance' showcase, all cabinet members backed the idea without much confrontation. 'Once the late PM introduced the idea, no one dared to challenge,' as one key informant pointed out.[9]

The LRT was thus a priority project for the government as it strived to demonstrate to the visiting African heads of state and to the people of Ethiopia the regime's commitment towards enhancing the image of Addis Ababa as the capital of Africa, as well as to reinforce the 'Ethiopian Renaissance' narrative that was getting political traction. In short, LRT had strong political backing from the highest levels of government. The urgency of completing the LRT project in a very short time-frame was promoted by the preparation surrounding the 2015 national elections. As one key informant succinctly put it:

> In addition to the social and economic significance of LRT for the residents of Addis, it is a political project that had symbolic meaning enhancing the renaissance of the country as well as helping the ruling party gain popular support.

Despite the efforts made in seeking an in-depth explanation, the swift government decision from implementing BRT to initiating the LRT remained a mystery. The late prime minister singlehandedly advocated for the emergence of LRT as a mega city project.

---

8   Interview with representative of AA city administration
9   Interview with a senior researcher/policy advisor to the government of Ethiopia

Discursive rationale

This study found that the interaction of two major factors contributed to the sudden abandonment of the BRT initiative in favour of the LRT in 2007. The first factor has to do with Addis Ababa's rapid population growth due to the dramatic growth of the Ethiopian economy, particularly in the capital and its surroundings. Addis Ababa's population is thought to be growing at an annual rate of 2.1% (Central Statistics Agency 2013). With the spatial expansion of the city, fuelled by expanding industries and other economic enterprises, more and more people were migrating to the capital in search of jobs and other economic opportunities. This expansion was further exacerbated by massive urban renewal projects initiated by both the federal and city governments. Since the 2005 urban policy, the city was busy clearing major slum areas in the inner city. As a result, 80% of inner-city dwellers who used to live in public housing were relocated into condominium apartments that were built in satellite cities, which have appeared in the outskirts of Addis since 2005.[10]

Relocated residents have been forced to commute long distances to and from the city centre where their work and social life are concentrated. As the city expands and creates satellite cities, a huge demand for transport is emerging that can no longer be satisfied with existing systems. Consequently, the government concluded that the BRT option was unlikely to meet the growing mobility needs of the fast expanding urban population. Instead, the federal government opted for the Light Rail Transit (LRT) option as the best solution given the changing dynamics of Addis Ababa and the surrounding regions.

Second, the government wished to modernise the city's image by introducing a modern mass transportation system, and that the LRT initiative fits very well with the evolving 'Ethiopia's Renaissance' narrative. Similar to the 'Africa Rising' narrative, the notion of 'Ethiopia's Renaissance' evolved internally while the country was celebrating the Ethiopian millennium nine years ago in 2007. Since then, the notion of 'Ethiopia Rising' has dominated the national development discourse, and is increasingly reflected in key strategic plans and documents, such as the Growth and Transformation Plan (I & II). For instance, the Growth and Transformation Plans (I & II) emphasise government financed mega infrastructure projects such as the 'renaissance dam' and industrial zones. The LRT represents one of the key mega projects that are designed to showcase the country's economic renaissance and the government's success in reducing poverty through accelerated economic growth and diversification.

Besides attractiveness, environmental friendliness was used as an important indicator for prioritising LRT as the most suitable form of public transport for Addis Ababa. Growing acceptance of the LRT among policymakers contributed to the

---

10 The city of Addis Ababa has been building condominium houses on the outskirts of Addis and established satellite neighbourhoods that can accommodate an average 15 000 households in areas such as Tulu Dimtu, Ayat, Bole Arabsa and Abdowolo. These new sites do not have transport mobility networks. And the city has been working hard to establish a mass transport service to and from the city centre to these new satellite sites.

fading away of BRT, although BRT would have been significantly cheaper than LRT.[11] This study found that arguments for LRT's capacity, attractiveness and environmental friendliness received more support than the initial investment cost that the LRT would incur. In other words, cost considerations were not given serious attention in the decision to go with the LRT.

The pragmatic stance that the government had taken in terms of LRT's capacity and environmental friendliness, the government of Ethiopia's ambitious plan to make Addis Ababa a global city have been major drivers for choosing AA-LRT over BRT. Perhaps this fits into the 'urban fantasies' that decision-makers are made to believe, such as 'Ethiopia is rising' (Terrefe 2020; Watson 2009)

The politics around LRT infrastructure investment

Once the LRT was recognised as a viable mass transit option with significant political backing and potential financing, the next stage of the process was the selection of its mode of delivery and construction. A conventional approach of 'design and build' was taken to choose potential contractors with prior experience in LRT infrastructure development. The Ethiopian government issued a Request for Expression of Interest, and companies from Russia, Italy, Turkey, India and China responded. It is striking what the geographic footprint of international interest is when such calls are issued. The preliminary selection process identified an Italian company based on its technical competence and prior experience in designing and building railways following EU standards. However, Ethiopia was challenged at that time by its capacity to finance the project in its entirety. According to one informant: 'For Ethiopia, it was not possible to secure financial resources from European countries, as the timing was when the European financial crisis emerged.'[12]

The rationale for the 'design and build' approach was twofold. First, it was clear that the LRT would require large financial investment that the Ethiopian government would not be able to generate on its own. Second, the country neither had prior experience in designing and building an LRT system nor adequately trained human resources for planning and executing such a project. Hence, the government deliberately sought a company that would bring both financial and technical resources. In the end, the government of Ethiopia decided to award the AA-LRT construction to the Chinese LRT turnkey developing contractor (China Railway Engineering Corporation [CREC]) after considering the company's experience in rail construction and its willingness to mobilise 85% of the financial cost of the LRT.

There was no debate or opposition to this decision due to the political backing of the LRT. The fast-track approach had several limitations. According to key informants, the 'design and build' approach by its very nature does not require precise planning in advance of construction, making it difficult for decision-makers to determine the actual project cost prior to its completion. For example, several amendments to the

---

11 ITDP estimates that BRTs are between four and twenty times cheaper than tram or light rail transit (LRT) and ten to a hundred times cheaper than metro.

12 Interview with representative of Addis Ababa City Road Authority (one of the board members for AA-LRT).

AA-LRT north–south and east–west routes were made during the construction phase, such as building additional bypasses, elevator shafts, which considerably inflated the investment costs. For instance, the construction of the LRT line is for a total of 31km, of which 23km is ground level rail; 7.33km is bridge construction, 0.9km underground tunnel. The 23km ground level line is fenced on both sides of the tracks.

Decisions regarding the bridge construction, creating an underground tunnel, and fence to separate the rail tracks were made after the start of LRT construction, again leading to an increase in construction costs. Furthermore, lack of proper planning introduced unintended social and economic costs. For example, the decision to fence off the rail tracks from the main road disrupted the urban fabric by blocking free pedestrian movement and cutting cars off from existing intersections and turning points. The LRT project also caused traffic congestion near train stations and at the new roundabouts where the LRT line is at ground level. Placing the LRT line between opposite traffic lanes has led to poor pedestrian safety, as pedestrians must cross through moving traffic while walking to and from the train stations. Furthermore, the average distance between LRT stations is 800 metres and pedestrians must watch out for both the fast driving cars on the road and the LRT when crossing. This makes crossing the LRT lines from one side to the other side of the road difficult for older people and people with disabilities. According to one informant, 'Since we did not have the design before the construction, we were not able to make relevant decisions in a timely manner.'[13] On 12 March 2017, *MailOnline* reported that the half a billion-dollar investment in public transport failed to curb Addis Ababa's traffic problems, featuring the headline, 'light rail fails to fix Ethiopia's traffic troubles'. The report went on to say:

> Electric light railway tracks soar over Ethiopia's capital Addis Ababa, a rare example of mass transit infrastructure on the continent ... But despite government promises, the roads below are still clogged with traffic 14 months after the light rail system's opening, and for many residents the city's network of overcrowded minibus taxis remain the only option. (*MailOnline* 2017)

During data collection, the current author observed how the lack of prior planning on the design of AA-LRT routes created enormous traffic in all roundabouts where the LRT line is on the ground level and near all train stations (see Figures 2 & 3).

Economically, LRT led to financial loss to individual business operators whose businesses face the fenced roads. The fence disrupts the normal conduct of business as communities are split apart. Furthermore, construction of LRT lines resulted in economic waste by the government. A report by the Ethiopian Institute of Architecture, Building Construction and City Development (EiABC 2015) identified major waste and costs incurred during the AA-LRT development, including the following:

----

13 Interview with key informant from the Addis Ababa City Road Authority.

Figure 2: LRT line-induced traffic jam around roundabouts

Source: Photograph taken by Meseret Kassahun March 2017

Figure 3: LRT-induced traffic jam near one LRT Station

Source: Photograph taken by Meseret Kassahun, March 2017

- A 40m wide road that was part of a BRT corridor and completed only in 2010 with a total cost exceeding 283.6 million birr (~USD 13.5 million) was demolished.
- The construction of the 8km LRT line from the CMC area to Mexico roundabouts involved the relocation of an 8km main water pipeline that provides water to over a million people from the Legedadi Dam. The total cost of the relocation of the pipeline was about 421 million Ethiopian birr (~USD 21 million).
- The AA-LRT line construction required relocation of electricity lines costing the Ethiopian Electric Power Authority 130 million birr (~USD 6 million).

Hence, a total of nearly USD 42 million was wasted that could have been used for other infrastructure or urban service provision. This could have been avoided if decision-makers had taken the time to assess the potential social, economic and financial consequences of the fast-tracked approach as well as if different actors had had a greater role in decision-making. Thorough planning using benchmarking could also have streamlined the process. For instance, countries such as Morocco have done well in constructing an efficient tram system instead of expensive LRT lines. As a result, the Casablanca tramway has been custom-built to facilitate free movement of passengers and significantly lessened traffic jams.[14] If the tram had been chosen, 'better traffic flow could have been achieved since tram lines/routes can be shared by other transport/mobility systems.'[15] For instance, in a guideline developed for the planning of BRT, Institute for Transportation and Development Policy (2007) asserts that BRT is a cost effective mechanism compared to LRT and can help cities to rapidly develop a public transport system while delivering quality service.

Accessibility, affordability and reliability of AA-LRT service

Although impossible to get an official report, attempts have been made to assess the experience of AA-LRT service users with the specifc emphasis on accessibility, affordability, and its reliability. Emerged qualitative data shows an average 135 000 residents use the LRT service per day.[16] A key informant reported:

> Although operated by the federal government, LRT daily ticket sells indicates that the 28 LRT cars transport 120 000–150 000 passengers daily.[17]

The LRT also provides multiple benefits such as time-saving to passengers as the LRT lines are fenced, and reduction in pollution as the LRT consumes electricity. In addition to the effectiveness of the LRT in terms of its benefit, assessing the effectiveness of the AA-LRT as a mass transit service needs to take transport users' preferences, the reliability of services, convenience, safety, comfort, accessibility, and affordability issues into consideration (Imam 2014). Similarly, Friman and Fellesson's (2009) extensive literature review suggests reliability, frequency, travel time and fare level, comfort and cleanliness, network coverage/distance to stop, and safety issues as relevant factors in customer evaluations of the public transport service.

Accessibility and affordability

FGD participants' experience in using the LRT and their overall assessment of the service is positive. In relation to its accessibility, study participants expressed their dissatisfaction that the LRT lines cover only certain areas. As shown above, in the AA-LRT map, the AA-LRT has only two corridors, these being, the East-West corridor that runs from Ayat to Tor-Hailoch and the North-South corridor that runs from Minilik. As a result of its limited connectivity to the different parts of the city, AA-LRT service users expressed their strong desire to see AA-LRT service in every direction of the city with better horizontal connectivity. Hence, its accessibility is only for people who are currently living near the LRT lines. This limits its accessibility for residents outside of the LRT lines.

---

14 http://www.railway-technology.com/projects/casablanca-tramway/
15 Interview with a senior urban development policy advisor, August 2016
16 Key informant from Addis Ababa Transport Authority Bureau
17 Key informant from Addis ababa Light Rail Transit Project office

When it comes to affordability, the most recurrent themes emerged from all FGDs were that the LRT is affordable, fast and covers long distance. An observation on the transport fee shows that the train tariff fee is significantly lower compared to other transport services such as city bus and mini-bus taxi fees for similar distance. The tickets cost two to six birrs (USD 0.08 to USD 0.20) depending on the distance of the trip. A discussion participant noted:

> The LRT is cheap. I could have payed more than 10 Bir for the trip via taxi from where I live (Hayat area) to the centre of the city. Now, I only pay 4 Birr.

Reliability of LRT service

Service users' perception of service frequency in relation to travel and waiting times, as well as frequency of departure was assessed and findings from FGDs consistently confirm that the LRT is a reliable and efficient service.

> In the city where you wait in line for an hour or two for taxis, the waiting time for the train is 15 minutes which impacts other parts of the city's economy positively.

Most FGD participants agree that the waiting time is on average 15 minutes during rush hours. However, there are times where service users experienced 40-minute delays (two FGD participants) and 50 minutes (one FGD participant). Furthermore, service users reported that they also witnessed a train arriving on time and not boarding passengers. This might be explained in terms of a dedicated train as 'Express Line' that might avoid some stations or a train that might have no space to board additional passengers. Furthermore, despite the dedicated power supply for the LRT, there were some incidents where the train stopped mid-trip and later announced to passengers that electric power was the cause. The challenge in relation to power disruption is also confirmed during key informant interviews. However, the integration of the city's major infrastructure and utility providers was instrumental to reducing the impact of electric power.

AA-LRT governance structure, institutional and human resource capacity

AA-LRT governance structure

The city of Addis Ababa is a federal government's capital and a city administration by itself. This offers opportunities for maximising the city's unique position in the country's urban development. Ethiopia's Urban Local Government framework guides the overall city development process and the city's legitimacy in collecting taxes and municipal revenues for its socio-economic development purposes. The city is mandated to provide major urban infrastructure and services.[18] The budget for these administrative functions is approved by the city council, and thus the city retains some decision-making power. This puts Addis Ababa in a better position than other Ethiopian cities.

Despite this presumed advantageous position, Addis Ababa is not fully exercising its administrative autonomy. The lines between its State and Federal functions are blurred due to excessive federal involvement. According to the World Bank and Cities Alliance (2015: 66), 'State government and Urban Local Government roles in the execution of state and municipal functions are not necessarily clear.' For example, the decision to construct the LRT was made exclusively by the federal government. Although providing transport service is the mandate of the city, AA-LRT does not fall under the jurisdiction of the city government of Addis Ababa. Ethiopian Railway Corporation (ERC) was established in 2008 based on Regulation No. 141/2007 and tasked with developing railway infrastructure and providing freight and passenger railway services in the country (Federal Democratic Republic of Ethiopia 2007).

According to key informants, the rationale for the establishment of an ERC independent of the old bureaucracy was threefold. First, the train network needs an independent regulatory body, which raises a couple of issues that need to be addressed by higher officials. Issues like whether or not to have one regulatory body for LRT and another for the ongoing and emerging national train networks that the country has embarked on. Second, the country did not have the technical capacity and experience in managing the day-to-day functioning of the AA-LRT. Third, the country had to find a way to cover the upfront infrastructure and operation costs. Hence, the ERC was established.

The political backing from the prime minister's office and the personal interest of the late PM in the LRT project warranted the creation of a management system independent of the normal government bureaucracy. The ERC, as an independent institution with strong political backing from the highest office in the land, was able to freely formulate and implement rules and regulations for the operation of railways in the country. The decision to have a single management and governance strategy in order to avoid red tape and unnecessary gridlock from the existing city and federal bureaucracy was instrumental in increasing the efficiency of the AA-LRT project. However, the establishment of ERC in 2008 introduced a gap concerning the role of the city government of Addis Ababa vis-à-vis AA-LRT management. A key informant from the city government of Addis Ababa noted:

> Our role was visible during the infrastructure phase of the project. It was the city administration that was responsible for providing land for the LRT lines. As a result, the mayor's office was active. We used to be involved and informed. Currently, in the operation phase, the relationship between the city

18 Basic urban infrastructure and services include: housing, land, water, electricity, telephone, road construction; road lights; drainage and sewerages; solid waste disposal systems; poverty reduction; maintaining vital statistics; certificates of marriage, birth and death; abattoirs; bus terminals and market places; combatting soil erosion, landslide disasters and environmental pollution.

administration and the AA-LRT project office as well as with the Board needs to be reviewed. Our present involvement is extremely minimal.[19]

As a federal project, the ERC is currently working on AA-LRT phase 2, that is, expansion of existing lines. In the current operational phase, the role of representatives of the board, including the city of Addis Ababa, is minimised: 'ERC is managing both the AA-LRT as well as other railway projects of the country. Structurally, ERC is accountable to the federal government, not to the city Administration.'[20] In operating AA-LRT, the ERC is dependent on international external institutions for infrastructure design, operation and maintenance.

The ERC is currently functioning with the support of two Chinese companies and a Swedish Road consultancy firm. The China Railway Engineering Corp (CREC) built the AA-LRT infrastructure. CREC is also partially involved in the current operation phase of AA-LRT. Another Chinese company called Chenzen Metro, which is experienced in the operation and maintenance of LRT, is contracted to manage the operation and maintenance of AA-LRT for the next five years. Significantly, the Swedish Road consultancy was hired to evaluate the work of the Chinese companies in all phases. Whether the AA-LRT will remain as a federally administered project for the foreseeable future is not clear. Questions remain whether the federal government will at some point hand over the day-to-day management and operation of the AA-LRT to the city administration. If the latter were to happen, city authorities will need time to prepare the appropriate legal, regulatory and management systems.

AA-LRT institutional capacity building

There were no railway engineers in the country prior to 2012.[21]

A critical look into the AA-LRT institutional setup shows that the nature of the project contributed to the government's decision about how the AA-LRT should be managed. As a new industry, LRT requires specific competences in order to successfully manage its day-to-day operations. The LRT idea was embraced in the absence of relevant professionals who could plan, implement and manage the project. As one informer put it, 'At that time [during the inception of LRT], the country did not have professionals on railway engineering. We also had no experience in managing LRT.'[22]

The establishment of ERC as an independent institution is not adequate to manage the AA-LRT in a sustainable way. Considering the complete lack of relevant skills in railway engineering and management expertise, the ERC relies on Chinese companies in managing the entire LRT design and operation process. Currently a Chinese company, Chenzen Metro, works under the AA-LRT project office to manage the day-to-day operation and maintenance of the AA-LRT. At the same time, the ERC

---

19 Interview with representatives of the Addis Ababa City Administration Mayor's Office, August 2016
20 Interview with representatives of ERC, August 2016
21 Interview with Railway Engineering Institute, Addis Ababa University, August 2012
22 Interview with Institute of Railway Engineering, Addis Ababa University

decided to establish a Railway Engineering Institute in the Technology faculty of Addis Ababa University in order to train engineers to be responsible for the management and maintenance of the LRT in future. According to one informant, 'There were no railway engineers in the country prior to 2012.'[23] This is a commendable move, as it would reduce the ERC's dependence on Chinese management and maintenance services in the long run. Hence, a two-year Master's of Science programme focusing on three fields of study at Addis Ababa University's technology faculty was opened. These fields include: civil railway engineering, mechanical or rolling stock engineering, and electrical engineering for railway systems. After signing a memorandum of understanding with the ERC, the institute enrolled 540 students in four cohorts. Since its establishment, a total of 58 students graduated in the railway civil, 55 in the mechanical or rolling stock, and 27 in the electrical engineering fields. 'All students are employees of ERC and will continue to work for ERC after graduation.'[24] This initiative demonstrates that Chinese experts are not meant to remain in the agency indedifinitely. Instead, local experts will progressively occupy operational and management roles in all aspects of the service.

Discussion

The political economy of Ethiopia's developmental state approach to governance clearly limited involvement of diverse actors during AA-LRT inception and implementation. The former Prime Minister Meles Zenawi's sole decision to impose the AA-LRT system on the city, despite the city administration's choice and perhaps the expert's well designed concrete plan to implement BRT, was a political decision. The government's grip on decision-making leaves no room for other visible and invisible policy actors to contribute to policy decisions. This reflects the uncontested 'democratic centralism,' a driving principle of the the the ruling party that guides its strategic day-to-day activities (Bach 2012; Vaughan & Gebremichael 2011). There is a notable absence of a 'level playing field' that would offer favourable conditions for organisations and civil society interest groups to negotiate and debate the merits of an urban project on the scale of the AA-LRT to maximise its benefit and reduce the negative social and economic impacts on Addis Ababa residents. The AA-LRT's emergence as the only viable transit system and the decisions taken during its implementation illustrate the idea of 'developmental patrimonialism' (Kelsal et al. 2010). According to Kellsal et al., developmental patrimonialism promotes personal rule. Hence, the ultimate decision made by the late Prime Minster Meles Zenawi in 2007 consistently confirms the role of 'personal rule' in guiding the city's infrastructure development and growth.

AA-LRT's governance structure and institutional system also demonstrate a top-down institutional arrangement and the decision-making based on embedded consensus within EPRDF's elite circle. As a result, open contestations and entertaining alternative policy ideas on how to provide an environmentally sound and economically beneficial mass urban transit system that would have averted the socio-economic chaos the AA-LRT project engendered were not allowed.

---

23 Interview with Railway Engineering Institute, Addis Ababa University, August 2012
24 Interview with AA-LRT project office

Top-down institutional setup

The AA-LRT demonstrates how a 'developmental state' can usurp the functions of local governments in the interest of optimising the delivery of urban services from its perspective. While the government has committed itself to decentralising decision-making to lower tiers of government, in reality, it bypasses these same local institutions or fails to consult them fully. Hence, the devolution of autonomy at local level government institutions remains unrealised. It would be fair to suggest that the requirements of strategic external actors, such as the Chinese investors, reinforce this pre-existing tendency. The federal government's decision to institute an independent railway corporation with a separate structure to be managed by the board rather than the city government of Addis Ababa, appeared as a pragmatic decision rather than adhering to and translating the country's established urban governance principles into practice. The narrative of good urban governance in key urban development initiatives is merely an alibi to cascade top-down decisions through embedded consensus at all levels. In this regard, the decision that was made in 2007 by the EPRDF elites to elevate the LRT service as the sole option to meet the city residents' transportation needs and showcase Ethiopia's 'rise' blurred existing urban governance structure and systems. Despite the city of Addis Ababa's autonomy and mandate to provide urban services such as a reliable, fast and affordable transport system, the top-down decision from the central government to introduce LRT has not to date created any controversy. The swift decision to introduce the LRT over the city's own preference to introduce a pilot BRT service perfectly shows the hierarchical power relationship between the federal and city governments. Furthermore, the federal government's sole decision on loan agreements with Exim Bank of China shows the limited autonomy of the city administration in terms of initiating and implementing socio-economic related development plans.

Urban governance based on 'embedded consensus'

The absence of any complex or dynamic interactions between policy actors is obvious within the 'developmental state' or 'developmental patrimonialism' approach to governance. What is interesting in the AA-LRT case study is that the AA-LRT's emergence faced no contestation, and its implementation did not raise debate between the national/federal and local level governance structures. There is no public document showing any conflict between the federal and city government bureaucrats throughout the entire political process. The consensus surrounding the introduction of LRT was seemingly absolute. The city administration expressed no concerns over the amount of investment neither for the initial LRT infrastructure development nor the ongoing operation and maintenance costs. In addition, none of the authority figures/elites questioned the relevance of the project as it led to financial waste of nearly USD 42 million. Although the loan agreement has its own grace period and maturity time, the city government of Addis Ababa was not involved in any of the negotiations and agreements pertaining to repayment of loans. Furthermore, the city administration did not undertake research into the feasibility of the project in terms of sustaining the service through revenue generation. The level of consensus and cohesiveness between the federal government and the city administration resonates' with Kelsall's (2011) neo-patrimonial 'embedded bureaucratic autonomy' of the federal government excluding other non-state actors including the private sector. The cohesiveness of the federal and the city government of Addis Ababa show the effectiveness of the regime's commitment to govern based on the principle of democratic centralism where the State and ruling party are one and the same. Top party leaders are the leaders of the country and focus only on State effectiveness in both policy decision-making and service delivery process. Hence, the structures that are instituted around the three tiers of governance (federal, regional and local level) are more symbolic than substantive.

Conclusion

The political economy of the state-society relationship within 'developmental state democracy' operates within the deeply entrenched bureaucratic centralism through which patrimonialism is harnessed. Hence, the system of governance does not promote dynamic interactions between various actors in line with the principles of good urban governance. Instead, the overriding concern is State effectiveness, which operates through embedded consensus and this seems the most likely way forward. AA-LRT's contribution in providing transportation for a significant number of Addis Ababa residents is commendable. Despite the effectiveness of the Ethiopian state in achieving the completion of AA-LRT construction in a few years to fit into the 'Ethiopian Renaissance' narrative, I argue that the absence of citizens, civil society organisations, and Ethiopian business involvement in the decision-making process is responsible for a huge amount of wastage. Had an authentic and genuine process of decision-making involving the federal government and the city authorities existed, a more cost-effective alternative form of transport services would have been proposed and debated without the federal government having to impose its will on the city government. The governance systems in place narrowed the space that could provide democratic checks and balances as well as feedbacks, which are fundamental in facilitating the social and financial efficiency of the LRT.

Furthermore, the government's ambition to reposition the city of Addis Ababa as a global city perhaps fits into the completely imported urban fantasies of which decision-makers were convinced in pursuing the 'Ethiopia is rising' and 'eco-friendly' project that also provided mass transit service (Terrefe 2020; Kloosterboer 2019; Watson 2014). As a result, local realities were ignored, and emphasis was more on the symbolic significance of AA-LRT as a mega city project that had helped the country get international attention. Moreover, the project has helped to provide affordable and reliable transport service although further research is needed to explore how the expensive modern mass transit has helped ease the city residents' transport need. Obviously, the desire to have modern transportation prevented decision-makers from averting LRT-induced financial wastage that could have been spared for other infrastructure developments. In fact, further research is needed to actually determine the cost and benefit of AA-LRT. The persistence of the government's decision to expand the LRT lines[25] without critically examining the unintended negative socio-economic impacts sufficiently explains the lack of transparent and accountable urban governance. Hence, the overall governance systems and structures in Ethiopia do not provide democratic checks and balances as well as feedbacks, which are vital to increasing the social and financial efficiency of LRT. External actors and their agendas are folded into these overriding dynamics, they are not determined by external actors.

Annexure I: Summary of study participants

Institutions	Number of participants
Government institutions*	12
Civil society groups	3
Research institutes	2
Focus group discussants	8

* Study participants from government institutions such as Ethiopian Railway Corporation, Addis Ababa Light Rail Transit, Addis Ababa City Mayor's office, Addis Ababa City Road Authority, Addis Ababa City Transport Bureau. Civil Society representatives are from (1) Addis Ababa Women's Association; (2) Addis Ababa Youth Association; (3) Ethiopian Cities Association. Research institute representatives are from Addis Ababa University, Institute of Technology, and department of Railway Engineering.

References

Addis Ababa and Special Zone. Development Planning Project Office (2013) Addis Ababa and the Surrounding Oromia Special Zone Integrated Development Plan (2014–2038): Draft Executive Summary. Addis Ababa: Addis Ababa Special Zone Development Plan Project Office (AASZDPPO)

Addis Ababa City Planning Project Office & Lyon Town Planning Agency (2012) Transportation challenges in a booming city: Coordination of the mass transit network and urban development in Addis Ababa. CODATU XV, 2012

Addis Ababa City Road and Transport Authority (2014) Feasibility and operational planning study of Bus Rapid Transit: Demand and forecasting report. Addis Ababa: Addis Ababa Transport Authority

Bach J-N (2011) Abyotawi democracy: Neither revolutionary nor democratic. A critical review of EPRDF's conception of revolutionary democracy in post-1991 Ethiopia. *Journal of Eastern African Studies* 5(4): 641–663

Caporaso JA & Levine DP (1992) *Theories of Political Economy*. NY: Cambrige University Press

Central Statistical Agency (2013) *Population Projection for Ethiopia*. Addis Ababa

Cheru F (2016) Emerging southern powers and new forms of South–South cooperation: Ethiopia's strategic engagement with China and India. *Third World Quarterly* 37(4): 592–610

---

25 According to a key informant, ERC has finalised PHASE II of LRT, and a USD 500 000 project agreement was signed with CREC.

CNN (2015) Ethiopia gets the first metro system in sub-Saharan Africa. http://edition. cnn.com/2015/10/14/tech/addis-ababa-light-rail-metro/

Creswell JW (2007) *Qualitative Inquiry and Research Design: Choosing Among Five Approaches*. Thousand Oaks, CA: Sage

Drake RF (2001) *The Principles of Social Policy*. London: Palgrave

Ethiopian Institute of Architecture, Building Construction and City Development (2015) Integrated and coordinated physical and transport infrastructure planning and development in Addis Ababa for safe and efficient mobility. Addis Ababa: Ethiopian Institue of Architecture and Building College

Federal Democratic Republic of Ethiopia (2007) Council of Ministers Regulation No. 141/2007 Ethiopian Railway Corporation establishment. Addis Ababa, Ethiopia

Fenta TM (2014) Demands for urban public transportation in Addis Ababa. *Journal of Intelligent Transportation and Urban Planning* 2(3): 81–88

Friman M & Fellesson M (2009) Satisfaction in public transportation: The quality paradox. *Journal of Public Transportation* 12(4): 57–69

Gebeyehu M & Tekano S (2007) Multi-criteria decision-making for public transportation development projects using analytic network process (ANP). *Journal of Eastern Asia Society for Transportation Studies* 7: 223–237

Harpham T & Boatang KA (1997) Urban governance in relation to the operation of urban services in developing countries. *Habitat International* 21(1): 65–77

Hendriks F (2013) Understanding good urban governance: Essentials, shifts, and values. *Urban Affairs Review* 50(4): 553–576

Imam R (2014) Measuring public transport satisfaction from user surveys. *International Journal of Business and Management* 9(6): 106–114

Institute for Transportation and Development Policy (2007) *Bus Rapid Transit Planning Guide*. NY: ITDP. https://www.itdp.org/wp-content/uploads/2014/07/52.-Bus-Rapid-Transit-Guide-PartIntro-2007-09.pdf.

Jemere Y (2012) *Addis Ababa Light Rail Transit Project*. Addis Ababa: Ethiopian Railway Corporation

Jones H, Clench B & Harris D (2014) *The Governance of Service Delivery in Developing Countries*. London: ODI. https://www.odi.org/publications/8329-governance-urban-service-delivery-developing-countries-literature-review

Kelsall T (2011) Rethinking the relationship between neo-patrimonialism and economic performance in sub-Saharan Africa. *IDS Bulletin* 42(2): 76–87

Kelsall T, Booth D, Cammack D & Golooba-Mutebi F (2010) Developmental patrimonialism? Questioning the orthodoxy on political governance and economic progress in Africa. *Working paper* No. 9. African Power and Politics Program/ ODI. https://www.odi.org/sites/odi.org.uk/files/resource-documents/appp-wp9-developmental-patrimonialism-questioning-the_orthodoxy-tim-kelsall-david-booth-july-2010.pdf

Kloosterboer MH (2019) The 'new' Addis Ababa: Shantytown or global city? An assessment of large-scale inner-city renewal, redevelopment and displacement for the construction of a 'new' Addis Ababa. PhD dissertation, Glasgow University

Lincoln YS & Guba EG (1985) *Naturalistic Inquiry*. Beverly Hills, CA: Sage

Lindell I (2008) The multiple sites of urban governance: Insights from an African city. *Urban Studies* 45(9): 1879–1901

Lyon Town Planning Agency (2011) Addis Ababa Support to 'B2' BRT project. Lyon.

MailOnline (2017, 12 March) Light rail fails to fix Ethiopia's traffic troubles. https://www.dailymail.co.uk/wires/afp/article-4305404/Light-rail-fails-fix-Ethiopias-traffic-troubles.html

Mcloughlin C (2014) *Political Economy Analysis: Topic Guide* (2nd edn.). Birmingham, UK: GSDRC, University of Birmingham

Melo MA & Baiocchi G (2006) Deliberative democracy and local governance: Towards a new agenda. *International Journal of Urban and Regional Research* 30(3): 587–600

Ministry of Finance and Economic Development (2006) Plan for accelerated and sustained development to end poverty (2005/06–2009/10). Addis Ababa, Ethiopia

Ministry of Finance and Economic Development (2010) Growth and Transformation Plan I (2010–2015). Addis Ababa, Ethiopia

Ministry of Transport (2011a) National transport policy. Addis Ababa: Ministry of Transport

Ministry of Transport (2011b) Transport policy of Addis Ababa. Addis Ababa: Ministry of Transport

Ministry of Urban Development, Housing, and Construction (2014) *National Report on Housing and Urban Development*. Addis Ababa: MOUDHC

Ministry of Works and Urban Development (2007) Plan for urban development and urban good governance. Plan for accelerated and sustained development to end poverty (2005/06-2009/10). Addis Ababa, Ethiopia

National Planning Commission (NPC) (2015) Growth and transformation plan II from 2015–2020. Addis Ababa: Ministry of Finance and Economic Development

Padgett D (2008) *Qualitative Methods in Social Work Research: Challenges and Rewards*. Thousand Oaks, CA: Sage

Speer J (2012) Participatory governance reform: A good strategy for increasing government responsiveness and improving public services? *World Development* 40(12): 2379–2398

Terrefe B (2020) Urban layers of political rupture: The 'new' politics of Addis Ababa's megaprojects. *Journal of Eastern African Studies* 14(3): 375–395. doi: 10.1080/17531055.2020.1774705

The Economist (2017, 31 August) Sub-Saharan Africa gets its first metro. https://www.economist.com/news/middle-east-and-africa/21665199-addis-ababa-has-opened-first-part-new-light-rail-system-sub-saharan-africa.

UN-Habitat (2002) The global campaign on urban governance. Concept Paper, 2nd edn. Nairobi: UN-HABITAT

UN-Habitat (2014) *Structural Transformation in Ethiopia: The Urban Dimension*. Nairobi: UN-HABITAT https://unhabitat.org/structural-transformation-in-ethiopia

UN-Habitat (2017) *State of Addis Ababa Report*. https://unhabitat.org/books/the-state-of-addis-ababa-2017-the-addis-ababa-we-want/

Vaughan S (2011) Revolutionary democratic state-building: Party, state and people in the EPRDF's Ethiopia. *Journal of Eastern African Studies* 5(4): 619–640

Vaughan S & Gebremichael M (2011) *Rethinking Business and Politics in Ethiopia: The Role of EFFORT, The Endowment Fund for the Rehabilitation of Tigray*. London: ODI

Watson V (2009) The planned city sweeps the poor away ...: Urban planning and 21st century urbanisation. *Progress in Planning* 72(3): 151–193

Watson V (2014) African urban fantasies: Dreams or nightmares? *Environment and Urbanization* 26(1): 215–231

World Bank & Cities Alliance (2015) *Ethiopia – Urbanization Review: Urban Institutions for a Middle-Income Ethiopia.* Washington, DC: World Bank

CHAPTER 12

Conclusion: African cities in the world of today and tomorrow

Göran Therborn & Alan Mabin

In African cities, the music is relentless – AbdouMaliq Simone, 2004

How do we imagine the past, present and future of Africa's cities? With what images of *the* African city might we choose to work? Is it Djenne, Mali, and its earth-walled grand mosque? Is it the postcoloniality of Bamako, contained in its avenues, post-independence buildings or fluid markets? Does the sweep of the waterfront of Luanda, and the murky, oily bargaining in its reemergent hotels capture the spirit of urban Africa? How does the focus change as the skyline of modern, central city Nairobi gives way to the garbage in its alleys or the decay in its buildings? Does the postmodernity of Johannesburg's suburban architecture reveal something exceptional, something repetitively global, or just possibly something of wider significance?

How do we think and read African cities? Are they mostly sites of chaos, or zones of sharp clashes between modernity and tradition? Are these the capitals of corrupt elites or the spaces of freedom and opportunity longed for across the continent? Do they offer promise of different futures or seem bound by colonial pasts and betrayed independence?

This book approached African cities through three perspectives: those of the national, the popular and the global. Here we reflect on and seek to refract through these themes, without claiming that we are at all close to exhausting the terrain.

The national

The nation came late to Africa, and usually in a form very different from the European. It was united, not by language, culture or religion, but by a common history of colonial occupation. Most, if by no means all, capitals and major cities were colonial creations, in many ways segregated from the rural African societies. Colonial cities were often referred to by the colonised as 'white villages.' However, in some other respects, many

African cities include an ancient, pre-colonial, pre-modern pattern of authority not found in cities of other continents, the authority of chiefs. Important, but very variable in resources and competence, as Philippe Ibaka Sangu shows us from Kinshasa.

The widespread colonial novelty of cities has stimulated a particularly strong African urban innovation of new capital city constructions. Gaborone in Botswana and Nouakchott in Mauritania had to be built because the new states had no urban colonial centre within its boundaries. Others have resulted from political choice, for various reasons and with diverse outcomes. Abuja has become the full political centre of Nigeria; Dodoma is rather a seasonal political capital of Tanzania. Yamassoukrou has survived the death of its patron and become a significant city of its own; but not the capital of Côte d'Ivoire, Abidjan. The new Ciudad de la Paz or Oyala in Equatorial Guinea is still under construction. Sometimes, existing smaller cities have been upgraded to capitals instead of the inherited colonial centre, like Lilongwe in Malawi and currently Gitega in Burundi. The contemporary construction of a new capital in Egypt, replacing ancient Cairo, might have drawn some inspiration from sub-Saharan Africa, but is actually more akin to Asian plans of de-congesting old capitals such as Tokyo and Seoul. With one difference: the military plan of a new capital for Egypt is unhampered by parliamentary politics and an independent judiciary, which in the end stopped or stymied (in Korea) the East Asian plans.

The ethnic diversity of African nations has not disappeared with urbanisation and modern class formation but remains a major force of structuring urban social and political relations, from dwelling concentrations and employment networks to electoral vote banks and occasional political violence. (See further the profound study of this by Noah Nathan 2019, centred on Accra.) As ex-colonial cities, African cities share the issues of decolonisation most immediately with Asian cities but also with the ex-settler states of Latin America, more than of North America and Australia where the native communities were almost exterminated, as well as of South Africa. Issues ranging from name-changing and commemorations to urban layout and planning. Above we have a previously little studied example of Yaoundé, presented by Jean-Pierre Togolo.

In Africa, as on other continents, the establishment of a nation-state could be a gradual, negotiated process or a rupture with the pre-national rule, more or less violent. Africa has had its experience of both, and urban monumentality remembering one or the other. Two nations and cities out of the former French empire express the alternatives with extraordinary clarity. The capital of the Republic of Congo is keeping its colonial name, Brazzaville, and the recent centenary of the arrival of the French-Italian officer Brazza and his expedition was commemorated in an imposing statue of him dressed rather like a pilgrim. In Algiers, by contrast, the statue of its colonial conqueror general Bugeaud has been taken down, and his square renamed after the leader of the anti-colonial resistance, Emir Abdel Kader, now tall on horseback with drawn sword.

The popular

There is a paradox of the popular impingement on African cities. On the one hand, it is obvious and overwhelming, as major parts of the cities are built and maintained by the people outside the establishment, the 'informal' settlements, housing the bulk of the population in many African cities. A legacy of the colonial urban duality, between the centre of the colonisers and the settlements of the colonised, between '*la ville*' and '*la cité*' in the Francophone colonies, a duality lopsidedly expanded after independence with the same centres overtaken by the new nation-states and their meagre resources and, on the other hand, the popular settlements now hugely swollen by massive urban immigration. Occasionally, popular informality erupts in massive, spontaneous rioting, for example, 'IMF riots' against imposed 'structural adjustment' policies, or against sudden governmental price hikes, like petrol prices in Nigeria.

As already cited in the Introduction, Garth Myers (2011: 198) noted '[s]trangely, political science seems only an occasional presence in African urban studies, when it ought to be a central field in our analyses, because these are such fascinating years for urban politics in Africa'. The conference of which this book is largely a product reflected that situation and trod lightly over popular political and related organisation. With notable exceptions, even (trade, industrial) union organisation escapes much scrutiny in the city literatures, and popular organising, whilst an ever-present theme, plays second fiddle to issues of administration, governance, planning and institutional matters. One searches indices in general volumes for the most part in vain for references to popular struggle, community-based organising and union activity. Yet popular movements have a long and significant history across the continent's cities.

However, cases of popular power in the 'formal' city are rare or even absent. Formal city power itself tends to be weak – 'the absence of a strong local state with a clear and unchallenged mandate to manage the city' is one of 'the leitmotifs of African urbanism today' according to Pieterse and Parnell (2014: 10). Formal popular power tends to require autonomous and city-wide popular organisation which is difficult in African cities, with their ethnic diversity and, in some instances, chiefs, their mostly embryonic or fragile class formation, and their pervasive patterns of Big Men patronage and clientelism, although 'populist' electoral strategies are sometimes employed by successful politicians (Resnick 2014). In some cities with developed institutions of local urban administration there can emerge local formal urban resistance and contestation of national policies more distant from local popular experiences and concerns. Margot Rubin gives us insights into such processes in Johannesburg and Ekurhuleni. On occasion, organising is along divisive lines, by language group, or other forms of ethnicity. Popular action dissolves into attacks on members of out-groups. The September 2001 events in Zaria, Nigeria provide one of many unfortunate illustrations (cf. Adetula 2005: 228).

In between the informal 'slums' and the institutional city power, there are movements struggling for basic urban services, like water in Mathare, Nairobi as studied by Wangui Kimar, and in the informal settlements themselves a kind of popular urban government may develop, as may also be spotted in Nairobi. One popular sphere common to Africa's cities is that of waste. Pickers on dumps and trolley pushers symbolise the enormity of engagement in this sector: but it seldom appears to lead to substantial social organisation, though there are exceptions, such as that briefly portrayed by Grest et. al. (2013: 128) in the case of Associação de Agua e Saneamento do Bairro Urbanização (ADASBU) in Maputo. But the emphasis in the literature remains one of governance, and relationships between largely individual even if substantial 'groups' of social actors and the state or government remain open to exploration. The trope that dominates is that of 'informal economic activity' rather than popular organising for change.

As Ngonidzashe Marongwe highlights in this volume, international urban popular movements too have their refractions in Africa, as in the case of the Occupy movements which began with targeting Wall Street in New York, mutating into Occupy African Unity Square in Harare.

The global

African cities have always been caught between the global and the local. In this way they are no different from the world's other cities. But the tension between the two seems especially acute in Africa. That tension expresses itself in a thousand ways, none more dramatic than the simultaneous attraction and repulsion of formal and informal ways of doing things.

How do Africa's cities fit in to the 'fragmented, hierarchical' features of Henri Lefebvre's 'geographies of globalisation'? or the 'satanic geographies of globalisation and uneven development in the 1990s'? (Brenner 1997)

African cities came late both to the first, national, and to the current, capitalist wave of globalisation. The continent was not part of the time when the globalisation of nationalism generated capital cities 'worthy of the nation' looking to Paris of the Second Empire. International Style Modernism was an inspiration to several figures of the first generation of African – as well as Asian – national leaders, like Nkrumah, for instance. But actual implementation was limited.

After the millennium shift, several African cities are now eager to enter the competitive field for global imagery and foreign attraction to real estate opportunities, business locations, and upscale conventions and tourism. Dubai appears to be the most popular model, although Singapore and Shanghai are also points of reference.

Skyscrapers are important indicators of this ambition, once a symbol of the rise to supremacy of US capitalism, after 2000, a world race, first of all between China, with East Asia, and the Arab Gulf states leading the trend. Africa is about to enter the fray. Kenya is leading for the time being. Carlton Centre in Johannesburg is, at 201 metres, still the tallest building in Africa, built in 1973; but the Kenyans show more drive to the top. Kenya's tallest completed building is the Britam Tower in Nairobi at 200 metres, but by 2020 the Pinnacle Tower is to be completed at 320m, and the 370m Palm Exotica in the beach resort of Watamu. Cairo is building an Iconic Tower slated to be 385m. In Nigeria, the political capital Abuja is vigorously competing for the skies with the economic centre, Lagos. Dar es Salaam and Luanda have recently started to build vertically, though still on a globally modest scale, with the Tanzania Ports Authority from 2016 at 157m and Luanda with its 2018 IMOB tower at 145m (www.skyscrapercenter.com). Like in the rest of the world, these developments seem driven primarily by local and national global aspirations, rather than by foreign investors.

A world-class city image usually has to include other elements than skyscrapers. In Addis Ababa searching for an imagery was, as Meseret Kassahun's careful study shows, a major reason for the adoption of an expensive light rail transit system in Addis, stopping the already started much cheaper Brazilian-type bus rapid transit. It may be added, though, that the second reason invoked, that the bus system would not be able to cope with the city's population growth and relocations, was probably correct. The most famous such system, that of Bogotá in Colombia, was soon overtaken by surging transport needs.

Waterfront developments are frequent features of recent urban upgrading ambitions, whether the water is a river, a lake or an ocean. In Luanda, it is of course the ocean at the Bay of Luanda, with its renamed Avenue of February 4 (in 1961, the start of the war of independence), across the ocean from the Avenida Atlantida of Rio's Copacabana. In her study of Luanda, Sylvia Croese also takes note of another aspect of current urban globalisation, the invention of traditions and the use of historical pastiche. The latter is here deployed in a strikingly post-national, globalist way: the new 2015 National Assembly building is modelled after a landmark of colonial Luanda, the (Portuguese) National Bank of Angola.

This century has started well in Africa and there is immense urban construction and renovation going on all over the continent, even in a failed state such as Kinshasa, Congo. However, African cities still have handicaps to overcome, stemming from their uncompleted tasks of nation-state consolidation and of popular upliftment in terms of rights, resources, and cohesive trust. Attempting to build a 'smart city' out of a city where half the population has no direct access to electricity is not very promising, or it may mean building a still more divided city of exclusions, as the chapter on Lagos points out. 'Gated communities' are another prominent feature of global cities, which entered postcolonial Africa in the late 1980s (Morange et al. 2012). The economically most developed African country, South Africa, already harbours some of the world's most unequal cities, an urban inequality on par with that of the planet as a whole (UN-Habitat 2008: 72; Milanovic 2005: 142).

However, as Agunbiade, Olaide, and Bishi also stress, the resurrection of Lagos in this century, out of chaos and decay, is an impressive example of creative urban leadership and innovative energy. The city's fascination with the Dutch star architect Rem Koolhaas, who studied it in the transition period of 1998–2001 is understandable, without sharing his peculiar perspective of hype and dystopia (Koolhaas et al. 2001: 652f).

There is, in addition, a scholarly and research connection with the global across Africa's cities. 'The conditions under which urban knowledges are produced are changing' (May & Perry 2005: 347). What do readings of African cities offer to understandings of African society, to reimagining Africa? What do they offer to thinking about and indeed, living in, cities across the world?

African cities form a marginal category in the global urban literatures, which mirrors the minor attention which African society at large receives in much 'global' literature – that is, western-sourced scholarship on the concerns of the contemporary world (Ferguson 2006: 25–27). Aidan Southall, despite his own history as African anthropologist, devotes no more than four pages to Africa in his global urban history *The City in Time and Space*. Peter Hall, celebrating *Cities in Civilisation*, implied that African cities are not very civilised. Every reader of this book will be aware of growing debates on this matter. But perhaps 90% of African urban publication (at least in English or French) is still north American and western European.

Of course, the book is based on a shared notion of the connectedness of African city life with points and patterns in and through other continents: something perhaps becoming more likely inversed to infuse writing the city in the northern hemisphere.

The major advances (with limitations) thus far have been made in a few historical studies, and in postcolonial literatures which form part of broader culturalist work. An indication of the possibilities can be found in a couple of pages provocatively titled 'Cosmopolis: de la ville, de l'Afrique et du monde'[26] (Malaquais & Marchal 2005). The postcoloniality of cities *including* London, Paris and Rome as well as those of Asia and Africa and (sometimes) Latin America seems more widely imbibed, though not endemic, in northern and western spaces of urban scholarship. At least there is now an elaborate foundation for thinking cities across the world simultaneously, as Anthony King, followed by more recent authors such as Jenny Robinson, have prominently demonstrated. In other words, African cities are becoming part of the global cannon of research and scholarship rather than being a curious and neglected backwater.

To close

African urbanisms are longstanding (Freund 2007; Coquery-Vidrovitch 1993, 2006). African cities were key points of interaction in their own regions and way beyond the continent for centuries. But once subjected to colonialism they became secondary to European and to other cities in their networks, Asian in some cases, and American later, perhaps Chinese in particular today. African cities also transmitted forms and images, materials and people, to cities of every other continent, over very long historical time. African cities also fostered resistance to colonial rule which ultimately broke them free – only to be submerged in new nation-states with generally nationalistic developmentalisms, over time once again subjected to western-centred linear development thinking which has only recently begun to vacillate. The cities nevertheless have continued and survived. They have faced, and still face, dangers of being swamped by 'imagineered' nationalism (within ex-colonial boundaries and frequently parasitic elites) and/or failed developmentalism (punted more or less vigorously since late colonial times with minimal understanding of city possibilities).

There is, though, a deepening sense, in Africa's cities as well as in the literatures concerned with them, that the cities will be more and more the place where Africa's futures are decided (Freund 2007: 196) – partly because urbanisation is much more than a century long process and it still has a long way to go with no certain result.

Africa is making its own, specific urban experiences and practices, and that is exemplified across all of the chapters in this volume. But it makes sense seeing them as refractions of tendencies and challenges common to urban modernity worldwide. The continent has just entered into the beginning of a large-scale urban transformation, promising a fascinating field of observation and learning to urbanists of the world for decades to come. The urban arm of the UN, UN-Habitat, was prescient in locating itself in Nairobi.

One of the exciting prospects of Africa is that it remains the least urban continent – thus Africa is the key continent of urban growth to come – along with parts of south Asia. Urban growth and change are being globally, as well as locally, shaped and there may be rising popular movements also reshaping trajectories. The urban obsessed politicians have not yet emerged, but their constituency may be forming – and it may

---

26 'Cosmopolis: On the city, on Africa, on the world'

not merely be a poor one. The rising cosmopolitanism of African cities; with their own knowledges and creativities which Africa did not have to wait to be given and will not wait to be given from beyond; the fluidities of African cities – which may in some respects prefigure an urban future of the world (Coquery-Vidrovitch 2006: 1118).

References

Adetula V (2005) Ethnicity and the dynamics of city politics: The case of Jos. In: AM Simone & A Abouhani (eds) *Urban Africa: Changing Contours of Survival in the City*. London: Zed and Cape Town: HSRC Press. pp. 206–234

Brenner N (1997) Global, fragmented, hierarchical: Henri Lefebvre's geographies of globalisation. *Public Culture* 10(1): 135–167

Coquery-Vidrovitch C (1993) *Histoires des villes africaines. Des origines à la colonisation*. Paris: Albin Michel

Coquery-Vidrovitch C (2006) De la ville en Afrique noire, *Annales. Histoire, Sciences Sociales* 61(5): 1087–1119

Ferguson J (2006) *Global Shadows: Africa in the Neoliberal World Order*. Durham and London: Duke University Press

Freund B (2007) *The African City: A History*. Cambridge: Cambridge University Press

Grest J, Baudouin A, Bjerkli C & Qunot-Suarez H (2013) The politics of solid waste management in Accra, Addis Ababa, Maputo and Ouagadougou: Different cities, similar issues. In: S Bekker & L Fourchard (eds) *Governing Cities in Africa: Politics and Policies*. Cape Town: HSRC Press

Hall P (1998) *Cities in Civilisation*. London: Pantheon

King AD (1995) Writing colonial space. A review article. *Comparative Studies in Society and History* 37(3): 541–554

Koolhaas R, Boeri S, Kwinter S, Tazi N & Obrist HU (2001) *Mutations*. Barcelona: ACTAR

Malaquais D & Marchal R (eds) (2005) Cosmopolis: de la ville, de l'Afrique et du monde. *Politique Africaine* 100. Paris: Karthala

May T & Perry B (2005) Continuities and change in urban sociology. *Sociology* 39(2): 343–347

Milanovic B (2005) *Worlds Apart*. Princeton, NJ: Princeton University Press

Morange M et al. (2012) The spread of a transnational model: 'Gated communities' in three southern African Cities (Cape Town, Maputo and Windhoek). *International Journal of Urban and Regional Research* 36(5): 890–914

Myers G (2011) *African Cities: Alternative Visions of Urban Theory and Practice*. London: Zed

Nathan N (2019) *Electoral Politics and Africa's Urban Transition: Class and Ethnicity in Ghana*. Cambridge: Cambridge University Press

Pieterse E & Parnell S (2014) Africa's urban revolution in context. In: E Pieterse & S Parnell (eds) *Africa's Urban Revolution*. London: Zed. pp. 1–7

Resnick D (2014) *Urban Poverty and Party Populism in African Democracies*. Cambridge: Cambridge University Press

Robinson J (2016) Comparative urbanism: New geographies and cultures of theorizing the urban. *International Journal of Urban and Regional Research* 40(1): 187–199
Simone AM (2004) *For the City yet to Come*. Durham: Duke University Press
Southall A (1998) *The City in Time and Space*. Cambridge: Cambridge University Press
UN-Habitat (2008) *State of the World's Cities 2008/2009*. Nairobi: UN-Habitat

List of contributors

AMR ABDELAAL, Takween Integrated Community Development, Cairo, Egypt

MUYIWA ELIJAH AGUNBIADE, Urban and Regional Planning, University of Lagos, Nigeria

HAJER AWATTA, Takween Integrated Community Development, Cairo, Egypt

SIMON BEKKER, Sociology, University of Stellenbosch, South Africa

HAKEEM BISHI, Research Manager, Lagos Trader Project, Nigeria

SYLVIA CROESE, African Centre for Cities, University of Cape Town and School of Architecture and Planning, University of the Witwatersrand, South Africa

LEILA GROENEWALD, Sociology, University of Johannesburg, South Africa

MESERET KASSAHUN, Research Associate, Social Work Department, University of Johannesburg, South Africa

WANGUI KIMARI, Mathare Social Justice Centre, Nairobi, Kenya

ALAN MABIN, School of Architecture and Planning, University of the Witwatersrand, South Africa

NGONIDZASHE MARONGWE, History and Development Studies, Great Zimbabwe University, Zimbabwe

OMAR NAGATI, Cairo Lab for Urban Studies, Training and Environmental Research, Cairo, Egypt

OLUWAFEMI OLAJIDE, Urban and Regional Planning, University of Lagos, Nigeria

EDGAR PIETERSE, African Centre for Cities, University of Cape Town, South Africa

MARGOT RUBIN, School of Architecture and Planning, University of the Witwatersrand, South Africa

SALWA SALMAN, Takween Integrated Community Development, Cairo, Egypt

PHILIPPE IBAKA SANGU, History and Sociology, University of Kinshasa, Democratic Republic of the Congo

MARWA SHYKHON, Cairo Lab for Urban Studies, Training and Environmental Research, Cairo, Egypt

GÖRAN THERBORN, Sociology, Cambridge University, United Kingdom

JEAN-PIERRE TOGOLO, Sociology, University of Dschang, Cameroon

Index